Knowledge Goes Pop

CULTURE MACHINE SERIES

Series Editor: Gary Hall
ISSN: 1743-6176

Commissioning Editors: Dave Boothroyd, Chris Hables Gray, Simon Morgan Wortham, Joanna Zylinska

International Consultant Editors: Simon Critchley, Lawrence Grossberg, Donna Haraway, Peggy Kamuf, Brian Massumi, Meaghan Morris, Paul Patton, Paul Rabinow, Kevin Robins, Avital Ronell

The position of cultural theory has radically shifted. What was once the engine of change across the humanities and social sciences is now faced with a new 'post-theoretical' mood, a return to empiricism and to a more transparent politics. So what is the future for cultural theory? Addressing this question through the presentation of innovative, provocative and cutting-edge work, the *Culture Machine* series both repositions cultural theory and reaffirms its continuing intellectual and political importance.

Published books include

City of Panic Paul Virilio
Art, Time and Technology Charlie Gere

Forthcoming books include

Anti-Capitalism: Cultural Theory and Popular Politics Jeremy Gilbert

Knowledge Goes Pop
From Conspiracy Theory to Gossip

CLARE BIRCHALL

Oxford • New York

English edition
First published in 2006 by
Berg
Editorial offices:
First Floor, Angel Court, 81 St Clements Street, Oxford OX4 1AW, UK
175 Fifth Avenue, New York, NY 10010, USA

Berg is the imprint of Oxford International Publishers Ltd.

Library of Congress Cataloging-in-Publication Data

Birchall, Clare.
    Knowledge goes pop : from conspiracy theory to gossip / Clare
Birchall.—English ed.
        p. cm.—(Culture machine series)
    Includes bibliographical references and index.
    ISBN-13: 978-1-84520-143-2 (pbk.)
    ISBN-10: 1-84520-143-4 (pbk.)
    ISBN-13: 978-1-84520-142-5 (hardback)
    ISBN-10: 1-84520-142-6 (hardback)
  1. Knowledge, Sociology of. 2. Popular culture. 3. Social
perception. 4. Gossip. I. Title. II. Series.

    HM651.B57 2006
    306.4'2—dc22

                                                                    2006009546

British Library Cataloguing-in-Publication Data

A catalogue record for this book is available from the British Library.

            ISBN-13   978 1 84520 142 5 (Cloth)
                       978 1 84520 143 2 (Paper)

            ISBN-10   1 84520 142 6 (Cloth)
                       1 84520 143 4 (Paper)

Typeset by JS Typesetting Ltd, Porthcawl, Mid Glamorgan
Printed in the United Kingdom by Biddles Ltd, King's Lynn.

www.bergpublishers.com

To RRS

for speculating on me

These are difficult times for 'modern' people who believe that there are proper sorts of knowledge, usually produced and disseminated in places like universities. Today, knowledges of various kinds are being produced at all sorts of places, and disseminated in all sorts of ways. Universities can no longer claim to be the sole guardians of knowledge, even of more or less academic knowledge, which is being produced as much outside the university as inside. While both the left and the right are challenging the status of certain ways of producing and presenting knowledge, the relations between expertise and the various forms of common sense are becoming increasingly conflicted. *Knowledge Goes Pop* jumps into the middle of this messy terrain, and offers an incisive and insightful analysis of both sides of the line dividing cultural criticism from popular knowledge. Hopefully, Birchall's book will set in motion a sustained and rigorous discussion of the place of 'knowledge' in the coming modernity.

Lawrence Grossberg, *author of 'Caught in the Crossfire:*
Kids, Politics and America's Future', Morris David
Distinguished Professor of Cultural Studies and
Director of the University Program in Cultural Studies,
University of North Carolina at Chapel Hill

Contents

Preface

WHY I WROTE THIS BOOK

A voice on late-night talk radio told me that Kentucky Fried Chicken injects its food with drugs that render men impotent. A colleague asked if I thought the FBI was 'in' on 9/11. An alien abductee on the Internet claimed extraterrestrials implanted a microchip in her left buttock. The front page of a gossip mag screamed 'Julia Roberts in Porn Scandal'. A best-seller suggested gender difference is so great, men and women may as well come from different planets. A spiritual healer claimed he could cure my aunt's chronic fatigue syndrome with the energizing power of crystals.

This book came out of a deep fascination with the popular knowledges that saturate our experience of everyday understanding and communication in the twenty-first century. I was struck by how we mediate and are mediated by popular knowledges, how they influence the way we position ourselves in the world and shape the way we imagine the world works. I wanted to call such phenomena 'knowledge' in order to remind myself of its relation to the more 'official' knowledges that also tell us who we are, what to believe, and how to conduct ourselves socially. From Michel Foucault's work, I knew that power relations are determined by knowledge, but I also wanted to think about the relations *between* knowledges in terms of power. Are popular knowledges, I wondered, marginalized by official knowledges? What challenge do they pose to traditional sites of knowledge production? Why does their presence cause so much institutional anxiety?

When I began to tell people that I was studying conspiracy theories (among other examples of popular knowledge) they responded in one of two ways. They either asked why on earth people believe in such 'nonsense' or grilled me for what *really* happened to Diana, JFK, or Martin Luther King. Was September 11 a set-up to legitimize the invasion of firstly Afghanistan and then Iraq? Is there such a thing as the New World Order? Does the Bilderberg group really pull the strings? They wanted me to tell them why these stories existed or if they were true. And in some ways it might have been easier to address these concerns. I could, with regards to the second concern, occupy myself with the veracity of particular statements produced within popular knowledges. (Was Diana really murdered? Do aliens actually abduct humans? Will this book improve my sex life? Have the latest celebrity couple truly broken up?) Let's face it, we are all capable of becoming absorbed by the details and this is part of the pleasure to be found in gossip, conspiracy theory, alien abduction narratives and the like. Some commentators have gone down this route, debunking certain theories and ideas perpetuated by these kinds of narratives.

Other commentators have addressed the first concern as to *why* people believe in 'false' or 'fragile' knowledge. Such approaches tend to perform symptomatic readings of popular knowledge in which the knowledge always takes the place of some psychosocial lack, or is read as a political act performed by usually disenfranchised agents. Francis Wheen, for example, in an article extracted from his book *How Mumbo Jumbo Overtook the World* writes, 'The new irrationalism is an expression of despair by people who feel impotent to improve their lives and suspect that they are at the mercy of secretive, impersonal forces whether these be the Pentagon or invaders from Mars. Political leaders accept it as a safe outlet for dissent, fulfilling much the same function that Marx attributed to religion' (2004: 12).

Indeed, there are all sorts of routes to answer the question 'Why do we turn to popular knowledge?' – via psychoanalysis, philosophy, history, or anthropology – but I wanted to write a book that could open up a different way of responding to popular knowledges: one that moves beyond the truth or falsity of statements produced by a particular knowledge and the question of why people might choose to invest in them. Working against the grain of much academic work on fan communities and the idea of empowered consumers (in my field of cultural studies especially), I wanted to focus on the knowledge believed in, rather than those who believe. That is not to say that I wanted to eliminate the 'subject' altogether as there is always a residual concept of subjectivity in discursive mechanisms but I did not want to make claims as to these subjects' intentions, desires, or reasons for belief. While I knew psychological motive and socio-political pressures would all inform a reading of popular knowledge's increased circulation and employment, I felt that focusing on what makes each popular knowledge possible in the first place would allow me to consider the relationship between 'official' and 'unofficial', 'legitimate' and 'illegitimate' knowledges. I thought that understanding these relationships was necessary for approaching some key events of our age. Having written this book, I still do.

With so many claims on what knowledge is and what it *should* be – exemplified not least by current international debates about school curricula (see Apple 2003) – I wanted to perform a timely investigation into the relationship between un-legitimated and legitimated forms of knowledge. Of course, thinking through this relationship threw up difficult self-reflexive questions about any knowledge in a disciplinary form – including cultural studies, the particular knowledge-producing discourse that I identified with – that I might mobilize to analyse popular knowledge. That is to say, I realized that the way in which I approached such cultural phenomena was crucial: if I approached popular knowledges according to an ideal of critical distance, say, positioning popular knowledges as the other of, foreign to, and outside legitimated knowledge, I would in effect already have decided in advance what these popular knowledges were. Indeed, although such an approach would have allowed me to pontificate about the political significance (either positively or negatively) of popular knowledges, position them as subcultural, or think about their role within everyday life (acts familiar within cultural studies), I would not have been able to think about the close relationship they hold to my own knowledge production. Taking this relationship into account would, I hoped, lead to a better understanding not only of why popular knowledges matter but also what kinds of strategies we can employ in order to gain this better understanding. In other words, as well as thinking about the role of popular knowledge in contemporary culture, I also wanted to think about what kind of cultural studies might be up to the job of thinking through the questions it raises about legitimacy and responsibility.

I have tackled the themes of this book through two main examples: conspiracy theory and gossip. I could have chosen to concentrate on a number of others, such as urban legends, the self-help rhetoric and pop-psychology that permeates talk shows such as *Oprah* (US Harpo Productions) and *Montel Williams* (US Paramount Pictures), or alien abduction narratives. While singular and unique, I felt that such knowledges could usefully be considered on a continuum. This whole book could be thought of as exploring the question of how to do justice to popular knowledge – how to analyse it responsibly in a tension between the universal (popular knowledge as a whole) and the singular (individual instances of popular knowledge). This meant making decisions about which examples to focus on. I could not study all forms of popular knowledge (although I wanted to open up more space for such work).

Besides, reading 'responsibly' would never be about producing exhaustive lists. And so, I had to make some decisions as to which forms and singular practices of popular knowledge (conspiracy theory, gossip) and case studies (such as Diana and September 11 conspiracy theories, and the gossip that permeated the lead up to the second Gulf War) I considered to be important and interesting. My selections, therefore, were informed by two aspects. Firstly, my desire to do justice to each example obviously placed a limitation on how many could be included. But, more pertinently, it seemed to me that conspiracy theory and gossip and their framings of knowledge were in urgent need of consideration at this socio-political conjuncture, when war is waged on little more than gossip, and interpreting information as calculated plot shapes a whole nation's future. These choices might have been different at another time. I hope in making these decisions about what to focus on, I have kept open the way for further investigations into other popular, or indeed, unpopular knowledges.

Mostly, I wanted to write a kind of 'self-help' book for the contemporary *zeitgeist* – characterized, I'd argue, by the making of decisions on the basis of knowledge that cannot be decided. Keep it with you at all times for you never know when talk radio will be talking again, when paranoia will inflect a colleague's voice, when everyone around you will turn to a way of knowing that you haven't yet learned to trust, or equally when your government will try to persuade you that their knowledge is not infected by its popular 'other'. It might not be a question of arming yourself against these cognitive effects, but of opening yourself to them. It might be disorientating; you may require some assistance; or at least desire some company...

Acknowledgements

I owe special thanks to the following people: Geoff Bennington for humouring me in the kindest way possible; Paul Smith for always raising the question of politics; Robert Smith for the spontaneous lectures while cooking; Gary Hall for persuading me that it might be a good idea to write a book and then helping me to see it through; Tristan Palmer at Berg for not asking me to write a textbook; my colleagues in Media and Cultural Studies at Middlesex University; Neil Badmington, Kay Dickinson, Jem Gilbert, Matt Hills and Paul Myerscough for being, at various points, receptive readers; and everyone who has listened and responded with patience and care to papers I have given at various conferences and talks.

In less academic matters, thanks are due to Roger Birchall and Christine Clarke for love and support; Lou Dodds for essential outdoor pursuits; Polly Russell for being in on the conspiracy before asking what it is; Matt Herbert, Lola Oliyide, Robyn Pierce, Caitlin Pitts and Richard Vine for good gossip; and Ms Millicent Rose for being so small.

Some of the material in Chapter 2 appeared in 1999 as 'alt.conspiracy. princess-diana: The Conspiracy of Discourse', *New Formations*, 36, pp. 125–40 and in 2002 as 'The Commodification of Conspiracy Theory' in Peter Knight (ed.) *Conspiracy Nation: The Politics of Paranoia in Postwar America*, New York: New York University Press, pp. 233–53. Parts of Chapter 3 have appeared in a different form in 2004 in 'Just Because You're Paranoid, Doesn't Mean They're Not Out To Get You', *Culture Machine*, 6 (http://culturemachine.tees.ac.uk/ articles/birchall.htm) and in 2004 as 'Economic Interpretation' in Rochelle Sibley and Charlotte Ross (eds) *Illuminating Eco: on the Boundaries of Interpretation*, Warwick Studies in the Humanities Series, Aldershot and Burlington: Ashgate, pp. 71–87.

This book could not have been written without a sabbatical funded by the Arts and Humanities Research Council and Middlesex University.

Clare Birchall

CHAPTER I

Know It All

Conspiracy theory, alien abduction narratives, astrology, urban legends, self-help rhetoric, gossip, new age practices. It is so tempting, when someone asks what popular knowledge is, to respond by listing some examples. But this doesn't really answer the question; it merely illustrates an answer that remains absent. It is easier to point to examples already penetrating everyday life than to come up with a list of hard-and-fast characteristics that can always be disputed. I don't intend this book to become a checklist that people can reference in order to ascertain the 'popular knowledge-ness' of one discourse or another. I recognize that there are as many differences as similarities between various forms of popular knowledge and that discourses will slide imperceptibly between the 'unofficial' and 'official', between the 'legitimate' and 'illegitimate', between the 'high' and 'popular'.[1] Though singular and unique, I do think that knowledges like the ones I began by listing can usefully be thought of on a continuum of popular cognitive practices that deny scientific rationalism and justified true belief as the only criteria for knowledge. In thinking of this continuum, I will be able to make a meaningful engagement with questions regarding the status of knowledge in general.

KNOWLEDGE-SCAPE

While I will ultimately challenge the terms outlined in Figure 1, I want to use it as a springboard for thinking about the status of knowledge as it is theoretically configured, experienced, or presented to us in everyday encounters. It might be helpful to think of this diagram as a visual representation of an historically rooted debate in the 'West' about different kinds of knowledge.

Lingering at the top right-hand corner of Figure 1 (Position A) lies 'justified true belief'. This formulation of knowledge can be traced back to Plato's *Theaetetus* written in 360 BCE in which Socrates is in dialogue with Theaetetus about the nature of knowledge. The logic of the 'justified true belief' account is as follows (*S* delineates the knowing subject, and *p* the proposition known). *S* knows that *p* if and only if:

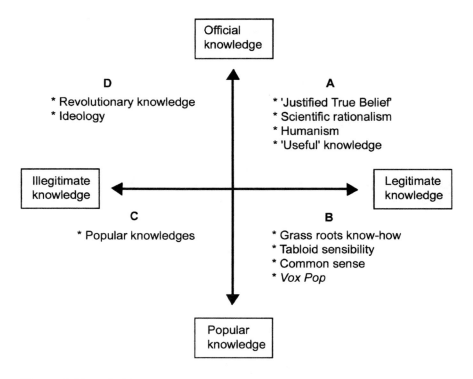

Figure 1 Knowledge-scape

- p is true;
- S believes that p; and
- S is justified in believing that p.

If something is false (say, for example, the proposition that Prince Charles wrote this book), we cannot know it: this would be to know no thing (nothing). So, the proposition has to be knowable as true. Of course, we can believe something without necessarily knowing it; it only becomes knowledge if we can establish its truth and justification. Epistemologically, belief does not refer to the idea of having faith, rather it indicates our assent to a statement's truth. Much attention in the dominant epistemological traditions has been given to the question of how justification can be ascertained and, latterly – since Edmund Gettier (1963) showed 'justified true belief' to be insecure or incomplete as a definition – what other criteria have to be in play for knowledge to be knowledge. Despite the many challenges to this definition of knowledge, I have situated 'justified true belief' as an example of the 'official' and 'legitimate' because of the force it has had and continues to have in 'common sense' understandings of knowledge.

Below the horizontal dividing line of Figure 1 (positions B and C) lie discursive phenomena more closely associated with the popular (whether this be in the sense of populist or mass circulation and participation). That which, albeit provisionally, falls into the category of 'legitimate' and popular (position B) can be traced back at least to the challenge put forward in the English Civil War to the divine right of kings, and, latterly, to the drive for universal suffrage. Whereas for Plato, those ideas that couldn't fulfil the criteria of knowledge were branded and devalued as opinion or *doxa*, in the tradition of what we could call democratic or Christian socialism, and populism of all political ilks, the knowledge of 'the people' is valued as being untainted by high office and therefore closer to truth. Such ideas see 'the people' and their knowledge as legitimate (*more* legitimate, even, than those in corrupting positions of power).

Broadly speaking, tabloids from both ends of the political spectrum (I am thinking primarily of the British press in this instance) such as the *Mirror* and the *Sun*, champion the 'man on the street' over politicians, large corporations and, more ambivalently, the law (particularly EU law, which is fashioned as being remote or insensitive to the concerns of the British people). This rhetoric, privileging the individual over the corporation or state, can be seen reflected in a surge of populist politics from the Conservatives and New Labour in contemporary Britain, in the admonitions of the 'nanny state' and advocacy of personal autonomy and choice. Elsewhere, populists who peddle their various politics in the name of the people include Australia's Pauline Hanson, Winston Peters in New Zealand, Jean-Marie Le Pen in France, Carl I. Hagen in Norway, William Jennings Bryan, Huey Long, Paul Wellstone, Howard Dean and John Edwards in the United States, Aung San Suu Kyi in Myanmar, Silvio Berlusconi in Italy, Jörg Haider in Austria, Lula in Brazil, Preston Manning in Canada and Hugo Chavez in Venezuela.[2]

Under the category of the 'legitimate' and popular, we could also situate 'common sense'. Usually notions claimed as unmediated, self-evident common sense (such as the possibility of agency, the difference between the human and inhuman, or what constitutes truth) are filtered down from humanism and are in actual fact highly ideological and situated. Such ideas have legitimacy in their own terms with regards to the dominant ideology and are popular in their standing. That is to say, they are widely disseminated and, in general, support the official ideas of that society (even while they might be voiced with different, more individualist, concerns).

Position C in the bottom left-hand corner of Figure 1 is traditionally ascribed to the phenomena that I am interested in for this book (though in some appropriative accounts that praise popular knowledges, such phenomena has been ascribed position B). Under this category fall all those knowledges that traditionally have not counted as knowledge at all: knowledges of an uncertain status; knowledges that have not been verified; knowledges that are officially discredited (for different reasons) but which still enjoy mass circulation. These would include gossip and conspiracy theory (the two main examples I consider in this book), but also those knowledges I began this chapter by listing. With regards to a definition, I will postpone any attempt until later and as I will have much more to say about this realm, I will move on swiftly to position D.

The top left-hand corner of Figure 1 is perhaps the most slippery position of all, or at least the one that exposes the instability of all the positions. The clearest example of a knowledge that is official yet illegitimate arises from Marx's conception of revolutionary knowledge. Knowledge that the working class is exploited is part of the official logic of capital and yet the expression of this knowledge is branded illegitimate by the ruling class. Exploitation is both part of the smooth running of industry, say, but it cannot be seen as a 'legitimate' idea to know because this might sanction resistance and revolution. Inequality and exploitation are 'legitimate' and official (position A) for those in power, but knowledge *of* them is framed as illegitimate in order to maintain the status quo. Position D, then, is the space of ideology. Here, discourses such as racism can be institutionalized (and official) and yet remain unacknowledged (illegitimate). Equally, in a slightly different formula, discourses like racism can be institutionalized (and official) and yet be exposed, dismissed and deemed illegitimate by another discourse, say liberalism or human rights. Either way, such discourses are positioned as illegitimate *and* official.

Figure 1 is something of a ruse (as is the as-yet unseen Table 1). I am not usually a fan of diagrams and tables because of their rigid appearance. The positions in Figure 1 are far from fixed and are dependent on external, contingent factors. All of the knowledges in position A, for example, could equally be in position D. What is illegitimate knowledge from one political position could be legitimate for another, depending on what legitimating criteria is drawn upon. I have, however, tried to provide a diagram that expresses the dominant ideology in the 'West' with regards to knowledge culture. The interventions that I will summarize and draw upon below arise from those disciplines that I feel to be the most helpful in preparing the ground to consider a particular dynamic evident in the diagram; namely, the tension between positions A and C. That is, I am interested primarily in questioning the relationship between knowledge that holds an officially 'legitimate' status and that which is considered to be of 'illegitimate' and popular status (at least from the vantage point of the 'official'). This is the tension that will organize the concerns of this book, though the other positions in Figure 1 will never be far from view and will occasionally take centre stage.

KNOWLEDGE NOW

When thinking through the contemporary conditions of popular knowledge, we would do well to remember that the exchange of knowledge on a mass level is nothing new. The rise of the print medium and of general literacy ensured a degree of knowledge exchange on a wide scale. Locally, of course, 'illegitimate' knowledges have always been exchanged. Yet, the velocity and scale of knowledge exchange in the Internet age is unique. Those local, 'illegitimate' knowledges now enjoy mass participation. But it is not only the speed and scale of dissemination that marks this situation out as particular to the late twentieth, early twenty-first century. The whole question and context of knowledge into which popular knowledge arrives is situated within an epistemological conjuncture. Moreover, the ground into which popular knowledge arrives determines the way it will be configured, what role it has to play, and what will be challenged by that arrival. The questions raised by popular knowledge are unique today because of the particular way in which the ground of knowledge is configured. We could schematize part of that epistemological conjuncture as in Table 1.

The linear construction of this table is misleading, not only because of the interdependent and porous boundary between each knowledge but because there is no intrinsic order or hierarchy of importance to these knowledges (although we are often led to believe there is). It also disguises the way in which definitions are disputed within particular discourses, let alone between them. Moreover, this table is by no means exhaustive. We could, for example, add religious knowledge and scientific knowledge, and no doubt the list could go on in an endless, somewhat Borgesian, taxonomy. It is not my intention to attempt such work here, but this table should at least hint at the way in which new definitions of knowledge have both symbolic and material repercussions. When the humanities' concept of knowledge is symbolically displaced by that proposed by the knowledge economy, for example, the institution the humanities' concept is attached to – the university – in turn has to adapt to that challenge (by being forced to respond to market pressures). This symbolic displacement has very real effects on the experience of higher education.

Let me look at this effect in the UK more closely (although similar policies concerning the knowledge economy have been proposed by most governments in the 'developed' world). The role of the university is integral to the vision of a successful knowledge driven economy as outlined in the 1998 Department of Trade and Industry (DTI) White Paper, *Our Competitive Future: Building the Knowledge Driven Economy.* It provides incentives for universities to develop links with businesses, to aid what is called 'knowledge transfer'. The signifier 'university' is borrowed by 'the university for industry' – an idea that has lead to the creation of a public-private partnership whose services are currently delivered by Learndirect. The emphasis here is on the (often online) delivery of business and IT-oriented skills. The focus is on the acquisition of tangible content, rather than the experience of learning and the development of transferable cognitive skills. The development of this alternative 'university' implies that the traditional university is somehow ill equipped to cater for the new knowledge economy. In fact, higher education centres have been working

Table 1

Form of Knowledge	Site of Production and Circulation	Means of Legitimation	Criteria
Knowledge economy	Industry; commerce; government policy; the economy; economics; management theory; sociology; the media	Free market economy; neoliberal/ neoconservative capitalism; appeal to new and 'inevitable' economic phase; the media	Commercial use and profitability; design and innovation; tacit knowledge with codified technical knowledge
Knowledge within the humanities	The university	Appeals to 'the university'; university endorsed awards; grants and bursaries; tradition	Intellectual use; internally established measures such as reason and scientific rationalism; that which yields cultural capital
Popular knowledge	Relatively unofficial and unregulated sites (e.g. Internet; face-to-face interaction)	Insider knowledge; paradoxical reliance upon 'official' accreditation; degree of risk or perseverance required to obtain information	Whether it has been dismissed, excluded or suppressed by any of the above.
Indigenous knowledge	Localized sites; 'home'	Tradition; culture; claims on the land	Repetition; that which is revered; often dogmatic; spiritually or agriculturally useful

with Learndirect to deliver these courses but there are still indications that the traditional degree programme is considered to be out of step with the needs of industry. Some of this is valid criticism, and many universities have attempted to address these problems through work placement schemes and modularization. But there are many reasons why academics are resisting this change in the focus of degree programmes and the aims of higher education institutions. These range from political objections (many disciplines are based on critiquing rather than supporting commercial culture), to pedagogic concerns (over what effects the corporatization of higher education has on teaching). Straight away we can see an incompatibility arising between the first knowledge in our table and the second.

It is not that the humanities' definition of knowledge is *wholly* different from knowledge that holds such a premium in the knowledge economy if, for the sake of argument, we take the former to be a philosophically derived definition of knowledge as a belief which is verified as far as possible and is subject to conditions of fallibility (the 'justified true belief' model). After all, scientific methodology, which is central to the knowledge economy, is based on such principles set forth by scientific rationalism: the idea that everything is rational and explicable through empirical observation and the consequent deduction of laws. However, the humanities are not generally interested in the economic utility of its knowledge (except in as much as the production and publication of ideas are pretty much essential to the furtherance of an academic career these days). Also, the *objects* of knowledge are very different between the knowledge economy and the humanities. The former is interested in scientific, technical, service-based, brand-oriented knowledge, and the latter in knowledge about history, culture and knowledge itself. These are not mutually exclusive interests (if they were, I would not be writing about them here – and, in fact, the cultural inflection of commerce has been widely commented on), but businesses take historical and cultural factors into consideration when developing or marketing a brand or product primarily in order to gain a competitive edge in the market. Knowledge in the humanities by contrast is valued for being intellectually rather than economically 'useful'.

Although the DTI White Paper claims that the knowledge economy 'is not just about pushing back the frontiers of knowledge' but also 'the more effective use and exploitation of all types of knowledge in all manner of activity', it is not clear how knowledges within the humanities, some of which are based on a tradition of critique and challenge, could be made economically useful in a direct way without fundamentally changing those disciplines (so that, for example, cultural studies gives way to practice and skills based media studies). Despite certain similarities in the configuration of knowledge, the knowledge economy and the humanities value knowledge for fundamentally different reasons. Given its predominance, it is inevitable that the knowledge economy will influence the future of the university and affect the appeal of different knowledges for students persuaded to think of themselves as customers in training to be 'knowledge workers'.

When it comes to knowledge, there is not an infinite space for different configurations to exist. Those that gain precedence will influence what it means to know; what kind of knowledge is culturally valued; how we learn; and who will have access to knowledge and power. What, we could ask, happens to the idea of knowledge, its meaning and place in the world, when the signifier 'knowledge' is taken up by a different, even rival, discursive practice? What role will the university play if it is no longer the main site of knowledge definition, legitimation, and production? These questions are not purely conceptual; they have very real effects on the funding of particular disciplines at degree and doctoral levels.

I think of this task as a never-ending, culturally and economically focused epistemological enquiry. It is in this epistemological conjuncture that popular knowledges exist.

THOSE IN THE KNOW

As a backdrop to thinking about popular knowledge, I want to highlight just some of the (relatively) recent academic approaches to knowledge that have helped me to understand how knowledge has been positioned in the humanities and what challenges popular knowledges pose to that positioning. And although I won't explicitly refer to some of this work again, being aware of it will, I hope, convey how my approach in this book has developed, and establish the ground upon which I want to build in the chapters that follow.

Michel Foucault

No foray into the concept of knowledge could be attempted without acknowledging a debt to Michel Foucault. Foucault was concerned with analysing governing epistemic structures. In the first instance, this took the form of an archaeological method that dug below and beyond the 'empirical content of specific knowledges' (McNay 1994: 510); beyond, that is, a list of findings and a record of the key figures – beyond what is known, towards a conception of a particular knowledge in terms of how subjects are configured and constituted by it – to get to the material conditions that shape a body of knowledge in one way rather than another.[3] In terms of the history of thought, this represents a shift from thinking in biographical terms, from privileging the 'knowing subject' (as a history of epistemology, for example, often does) towards 'a theory of discursive practice' (Foucault [1966] 1992: xiv). Foucault knew that this was contentious: 'Can one speak of science and its history … without reference to the scientist himself – and I am speaking not merely of the concrete individual represented by a proper name, but of his work and the particular form of his thought?' (Foucault [1966] 1992: xii). He claims to not want to 'deny the validity of intellectual biographies, or the possibility of a history of theories, concepts, or themes' but rather to look beyond the 'customary boundaries' to 'systems of regularities that have a decisive role' in the history of a particular body of knowledge (Foucault [1966] 1992: xii–xiv).

In time, Foucault's archaeological approach gave way to or transformed into a genealogical method that enabled him to give a fuller account of the role of power within the process of knowledge production. Of primary concern in genealogical texts such as *The History of Sexuality* ([1976] 1978), and *Discipline and Punish* ([1975] 1977) are the ways in which discourses produce and organize knowledge according to institutionalized (but not necessarily top-down) power relations. Power in these genealogies is not simply repressive. Rather, power is at work in all social relations and can produce new roles and behaviour as well as controlling others. Foucault writes, 'Power must be analysed as something which circulates, or as something which only functions in the form of a chain' (1980: 98).

All of which shapes an understanding of any knowledge, popular or otherwise. And while I am not about to produce a Foucauldian study of popular knowledge in the chapters that follow, there are several Foucauldian insights that are relevant to my project. What do we need to know about Foucault's work in order to think about popular knowledge?

1   *His formulation 'power/knowledge'*. Evident in both the archaeological and genealogical methods (which some critics see as just two configurations of the same method) this is a concern with why certain knowledges are invested in and others fall to the wayside. The truth and dominance of one statement is established, for Foucault, at the expense of other – often equally valid – statements. He uses the signifier 'power/knowledge' to think through the process of why some knowledges come to light and others do not. When I turn my attention more fully to popular knowledges, I want to retain this idea that contingent forces allow only some things to become known. I would also want us to extend this, moving outside of Foucault's concerns somewhat, to think about why some knowledges are ratified and official whereas others are left to be taken up in popular culture – which, while engendering it's own 'legitimacies' and standards, can still, in comparison to 'official' knowledge, be considered 'unofficial'.

2   *The way in which Foucault fashions the relationship between knowledge and power*. This obviously draws on what we have just said about 'power/knowledge'. What I want to stress here is that, after Foucault, knowledge cannot be thought outside of power relations. But power, here, is not simply an

oppressive force. Rather, Foucault contends (mainly in *The History of Sexuality, Volume I*) that power can also be productive, allowing for new forms of behaviour and resistance. This makes for a chainlike concept of power, moving through all social relations, as opposed to just a top-down relation. The advantage of Foucault's thought over, say, economic determinist accounts, is that, as McNay writes, 'the idea that all thought is in the service of dominatory regimes cannot adequately explain how conflicting perspectives may arise in the same regime. Nor does it explain the emergence of counterfactuals or how knowledge is necessarily distinguishable from the rationalized systems through which society is ordered' (1994: 64). All of which has important ramifications for me here. Firstly because a variety of political positions can be detected in different examples of popular knowledge; and secondly because popular knowledges are not simply subjugated by more 'legitimate' knowledges. The power invested in a 'legitimate' discourse, while delimiting what can be said and done within it, also makes other, even sometimes openly oppositional or resistant discourses possible. At times, I will present popular knowledges that give rise to statements that resist other more 'legitimate' knowledges; at others, more compliant statements will be evident.

3   *His concept of 'discourse'*. Foucault admits (as early as the 1969 *Archaeology of Knowledge*) that his use of the term 'discourse' fluctuates: 'treating it sometimes as the general domain of all statements, sometimes as individualizable groups of statements, and sometimes as a regulated practice that accounts for a certain number of statements' (Foucault [1969] 1994: 80). In this way, the concept shifts between different conceptual levels, beginning with the most general, to include all instances of signification. This gives way to a more specific or bounded formulation to indicate a collection of particular utterances. Finally, in its most radical guise, 'discourse' refers to the unwritten rules that determine the boundaries of a knowledge. As Robert Young explains, Foucault encourages us 'to analyse not simply what was thought or said, per se, but all the discursive rules and categories that were a priori, assumed as a constituent part of discourse and therefore of knowledge, and so fundamental that they remained unvoiced and unthought' (1981: 48). The shift in focus is from knowledge as a transcendent entity held in a repository for later retrieval, towards thinking about the conditions of knowledge *making*. Foucault's work, that is, reminds us that the word 'knowledge' was once used as a verb (see Lloyd 2005: 197).

In locating discursive formations, Foucauldian analysis avoids being a history of ideas:

Whenever one can describe, between a number of statements, such a system of dispersion, whenever, between objects, types of statement, concepts, or thematic choices, one can define a regularity (an order, correlations, positions and functionings, transformations), we will say ... that we are dealing with a discursive formation – thus avoiding words already overladen with conditions and consequences, and in any case inadequate to the task of designating such a dispersion, such as 'science, 'ideology', 'theory', or 'domain of objectivity. (Foucault [1969] 1994: 38)

Foucault, then, fashions the concept of discourse in order to be able to identify a series of statements linked not by content but by a rule of formation – 'The rules of formation are conditions of existence (but also of coexistence, maintenance, modification, and disappearance) in a given discursive division' (Foucault [1969] 1994: 38). A discourse, for Foucault, plays an integral role in the formation of a discipline, determining the kind of statements that can be made within it. But a discourse also determines a set of exclusionary procedures that delimit the objects under study. If a statement does not adhere to a given discursive paradigm, it risks being deemed illegitimate.

We could say that a discourse is the mechanism by which information is translated into knowledge (a working formulation that is only permissible if we accept that the information to be translated is never 'pure' or unmediated to begin with). It is this notion that I want to take forward, positioning popular knowledge as a discursive formation (though not a discipline) that is characterized by a collection of statements and texts produced in different (para)institutional contexts that give rise to ideological formations. As such, popular knowledge has its own rules of formation that determine how knowledge is produced within it. But popular knowledge is also that which has been excluded from other, more 'legitimate', discourses by practices embedded within rationalist institutions.

4 *Foucault's study of marginal texts and informal knowledges.* It is worth noting that, when studying the deep structures of knowledge during his archaeological phase, Foucault broke with the conventions of historical research to consider both formal and informal knowledges. Prompted by the concerns of this book, I might be tempted to think of this in terms of popular knowledge but Foucault was focused on producing a history of science that pays as much attention to the 'softer' sciences 'that concern living beings, languages, or economic facts' as to more 'rigorous' or 'noble' sciences like 'mathematics, cosmology, and physics' (Foucault [1966] 1992: ix). Yet his endeavour – to establish that even 'the practice of old beliefs, including not only genuine discoveries, but also the most naïve notions, [obey], at a given moment, the laws of a certain code of knowledge' (Foucault [1966] 1992: ix) – emphasizes the importance of understanding the structure of less formal knowledges and their relationship to formal knowledges. Through this process, the 'frontiers [between different types of knowledge] are redrawn and things usually far apart are brought closer, and vice versa' (Foucault [1966] 1992: x).

Equally, Foucault's focus on non-canonical texts sets a helpful precedent to studies such as mine (and resonates with the project of cultural studies in general). His texts take into account cultural and discursive phenomena that others saw as marginal, like documents concerning child masturbation, or paedophilia. As well as encouraging us on our travels into the under-analysed arena of popular knowledge (at least as a distinct area of study), this non-canonical focus alleviates some of the concern over working on knowledges that, in some cases, do not themselves yet have canonical texts as such.

5   Overall, I want to take forward *Foucault's way of thinking about the discursive conditions of production for and rules of constraint upon a knowledge-producing discourse*. His emphasis on how Enlightenment thinking codified and policed knowledge through discourses will be helpful for thinking about the anxiety popular knowledges can prompt and the familiar charges of irrationality that they receive.

The Sociology of Knowledge

From the sociology of knowledge I want to highlight the prevailing idea (one which we have already seen at work in Foucault) that knowledge is socially constructed and determined. As E. Doyle McCarthy recognizes, '*knowledge* is best conceived and studied *as culture*, and the various types of social knowledges communicate and signal social meanings – such as meanings about power and pleasure, beauty and death, goodness and danger' (1996: 1). In this cultural guise, knowledges can give rise to new behaviours and objects. The sociology of knowledge, then, considers the effect of society on knowledge and the social construction of knowledge – in other words, how society shapes knowledge *and* how knowledge shapes society (in terms of social reality). The usefulness of such an approach, of course, is to recognize all knowledges, both official (such as scientific knowledge) and unofficial (such as folklore) – as genres of socially (and geographically) situated knowledge.

Significantly, the sociology of knowledge has placed itself within the discursive field, recognizing the discipline as one knowledge among others. Doyle McCarthy writes:

the lasting value ... of the sociology of knowledge is its capacity to draw attention to itself as part of its own enquiry: to enable us to scrutinize the current "turn to culture", both in society and in social science; to grasp – with more than an ounce of critical detachment – the effects that social scientific ideas and methods have on contemporary life; to ask how knowledge of culture and its operations can operate as a form of domination, since it is a resource from which many peoples are excluded. (1996: 107)

So in this book I will invoke cultural studies and theory as knowledges and, therefore, as culture. But as the above quotation suggests, I need to recognize that these knowledges are of a different order to other cultural forms (even other socially situated knowledges). We cannot allow the idea that 'all knowledge is cultural' to blind us to the fact that some cultural forms are more specialist than others. Many of the concerns central to the sociology of knowledge, then, will also be important here. However, some sociological concerns – such as a consideration of which social groups are more susceptible to belief in some knowledges over others – will be sidelined, for reasons that I will explain below. The main difference will be one of methodology. Whereas the sociology of knowledge relies largely on ethnographic studies (whether positivist or interpretative), this book will be concerned primarily with 'textual' mediations of popular knowledge whether virtual, televisual, journalistic, or literary.

Anthropology

The sociology of knowledge has been concerned with broadly (applied) philosophical questions around the nature of knowledge (which can, but do not necessarily, address the object of study here – popular knowledge) but folklorists have concerned themselves with producing a record of every aspect of knowledge transmission in informal settings. Folklorists, therefore, have been interested in much of the same material that I am looking at in this book. The novelty of *Knowledge Goes Pop* is perhaps, then, not in the objects looked at but in the way of looking at them. Folklorists have produced accounts and analyses of all kinds of discursive formats such as jokes, urban legends, fairy tales, proverbs, blessings and curses, customs, lullabies, riddles, catchphrases, gestures, greetings, and superstitions. They have also extended their interests to extranarrative objects such as costumes, art and crafts, dance and music. But folklorists are also interested in how these elements form a whole way of life. Jan Harold Brunvard explains:

> Folklore manifests itself in many oral and verbal forms ('mentifects'), in kinesiological forms (customary behaviour, or 'sociofacts'), and in material forms ('artefacts'), but folklore itself is the whole traditional complex of thought, content, and process – which ultimately can never be recorded in its entirety; it lives only in its performance or communication, as people interact with one another. (1968: 9)

Traditional folklorists have been very concerned with what such elements of folklife can tell them about group identities. Ellen McHale writes:

> traditional forms of knowledge are learned informally within a one-to-one or small group exchange, through performance, or by example. In all cases, folklore and folklife are learned and perpetuated within the context of the

'group', for it is the shared experience which shapes and gives meaning to the exchange. (1994: 2.1)

Robert Baron and Nicholas Spitzer read folklore as that which takes place in private – 'shared by groups in informal settings' (1992: 1–2) – but which publicly express a collective identity. While there is by no means a consensus on what defines folklore, one of the reasons for examining such phenomena outside of this body of work, I think, lies in the desire to move away from the emphasis on group dynamics. What is interesting about popular knowledges, I want to suggest, is that they seem to transcend geographically located groupings with a self-replicating structure that defies an ethnography of one-to-one communication. There are folklorists who take on board contemporary culture and technology but, as a discipline, it is largely dominated by painstaking records of individual examples of folklore, the danger being that while the object is different every time, the conclusions can be surprisingly routine.[4]

Barre Toelken actually posits folklore as that which resists mass mediation: 'In spite of the combined forces of technology, science, television, religion, urbanization, and creeping literacy, we prefer our close personal associations as the basis for learning about life and transmitting important observations and expressions' (1979: 25). He configures techno-globalization as a force that threatens folklore, rather than rethinking folklore as able to incorporate the characteristics of globalized culture. He goes on to write, '[folklore's] primary characteristic is that its ingredients seem to come directly from dynamic inter-actions among human beings in communal-traditional performance contexts rather than through the rigid lines and fossilised structures of technical instruction or bureaucratised education, or through the relatively stable channels of the classical traditions' (Toelken 1979: 28–9). In this definition, Toelken opposes informal face-to-face communication to instruction that seems at a remove from these lived practices either because it is mediated or because it is organized into a formal body of knowledge as part of a wider idea of education.

Despite these reservations, the study of folklore serves as an important precedent for the current study. Veteran folklorist Richard M. Dorson (1968) describes folklore as the hidden submerged culture lying behind the shadow of official civilization. Brunvard writes, 'Folklore is the traditional, unofficial, noninstitutional part of culture' (1968: 8–9). These descriptions certainly point towards the relationship between 'official' and 'unofficial' knowledges that I want to observe, while perhaps underestimating the popular, often mass mediated or mainstream, nature of this 'unofficial' culture.

As with the sociology of knowledge, my concerns will depart from these anthropological accounts in methodological terms. While ethnographic work used to analyse local, community-based communications and teachings is invaluable in understanding and recording cultures, I want to move beyond what people say about their culture, or even beyond what we can deduce from what people *don't* say about their culture (through interpretative, psychoanalytic readings), to an approach which considers, via 'textual' manifestations, the conditions which enable us to say anything, to *know* anything, about our culture *in the first place*.

Pedagogy and Knowledge

Nowhere is the question of what should occupy position A in Figure 1 as hotly contested as it is with regards to education. The organization of knowledge in educational contexts (the kinds of knowledges that should be given precedence and the amount of time that alternative viewpoints should be given) has particularly been a concern for studies in pedagogy and policy making. On the conservative side, there is a concern that real knowledge has given way to a form of political correctness in schools (see Ravitch 2000) while on the other, more liberal side, concern is expressed over what counts as this 'real knowledge' in the first place (see Apple 2003). By no means exclusive to this body of work, questions abound concerning the politics of knowledge. As Michael W. Apple observes, these questions arise from the fact that, 'Out of the vast universe of knowledge, only some knowledge and ways of organizing it get declared to be legitimate or "official"' (2003: 7). As a telling example, we only need to think of the controversy in the UK and the US over teaching creationism (as opposed to evolution) in schools.[5]

In some ways, I am coming at the question of knowledge from a similar angle (though with ultimately different concerns). For example this book is also concerned with the mechanisms by which some knowledges are deemed 'legitimate' and others 'illegitimate'. I, too, will be looking at the arrogation of power with regards to knowledge production and endorsement. Work in education (particularly the sociology of curriculum) is concerned not only with a democratic ideal of education (how to empower via knowledge transmission) but the idea that power resides in the authority to dictate what knowledge is. In other words, it is all very well congratulating ourselves (in 'developed' states) on having education systems open to all, but it is also necessary to think about what kind of knowledge will be taught and what that means to the status of, and relationship to, knowledge *per se*. Hence, as Apple writes:

> official knowledge is the result of conflicts and compromises both within the state and between the state and civil society. This involves complex issues of political economy, of cultural politics, of the relationship between cultural legitimacy and state regulation, and of the ways in which and through which identifiable social movements and alliances form. (2003: 7–8)

In line with *Knowledge Goes Pop*, Apple recognizes that official knowledge should not be focused on to the detriment of popular knowledge:

To do so would be a very real error, since popular knowledge is crucial in the formation and legitimation both of identities and of what counts as "real" knowledge. Indeed, popular knowledge serves as the *constitutive outside* that causes other knowledge to be called legitimate. The ability of dominant groups and the state to say that something is real knowledge is contingent on something else being defined as merely popular. For this very reason, the popular itself is actually closely linked to the state in often unseen ways and hence cannot be ignored. (2003: 11)

Apple's observation regarding the relationship between 'official' and popular knowledges, along with his recommendation to look more closely at popular knowledge to understand more fully the cultural and political role of knowledge as a whole, will serve as useful prompts (and props) for *Knowledge Goes Pop*.

Cultural Studies of Knowledge

Raymond Williams' much-cited definition of culture as not only 'the arts and learning – the special processes of discovery and creative effort' but also 'a whole way of life – the common meanings' ([1958] 1997: 6) announces cultural studies as interested in everyday acts of cognition. (What kind of 'whole way of life' would be devoid of some form of knowing?) This is not to claim cultural studies as the only pioneer in the study of popular knowledge (I have already hinted at the long history of anthropological studies in folklore and at philosophical precursors such as *doxa*) but it is to recognize that cultural studies, without naming its object as such, has always involved itself in the nature of specialist and everyday knowledges and how we use them to produce, consume and interpret the culture around us. As with sociological perspectives, not only is knowledge a form of culture here, but culture itself is a form of knowledge: we could say that cultural objects mediate knowledge and confer knowledge upon us. As Tim Dant puts it, sociology and cultural studies have produced studies into 'the embodiment of knowledge in cultural products' (1991: 2). Such a concern might have only become explicit or apparent in more recent years. Evidence of this can be found in the inclusion of an entry for 'knowledge' in *New Keywords* (2005) edited by Tony Bennett, Lawrence Grossberg and Meaghan Morris: a re-writing of Raymond Williams' classic text in which he passes over 'K' without pause.

In early cultural studies coming out of a socialist tradition, a Marxist concern over false consciousness dominated the discussion. Subjects had, it would seem, an inaccurate picture of society; they adopted 'official' knowledge (or the popular, 'commonsense' knowledge – from position B in Figure 1 – which supports the 'official' knowledge) about their place in the world, naturalizing social inequality and the subjugation of the working class. But cultural studies has now shifted from the assumption that subjects harbour the 'wrong' kind of knowledge, towards a desire to locate practices which display the 'right' (at least in progressive terms) knowledge: towards, that is, knowledges displaying resistance to the dominant ideology. An interest in subcultures, for example, has given cultural studies the occasion to focus on oppositional forms of signification and knowledge.

This writing about alternative and subcultural practices and ways of knowing extends from the sociological work of the 'Chicago School', through to the cultural studies approach of Birmingham's Centre for Contemporary Cultural Studies, and beyond. Such literature has usefully placed non-'mainstream' social practices onto the agenda and theorized the relationship between such practices and the 'parent' culture as well as mass culture. The political meaning and, often, resistance to be found in the signified values and alternative consumption modes of subcultures have been a guiding theme in subcultural studies since the Birmingham School's collection, *Resistance Through Rituals* (Hall and Jefferson 1976). The dominant mode of analysis, subsequently problematized and challenged by later theorists, seemed to begin from the subculture and work backwards in order to find a socio-political explanation for its emergence.[6] In this way, subcultures were very much seen as symptomatic of a social ailment: racial inequality, say, or an emasculated, unemployed underclass.

Popular knowledges like conspiracy theory or alien abduction narratives might once have fit the definition of a subcultural knowledge. The emergence of a conspiracy 'scene' that I will detail in Chapter 2 supports this view. And yet, seeing conspiracy theory like this – concentrating on its fringe status – overlooks the central role conspiratorial fears have played in mainstream political life for centuries. This other manifestation complicates the idea of an 'alternative' subcultural concern. In addition, the increased proliferation and rise in popularity of even its 'fringe' manifestation calls for a more nuanced configuration of its relationship to other discourses. In thinking along a continuum of knowledge practices – so that gossip is investigated alongside conspiracy theory – the commodification of previously 'fringe' practices is not the dominant narrative here. Some of the knowledges I am interested in have always been popular. And yet the development of new communication technologies has perhaps intensified their predominance.

Recent subcultural studies have asked if the category 'subculture' should even be retained in today's commodified, commercialized, pick-and-mix culture (see Bennett and Kahn-Harris 2004). Such unease with that category prompts me to justify the use of my own – 'popular knowledge'. I have constructed this category 'popular knowledge' only in order to deconstruct the opposition often created between popular knowledge (even if it is not named as such) and more legitimated modes of knowing.

Just as recent work in subcultural or 'post-subcultural' studies has called for a different approach to be taken – one that pays attention to the myriad, complex ways in which subcultural identifications are experienced, produced and consumed – I would argue that the 'popular' of 'popular knowledge' requires a different set of questions to be asked from those posed by classic subcultural studies. That is to say, if the old questions are not even right for subcultures anymore, they are even less appropriate for popular knowledges (a category that shares some characteristics of the 'subcultural', but departs from that identification in important ways). This is why I will try to move beyond a tracing back of each knowledge's origins (while recognizing that such narratives are compelling), and beyond ascertaining the socio-political meaning of each instance of popular knowledge (or popular knowledge as a whole).

I could be accused of replicating the binary opposition set up by subcultural studies. The fringe and mainstream in this book gets replaced with the popular and official. However, I will try hard to show the instability of such binarisms, whether based on the idea of a romanticized 'fringe' or self-contained 'official'. The popular, after all, confers its own kind of legitimacy, its own (popular) cultural capital. Moving away from a romanticized notion of subcultures, other studies, like those of fan cultures, have acknowledged the possibility that subjects might in fact identify with mainstream, rather than marginal or oppositional, ideology and knowledge.[7] In addition, the emphasis in cultural studies on those knowledges produced by historically 'marginalized' or disenfranchised groups (whether through their race, gender, sexuality, ethnicity and so on) have produced valuable contributions to our understanding of the relationship between knowledge, identity, and nationhood. The study of cultural knowledges and knowledge cultures, therefore, has evolved through different phases, and has been punctuated by various interpretations of what those knowledges might mean politically.

In terms of work on specific popular knowledges, a few are of particular note. Andrew Ross' *Strange Weather* (1991) and Paul Heelas' *The New Age Movement* (1996) consider so-called 'new age' practices. Jörg R. Bergmann's *Discreet Indiscretions* (1987), Patricia Meyer Spacks' *Gossip* (1985), and part of Patricia Mellencamp's *High Anxiety* (1992) all approach the phenomenon of gossip. Rosemary J. Coombe's essay, 'Postmodernity and the Rumor' (1992) considers the challenges rumour can pose to brands; while Patricia Turner's extended study, *I Heard it through the Grapevine: Rumor in African-American Culture* (1993) considers the racial politics of informal modes of exchange and urban legends. Conspiracy theory has also received a fair amount of attention: see, for example, Peter Knight's *Conspiracy Culture* (2000), Mark Fenster's, *Conspiracy Theories* (1999), and Parish and Parker's edited collection, *The Age of Anxiety: Conspiracy Theory and the Human Sciences* (2001). Alien abduction narratives feature directly in Jodi Dean's *Aliens in America* (1998), and as part of a highly interesting study of the post-human in Neil Badmington's *Alien Chic* (2004). Yet these studies do not set out to draw comparisons between popular knowledges, as I aim to in this book. Despite its shortcomings, John Fiske's *Power Plays/ Power Works* (1993) is the closest cultural studies has come to a theory of how popular knowledges work.

Fiske primarily uses the term 'popular knowledge' in *Power Plays/Power Works* to delineate how fan cultures create knowledges and beliefs that deny the status of scientific rationalism as the only way of knowing. Fiske claims:

> Despite [its] monopolist ambitions [scientific rationalism] has to recognise, however reluctantly, that other knowledges exist and contradict it, so part of its strategy of control is to define the realities known by other knowledges as 'unreal' and therefore not worth knowing. (1993: 181)

The wide range of beliefs (such as superstition) and experiences (such as *déjà-vu* or even coincidence) that scientific rationalism cannot wholly account for, maintain a complex relation to it. According to Fiske's model, scientific rationalism must at once recognize and reject that which it cannot explain. Some phenomena, then, is expelled and left to take form in an alternative kind of knowing. Fiske is also keen to point out that popular knowledge cannot afford to ignore the official knowledge:

> A popular knowledge is, then, never essential or self-sufficient, but can exist only in relation to official knowledge. This relationship may range from one of accommodation or excorporation to one of as great a difference or distance as possible. (1993: 198)

Popular knowledges, in this way, ape more legitimated knowledges (mirroring their legitimating strategies, for example). Fiske describes scientific rationalism as 'uni-accentual', that is to say, 'it does not serve its interests by accommodating subordinate knowledges, but by repressing them' (1993: 182). According to Fiske, popular knowledges, on the other hand, are 'multi-accentual' in that 'they cannot escape the knowledge that attempts to repress and invalidate them: they can only exist in relationship to it and never exist in autonomous independence of it' (1993: 182). But I want to argue that popular knowledges are not only dependent upon the 'official' discourses that might seek to repress them in various ways, as Fiske claims, but that 'official' discourses are also 'reliant' upon popular knowledges.

As has been pointed out many times before, Fiske's attendant populism can present problems. Jim McGuigan accuses Fiske of focusing 'more or less exclusively on "popular readings", which are applauded with no evident reservations at all, never countenancing the possibility that a popular reading could be anything other than "progressive"' (McGuigan 1992: 72) Indeed, Fiske's insistence on the resistant role that popular knowledges can play in transforming the notion of passive consumers into active producers is probably over-optimistic, and ignores the more multi-faceted political axis on which knowledge operates (popular knowledges can be highly complicit with the dominant ideology as well as resistant). Having said that, Fiske's study does set an important precedent for this book in that it recognizes the way in which popular knowledges question paradigms of legitimacy and authority.

DANGER OVERHEAD: DEFINITIONS AT WORK

It becomes clear from the discussion above that it is impossible fully to analyse popular knowledge without issues arising that concern knowledge in general. In fact, in the sociology of knowledge, there is no special term to delineate what I am here calling popular knowledge. Rather, these knowledges are simply discussed as one form of socially situated knowledge among others. As Doyle McCarthy explains, knowledge in sociology means:

> knowledge-of-reality or whatever information and ideas inform what we hold to be real and true about our worlds and ourselves. Knowledges are those organized and perpetuated ways of thinking and acting that enable us to direct ourselves to objects in our world (persons, things, and events) and to see them *as* something. (1996: 22)

Obviously, the ways of knowing that I describe in this book enable us to manage and organize the material world – they construct our social reality. Knowledge is, then, as Doyle McCarthy writes, 'any and every set of ideas and acts accepted by one or another social group or society of people – ideas and acts pertaining to what they accept as real for them and for others' (1996: 22). Likewise for Dant, knowledge is *'the construal of relations between abstract entities that are taken to represent communication and that can be used by them both to understand their experience of the world and to guide their actions'* (author's italics) (1991: 5). In light of this levelling of the playing field (in which popular knowledge is just another socially situated knowledge), why would I want to suggest a distinct way of thinking about popular knowledges? Why would I insist on the specificity of popular knowledge? What is popular about popular knowledge? How does the 'popular' modify what sociologists have been saying about different forms of knowledge?

In one sense, there is nothing at odds with the formulation to be found in the sociology of knowledge and my term, popular knowledge. My usage of 'popular knowledge' does not deny that forms of knowledge are socially produced and contextualized. But in another sense, I want this term to indicate a resistance to a flattening out of all knowledges. I want it to point towards both the continuity with knowledge in general (why else use the term 'knowledge'?) and the discontinuities that set it apart and demand a particular mode of analysis that can raise questions about the status and authority of knowledge. When a notion of knowledge is extended to include popular knowledges (or whatever they are called in various disciplines), the idea of knowledge itself is more often than not left unchanged by the encounter. To be sure, thinking about all forms of knowledge, including scientific knowledge, as socially constructed has been a radical gesture in epistemological terms. But we would not want such relativism to underplay the singularity of particular kinds of knowledge and what they can tell us about the whole field of knowledge. Knowledge as a concept is forced to shift when previously external discourses make claims upon it. If the centre of knowledge shifts – if the way it is produced, consumed and legitimated changes – it is difficult to see popular knowledge as just one more form of knowledge, because knowledge itself will have altered in the process.

In the sociological understanding of knowledges, then, there is perhaps too little specificity. In some ways, the opposite problem is evident in Fiske's study, which risks making popular knowledge seem more subversive, more distinct, more singular than perhaps is justified. Fiske's concentration on the oppositional nature of his version of popular knowledge to scientific rationalism and 'the establishment', as Fiske calls it, belies the way in which popular knowledges borrow from more established discourses in the attempt to legitimate themselves. (Why else would gossips appeal to direct knowledge of the event being relayed and conspiracy theorists claim access to an anonymous but authoritative source?)

To get to a definition, I could think about what different popular knowledges have in common. Psychologically they may serve different functions. Formally, they may employ or display differing discursive traits. Politically, they might question or support dominant ideological modes. Nevertheless, they all offer understandings of the world not bounded by (although certainly in various kinds of relation with) 'official', legitimated knowledge. In addition, these popular knowledges are often produced outside of (and yet, as we shall see in later chapters, surreptitiously used within) the 'official' sites of knowledge production – the university, government, the law. They are popular, not only because many of them are pop*ulist* in nature, but also because they represent attractive ways of knowing that are open to a wide range of people (though this is of course dependent on access to media and socio-cultural engagement). These knowledges do not require formal training (indeed, we may enjoy popular knowledges precisely because we already feel well versed or 'trained' merely through exposure to particular cultural forms and texts) and form a common part of our popular cultural landscape and currency. They are ways of knowing that circulate via word of mouth, television, talk radio, the Internet, tabloids, magazines and so forth, rather than verified, peer-reviewed academic journals, books or more 'serious' or 'elitist' forms of cultural output. Such modes of exchange and proliferation are not incidental to these knowledges but play an integral role as they shape, organize, create, recreate, promote and deliver them.

As a provisional working definition – one informed by the many disciplinary interventions so far discussed – I want to put forward the following (some elements of which I have yet to qualify): popular knowledges are discursive forms of popular culture (and all that this term indicates about the complex relation between both folk and mass culture) that systematize and contextualize ideas about the world and specific events. They often require no specialist training, although participants become versed in discursive 'rules'. They retain an ambivalent relationship to more legitimated ways of knowing; and display both general and singular properties. More important than producing a working definition, however, and what I want to finish this section with is the need to stress that the issue of what popular knowledge is must remain open and undecidable (as must the question of what knowledge 'is'). A final definition will elude us, even at the end of this book, not least because our very encounter with popular knowledge will shift any ground from which we might re-*cognize* it.

SOMETHING DIFFÉRANT

I have deliberately avoided positing a Big Theory about popular knowledge. But believe me, there are plenty of them about. Francis Wheen, for example, broadly argues that the kinds of knowledges that I am discussing in this book arise out of a turn away from Enlightenment rationalism. He writes, 'By the end of the 20th century ... there were countless indications of a general retreat from reason – the search for millennial portents, the revival of interest in Nostradamus ... the Gaia craze, the appearance of horoscopes in even serious broadsheets, the flood of books about angels, fairies, Inca secrets, Egyptian rituals and secret Bible codes' (Wheen 2004: 12). As I have already mentioned in the Preface, this 'new irrationalism', as Wheen sees it, results from a feeling of disempowerment: it is 'an expression of despair by people who feel impotent to improve their lives and suspect that they are at the mercy of secretive, impersonal forces whether these be the Pentagon or invaders from Mars. Political leaders accept it as a safe outlet for dissent, fulfilling much the same function that Marx attributed to religion' (Wheen 2004: 12). Such is the force of this irrationalism that populist politicians – those who have a relative amount of power within the system – have begun to ape the public's obsession with irrationalism and the primacy of feeling and emotion. The politicians feel that they cannot afford to ignore the dominant communicative mode – they want to be a part of this collective experience – but in doing so, place at risk the primacy public figures are supposed to give to universal reason or conscience, over egoistic reason or self-love (Wheen 2004: 17).

And if you don't like the sound of that, you could read Fredric Jameson's work, which posits conspiracy narrative (and film in particular) as taking 'a wild stab at the heart of' the collective effort 'to figure out where we are and what landscapes and forces confront us in a late twentieth century whose abominations are heightened by their concealment and their bureaucratic impersonality' (Jameson 1992: 3). In a different essay, Jameson stresses that conspiracy 'is the poor person's cognitive mapping in the postmodern age' (1988: 356) induced by the insecurities and inequalities of late capitalism. Jameson thinks about conspiracy narratives as attempts to represent or map out the ever elusive social totality. Whereas for Wheen the turn to popular knowledges is indicative of a systematic turn away from rationality, for Jameson, it is a symptom of an overwhelmingly complex and subjugating landscape.

Both arguments persuade. Yet, the way in which they present popular knowledges as the result of an increased premium on feelings, or a symptom of postmodern confusion – and more widely as a symptom of disempowerment – is only part of the story. As will become a recurring argument in this book, symptomatic readings of this kind are guided by an idea or ideal of politics that itself often remains unexamined. Wheen and Jameson's analyses begin from a point that 'knows' what the political is. The political remains stable, while subjects either get distracted from politics by emotionally led irrationality (Wheen), or inadequately attempt to map the political landscape (Jameson). If popular knowledges are seen only in already decided political terms (and Big Theories, by virtue of their size, tend to grapple with big political issues), where the worth of the political intervention is pre-determined according to a political ideal, there is little room for thinking about our own relation to those knowledges and how this in turn might question the tropes of knowledge and politics.

More interesting, in my opinion, is the way in which popular knowledges exceed or complicate this (whether positive or negative) narrowly defined political interest in popular practices and texts. For popular knowledges can appear (to varying degrees in different contexts) *both* politically engaged *and* deeply ineffectual in the realm of democratic politics. The oscillation between the serious nature of popular knowledges and their more ironic and playful elements is important to any 'Theory' or account of popular knowledges. It makes it difficult to pronounce upon their import, role, or function in the world. They are constantly shifting.

I think the play between the serious and playful is partly a result of popular knowledges being a form of popular culture – something that has gone unrecognized in the sociological approach, for example. 'Knowledge' suggests the serious role popular knowledges play; the 'popular' points towards an appealing entertainment. Placed together, however, we should be reminded that such meanings are not mutually exclusive. We can play with knowledge; the popular can resonate seriously. Thinking about popular knowledge in this way means being concerned not only, as sociologists Peter Berger and Thomas Luckmann claim, 'with whatever passes for "knowledge" in a society, regardless of the ultimate validity or invalidity (by whatever criteria) of such "knowledge"' (1966: 3), but also keeping in mind (though not necessarily discussing in 'traditional' cultural studies ways) the mechanisms by, and circumstances in which such knowledges are produced and consumed. In each chapter I spend some time outlining the role of my examples as forms of popular culture. What is striking in each case is the way popular knowledges force us to reformulate (by now out-dated) framings of popular culture as *either* mass or folk culture. I propose that we have to start thinking about popular knowledge at both a local *and* global level; as both 'home-made' folk culture *and* mass-produced culture; and as both a pragmatic, social tool *and* an entertaining, pleasurable practice or product. It means keeping such binarisms in tension.

For example, the central position of celebrity gossip within the entertainment industry with a burgeoning market in celebrity magazines such as *Heat, Hello!* and *OK*, and the commodification of conspiracy theory as a central trope within mainstream television and film, both point towards the inadequacy of discussing popular knowledge as only a form of latter day home-made folk culture. Rather than characterizing the mass media as an industry that appropriates and exploits popular knowledge, the impossibility of locating the origin of a popular knowledge (where, for example, do urban legends come from?) means that it is always already separated from any author it might be thought to 'belong' to. The romantic characterization of an empowering, localized folk culture is therefore radically upset. Equally, however, the commodification of popular knowledge and the effect of exporting it to new contexts should not be considered as a simple act of cultural imperialism or appropriation, but as a process of proliferation often secured by the self-replicating structure of popular knowledge itself. Gossips, for example, are never sated. The revelation of secrets (true or untrue) does not satisfy – the desire to reveal or receive simply gets deferred elsewhere, searching for new material in an endless exchange of signifiers parading as signifieds.

In short, popular knowledge problematizes the terms by which popular culture has been discussed and the concept of politics such discussion often implicitly relies upon. The emphasis in much cultural studies to read popular culture as a site of ideological contestation or identity negotiation – makes a number of assumptions about the politics of popular culture, assumptions that I think are questioned by popular knowledge in various ways. Not least because popular knowledge prompts us to self-reflexively consider the conditions of our own knowledge-producing discourse of cultural studies and its anxieties (including, and this will be important for what follows, the anxiety caused by any apparent theory/praxis divide).

To explain what I mean by this, I want to turn to a certain 'resistance' in some quarters to thinking through the conditions and assumptions of one's own discipline that Wendy Brown identifies in her provocative chapter, 'Moralism as Anti-politics', from *Politics Out of History* (2001). Brown describes how both leftists and liberals have not been able to give up the figures of the sovereign subject and neutral state: 'The consequences of living these attachments as ungrievable losses – ungrievable because they are not fully avowed as attach-ments and hence are unable to be claimed as losses – is theoretical as well as political impotence and rage, which is often expressed as a reproachful political moralism' (Brown 2001: 21). One of the culprits often cited by left moralists, she claims, is among other things, post-structuralist theory – a theory that, I will go on to argue, allows us to ask the questions that popular knowledges prompt. Post-structuralist theory is lambasted for its 'failure' to tell the left what to value and what to fight for (Brown 2001: 29). In fact, she claims, the identity of the moralist is 'staked against intellectual questioning that might dismantle the foundations of its own premises' (Brown 2001: 30). Thus, seemingly radical politics including multiculturalism 'often transmogrify into their opposite, into brittle, defensive, and finally conservative institutions and practices' (Brown 2001: 30–1). Which should in no way be mistaken for reactionary, anti-political correctness. Her point is much more challenging.

To illustrate her argument, Brown recounts the hostility of her colleagues to a radical critique of institutionalized women's studies. She found her colleagues to be entirely resistant to a self-reflexivity that fought against the now naturalized boundaries of their discipline and newly essentialized identities that they had previously fought against, like 'woman'. Everything that had been such a mark of contestation for women's studies in the 'beginning' has now solidified into its conservative opposite. This, for Brown, is because left academics, instead of facing the disorientation and loss experienced when trying to analyse the sources of social injustice, 'posture as if we were still fighting the big and good fight in our clamor over words and names' (Brown 2001: 36). In other words, the fight is fought over the wrong issues: the fight is kept alive, but the goal is long since obscured. Here, moralizing takes the place of mourning or critique.

A similar logic, I want to suggest, is at work in some strands of cultural studies. Whether we see it in identity and cultural politics as Brown does, or in the recurrent calls to the serious business of 'real' politics – through a (re)turn to various configurations of political economy approaches, or demands for urgent action. The political imperative prompted by post-September 11 domestic and foreign policy in the UK and US (including infringements of civil liberties, increasingly hostile attitudes towards immigration and the waging of legally unsanctioned war) means that self-reflexive theorizing is currently being given a short shrift by many factions within cultural studies and beyond. Bruno Latour asks in *Critical Inquiry*, 'Is it really the task of the humanities to add deconstruction to destructions?' (2004: 225). At the 2004 Crossroads in Cultural Studies Conference in Urbana-Champaign, one delegate literally shouted at the audience that theory was no longer applicable in this time of war. And while this is understandable and mostly forgivable (we all feel an *urgency*, a *crisis* even), a protection of left-wing ideals and ideas as if they were the same as those pre-September 11, or pre-Bush, or pre-New Labour, results in unthinking moralism of the kind Brown describes.

In this moment, we become frustrated with questions of a meta-nature, we become anti-intellectual, anti-speculative and anti-theoretical. There is a strong temptation, in this climate, to dismiss speculation as procrastination. I want to suggest that this taking of the 'moral high ground' is not the only position to adopt in response to the current conjuncture. It may not be the most productive, nor even, and I will explain what I mean by this in a moment, the most *political*.

If cultural studies is to be up to the job of understanding popular knowledges, it has to consider the consequences of moralism displacing theory. Some theory, what I will later come to think of as 'radical speculation', offers a more, not less, responsible position from which to 'do' cultural studies.

So why isn't moralism as political as it might feel? Brown writes:

> If the contemporary Left often clings to the formations and formulations of another epoch, one in which the notions of unified movements, social totalities, and class-based politics were viable categories of political and theoretical analysis, this means that it literally renders itself a conservative force in history – one that not only misreads the present but instils traditionalism in the very heart of its praxis, in the place where commitment to risk and upheaval belongs. (2000: 26)

Moralism is nostalgia: it performs a politics appropriate to a different age. This does not mean that left politics are defunct but it does mean that we need to be constantly vigilant about stagnation and obsolescence. It means that we cannot take our 'politicalness' for granted. It is not always clear in this context what 'being political' means. If we say that a 'political' approach is supposed to ground one's analysis in a materialist concern with history, we could question the 'political-ness' of an approach that fails to closely examine the material, historical conditions of politics *today*. Politics, in this revised sense, is a commitment to re-examining the context, and if that context demands a reconfiguration of 'the political', then that is the most 'political' thing to do. Brown points out that traditionalism pre-empts any possibility of risk, and it is the risk of admitting our closeness to popular knowledge that I want to think through in this book. For it is risk – a speculative gesture that cannot guarantee a return and thus resists a neo-liberal discourse of utility – that might prove more 'political'.

How has this turn towards political and cultural economy come about in cultural studies? In recent years, there has been a move nearer to questions of the economy as a way to better understand the political, and indeed cultural, moment. Whereas once the expressive texts of popular culture seemed to offer sites of contestation and struggle, today that cultural struggle is found in more explicitly political and economic spheres. And so, cultural studies practitioners like Lawrence Grossberg are no longer looking towards popular culture – towards rock music, television, Hollywood film, dance culture and so on – for the agent of change because it 'does not appear to be playing the same central role. It is not where change is being organized and experienced, and it is certainly not where resistance is being viably organized' (Grossberg 2004). Culture itself is going through a major shift, it 'is rearticulated and relocated, in which the "center" of culture itself – its work as it were – has moved'. This cultural shift, he proposes, means that 'people are experiencing politics and economics as the primary field of change, and as the primary experience of change itself.' While Grossberg is careful to point out that these two realms, the cultural and the politico-economic are not distinct entities (the latter is articulated to the former, he writes), he does think that cultural studies should turn its attention to political economy, albeit a political economy connected to culture in intricate ways.

This move away from the culture of the popular to that of politics and economics has been accompanied by a wider shift in cultural studies generally towards sociology and political economy and what Paul du Gay and others have called 'cultural economy' (see Amin and Thrift 2004; Du Gay and Pryke 2002; Merck 2004; Hesmondhalgh 2002) as an attempt to relocate politics in the new modernity. This increasing socio-economic drive is characterized by a move away from 'Theory' in general and so-called 'post-structuralist' theories like deconstruction in particular in a mistaken belief that they are concerned with textuality as opposed to the lived material culture of politics. The speculative workings of theory are often seen as an indefensible luxury in the current conjuncture. The apparent attention to textuality misses the action.

If deconstruction needed 'defending', I would start by pointing out that it is in no way interested simply in 'textuality' as opposed to 'material reality', in the way detractors accuse. In fact, deconstruction allows for a more productive way of understanding this opposition, because it doesn't take for granted or leave unquestioned oppositions like text versus materiality, fiction versus reality, culture versus economics, theory versus politics. That is to say, such ideas of doing 'real practical politics' are not outside theory; they are just poor theory because the theoretical dimension – the fact that 'practical politics' is always already in some sense made possible by theories of the political – is left unacknowledged and so un-addressed. Such a defence, however, might lead me into problems. I could myself be accused of opposing one set of ideas and approaches (deconstruction, post-structuralism, theory) to another (sociology, politics, ethnography) in a way I am accusing others of doing with regards to oppositions like textuality versus materiality. This would replicate the closure(s) and corners of moralism that I see some strands of cultural studies facing.

Thus, a turn simply to theory would not have the politically and disciplinary disruptive effect I think is needed here. To have some chance of success in this respect I want to explore the possibilities of athetic speculation, the chance of moving beyond the *praxis* versus theory divide without positing just another theory (which would fall down on the side of theory and fail to question the 'versus'), or equally without putting forth just another call for action. I want to look at popular knowledges in order to interrupt this process. For we can see popular knowledges at the heart of both important contemporary political events and the academy also.

Through attention to popular knowledges, I hope to explore forms of questioning that are intellectually, institutionally and politically challenging. The point of such work is to keep the question of knowledge, and therefore of politics – of what it is, of what it can do, and all of its associated questions about power, authority, legitimacy, responsibility, and representation – open. This means that the question of what the politics of cultural studies is will also remain open, offering an alternative to the closure(s) and corners of moralism. For popular knowledges prompt self-reflexive questions about what legitimates cultural analysis or interpretation. They make it difficult, I argue, for us to assume what the political is and to take for granted the solidity of our own position from which we might make judgements or analyses (in other words, the solidity of the position from which we produce *knowledge*).

I want to look at popular knowledges, rather than say concentrating on theory, then, because of the former's explicitly uncertain, unstable status. Theory, while lambasted by some, would still perhaps fit into the category of 'legitimate' discourse, and, as I have already pointed out, championing theory could lead us into as many closures as moralism.[8] I need something far from moralism if I am going to disrupt, pause, question. And while in terms of content, popular knowledges can be moralism *par excellence* – gossip and conspiracy theory, after all, often contain expressions of moral outrage – in terms of form, as will become clear throughout this book, it disrupts the kind of political moralism Brown has described through an inherent undecidability.

It is with similar concerns to my own that Gary Hall writes:

It is noticeable that whereas so-called 'legitimate' discourses and forms of knowledge, those that either fall within or can at least be ascribed to recognized disciplines – literary studies, sociology, social policy, politics, economics, philosophy, history, communication and media studies, etc. – have been privileged and included in cultural studies' interdisciplinary canon, those 'less legitimate' discourses and forms of knowledge – hypnosis, for example – that have not been encapsulated by the 'established' disciplines have tended to be excluded or ignored. (2002: 15)

I would place popular knowledges like conspiracy and gossip alongside Hall's example of hypnosis as a form of knowledge that has been excluded from the cultural studies canon (not as objects, maybe, but certainly as forms of knowledge that already work 'within' cultural studies). Hall calls for us to open a space for thinking about 'what Derrida at one point calls "less visible, less direct, more paradoxical, more perverse" discourses – discourses that cultural studies can begin to appreciate only if it is prepared to radically rethink its identity' (Hall 2002: 15, quoting Derrida 1992a: 198). He chooses new media technologies as one of these discourses, but my example of popular knowledges also works here and requires the radical rethink he has identified.

Of course a question needs to be answered here. Why would I want to bring cultural studies and popular knowledges closer together at all? Well, for a start, although this may at first glance appear a circuitous route to answer the question, it's surprising how often the problems of cultural studies and cultural critique are articulated in relation to popular knowledges. For example, in his essay 'Why has critique run out of steam?' Bruno Latour airs his concerns regarding the state of critique through the terms of conspiracy theory:

> what's the real difference between conspiracists and a popularized, that is a teachable, version of social critique inspired for instance by a too-quick reading of, let's say, a sociologist as eminent as Pierre Bourdieu ... In both cases, you have to learn to become suspicious of everything people say because 'of course we all know' that they live in the thralls of a complete illusion [as to] their real motives. Then, after disbelief has struck and an explanation is requested for what is 'really' going on, in both cases again, it is the same appeal to powerful agents hidden in the dark acting always consistently, continuously, relentlessly. Of course, we, in the academy, like to use more elevated causes – society, discourse, knowledge-slash-power, fields of forces, empires, capitalism – while conspiracists like to portray a miserable bunch of greedy people with dark intents, but I find something troublingly similar in the structure of the explanation ... Of course conspiracy theories are an absurd deformation of our own arguments, but, like weapons smuggled through a fuzzy border to the wrong party, these are our weapons nonetheless. In spite of all the deformations, it is easy to recognize, still burnt in the steel, our trade mark: MADE IN CRITICALLAND. (2004: 229–30)

Here, conspiracy theory is positioned as a parodic repetition of cultural critique. In Latour's scenario we experience it like the uncanny: it is both familiar and unfamiliar, it returns to us as simultaneously ours and not ours, it's presence disturbs because it delivers, as Nick Royle puts it, 'homeliness uprooted' (2003: 1). But rather than use the analogy to discredit critique, we should use this uncanny encounter with our own 'weapons' to consider the 'fuzzy border' that separates them. Such fuzziness might suggest, not that those weapons are flawed in some way; instead, the possibility that popularized, 'teachable' versions of critique can give rise to popular knowledges like conspiracy thinking merely puts their close relationship on display – a relationship that consequently clearly needs to be thought through. Latour worries that critique has gone too far; that, to put it in the language I will be using in relation to gossip and theory later, our speculations have produced a return that we did not anticipate. Now, it may well be that theory's tools have been taken up by the right and used against us (Latour gives the example of US Republicans emphasizing the scientific instability of global warming to excuse their damaging environmental policies), but if we respond to this by reiterating the difference, by reinforcing the border between 'legitimate' and 'illegitimate' critique, we will have lost what is potentially subversive, radical, or 'political' about this relationship.

NO BUSINESS LIKE KNOW BUSINESS

In this book, I turn to thinkers like Jacques Derrida and Jean-François Lyotard because they provide a rigorous means of analysing how discourses and forms of knowledge are marginalized by dominant forces in a way that exposes the self-authorizing structure of all narratives and knowledges. Rather than accept and propagate rules and criteria for distinguishing between knowledge and gossip, or 'real' politics and theory, Derrida's work looks towards *a priori* conditions that precede such locally derived and enforced distinctions. Rather than being judgmental itself, deconstruction seems to allow us to focus on, as Derrida writes, 'judging what permits judgment, of what judgment itself authorizes' (2002: 231). This is why deconstruction will accompany me in a discussion of what it is about knowledge *per se* that makes popular knowledges possible. This, in turn, will enable me to think through the question of cultural analysis – of how we should approach culture.

Although I call upon post-structuralism more than existing work in cultural studies to help me read popular knowledges, this book is nevertheless also intended to encapsulate the spirit of cultural studies. I mean this not in the sense of sitting easily within a cultural studies oeuvre or recognized methodology but in the way Gary Hall describes it: that the most cultural studies thing to do is to question the decision of what both politics and cultural studies are (2002: 6). I don't want to be made to 'do away' with cultural studies just because my questions are slightly different from those that are usually posed; rather, I want to find out what these questions mean for popular knowledges and cultural studies both. In its openness to cultural phenomena and willingness to challenge the dominance of particular knowledges, cultural studies is exactly the 'place' for the current study to live (even if my landlord might grumble a little about the mess and noise). Crucially, I want to ask not only what cultural studies can tell us about popular knowledges but what popular knowledges can tell us about cultural studies. I have therefore set out to show

- why popular knowledge is important to look at in the twenty-first century;
- why cultural studies is well-placed to address this phenomena; and
- that what is known as 'Theory' has an important role to play in cultural studies' analyses of not only popular knowledges, but all cultural practices, products and artefacts.

The self-reflexive element of my analysis raises some important issues for us. Self-reflexivity might always appear as an appeal to 'legitimacy' – and risks replicating a strategy I will be challenging in the chapters that follow. However, by placing ourselves in the field of knowledge – thinking about the status of cultural studies, for example, as a form of knowledge – the hope, of course, is that we will have learned something *from* popular knowledges rather than just *about* popular knowledges.

Self-reflexivity, at least the kind that goes beyond situating oneself in the field to think about the conditions of possibility of that field, is a way of making one's project more robust, more situated and more interesting, but not necessarily more *legitimate*. When I read work that employs self-reflexivity and considers the conditions of possibility of their own project, it might make it more appealing to me, and yes, it might mean that I take more note of it than a study that fails to address these questions. But what is more 'legitimate' for me (if we insist on using this term) is part of a strategy to expose and question the arrogation of power rather than perpetuate it.[9]

I therefore want to defend self-reflexivity as more than box-ticking on our way to producing a 'legitimate' project. I want to stress the very real dangers of not being self-reflexive, particularly when dealing with the subject of this book – knowledge.

What would it mean, for example, if I were to talk about popular knowledge without thinking about its relationship and implications for my own field of knowledge – cultural studies and theory? It would mean, I think, underestimating not only the people who turn to popular knowledges, falling foul of accusations of false consciousness and the like, but also, as I will argue, the conditioning role that popular knowledges play in more legitimated knowledges. If I ignore the relationship between my own knowledge and the ones I am looking at here, I will not have understood either fully. So it is not a question of legitimating the project *through* self-reflexivity – not least because attention to the content of my argument will redefine the role and possibility of legitimacy itself. There is no contradiction here. The self-reflexivity employed in this book (and I can't vouch for *all* uses of self-reflexivity) can only seem like an appeal to legitimacy if the way in which that self-reflexivity forces us to rethink legitimacy has not been heeded.[10]

Besides, the criteria by which academic projects are deemed 'legitimate' or not are far from stable. Enough expressions of frustration with theoretical 'navel gazing' instead of 'real' political action have been aired for me to believe that self-reflexivity could also be the opposite of a legitimating strategy for many within cultural studies and other disciplines. If legitimacy is that which is lawful, right or proper, self-reflexivity has an uncertain, highly context-specific relationship with those signifiers (as do theory and speculation, for that matter). It is this somewhat relative, or at least, locally produced status, that has led me to prefer the terms 'legitimated' and 'legitimized' at various junctures in this book, or else to use quotation marks to suggest the same effect: reminding us that institutions or discourses *confer* legitimacy, that legitimacy is reproduced and ratified culturally, and that it is in process, something that is never fixed or finished, but which constantly has to be constructed and produced.

Cultural studies, as an interdisciplinary discourse that often finds itself marginalized by more 'legitimated', 'privileged', or 'traditional' discourses, is well placed to raise the question of legitimacy. It can only do this, however, if it is prepared to put at risk any investment it has in the continuing notion of the legitimate. This means, not only risking any hard-won legitimacy or institutionalization within the academy, but also opening up the notion of politics that underlies the project to investigation. Above all, it means, recognizing its own use of legitimating strategies (the appeal to 'real' political action, say), and the complex relationship between modes of knowing. Such work may involve admitting that knowledge does not enable us to *know* very much at all. We may, that is, be so concerned with legitimating one project or another via the status of 'knowledge', that we fail to see what exclusions occur for that status to be attained. Defenders of knowledge might try to exclude non-knowledge, but cannot: I will show throughout this book that they have always already failed in the endeavour to maintain purity in this respect.

In the following chapters, responding to conspiracy theory and gossip in turn, I want to both acknowledge the singularity of the popular knowledge under study, and discuss each knowledge in relation to not only other popular knowledges and knowledge in general, but cultural studies in particular.[11] In considering this relation to cultural studies, it will become apparent that I am using the terms 'conspiracy theory', 'gossip' and even 'popular knowledge' strategically. That is, they become avatars for the undecidability of knowledge, for the instability of knowledge, for the alterity that resides 'within' knowledge. They are ways of thinking through the excess that knowledge cannot contain but such strategic naming can never be sealed off from this process. We cannot, that is, fully *know* these popular knowledges: something will escape them, exceed their own logic and our cognitive apparatus. That is what keeps analysis and knowing open.

CHAPTER 2

Just Because You're Paranoid, Doesn't Mean They're Not Out to Get You

I closed the last chapter by claiming that I intend to acknowledge the singularity of popular knowledges. In this chapter I want to look at conspiracy theory as a particularly interesting example of popular knowledge. To do this adequately, I will examine conspiracy theory in several stages. Initially, I want to look at the contemporary conspiracy scene and its recent history. I will then address the commodification of a particular 'pop cultural' manifestation of conspiracy theory and the level of investment it invites. This contextualization will give way to two case studies of events that prompted many conspiracy theories – the death of Diana, Princess of Wales, and the events that took place on the 11 September 2001 in New York and Washington (commonly referred to as simply 'September 11'). I want to consider the press's response to the conspiracy theories firstly in order to find out how the idea of the legitimate and illegitimate is played out in the public realm; secondly, to see how popular knowledges produce and negotiate the stories that nations tell about themselves; and thirdly, to detect a shift in the place of conspiracy theory in the post-September 11 cultural climate.

YOU CAN RUN, BUT YOU CAN'T HIDE: CONSPIRACY'S CONTEXTS

As popular knowledges go, conspiracy theory is certainly a resilient example. Fears of conspiratorial events have arisen with surprising regularity. Today, it is hard to picture a contemporary scene, particularly in American and 'Americanized' contexts, in which conspiracy theories (whether they prove true or false) do not feature. This is certainly true in post-September 11 America in which paranoia has become a political tool for George W. Bush and a mode of (at least symbolic resistance) for those who oppose him. Events on September 11 and since have provided more than enough grist to the conspiracy mill, ensuring the continued presence of conspiracy theories from every faction imaginable: from the Middle East concerning the 'West'; from Bush concerning al-Qaeda, bin Laden, Saddam

Hussein and 'terrorists' in general; and from global citizens sceptical about the Bush government's role in and reaction to September 11. Jodi Dean thinks that the ubiquitous nature of conspiracy theory is because its two central ideas – 'that things are not what they seem and everything is connected' – are also 'the primary components of how we think about and experience the information age' (2002: 48). Peter Knight echoes this, but thinks that the links are much wider: 'Everything Is Connected could function as the operating principle not just for conspiracy theory, but also for epidemiology, ecology, risk theory, systems theory, complexity theory, theories of globalization, boosterism for the Internet, and even poststructuralist literary theories about intertextuality' (2000: 205).

Though the high 'pop cultural' moments of conspiracy (exemplified by 1970s films such as Alan J. Pakula's *All the President's Men* (1976) and *The Parallax View* (1974)) and conspiracy theory (particularly television shows such as *The X-Files* (1993–2002) and 'Dark Skies' (1996–7) in the 1990s) might have waned (at least in terms of fictional representations), it is clear that conspiracy theories are now part of our collective response to local and global events.[1] *The X-Files*, and its imitators, may have stopped running – we may have stopped watching conspiracy being plotted every week – but conspiracy theory still has currency. In fact, it is *more* available as a knowledge having been through a period of intense exposure and a process of commodification (about which I will say more below). Conspiracy theory's ways of knowing, if Dean is right, are supported by our encounters with information flows. This technological reinforcement of an alternative paradigm of knowing presents new challenges for how we think about knowledge, and how we think about our own investments in knowledge.

Because of the popularity of conspiracy theory, we more than likely already have a sense of what it is. Nevertheless, before I venture further, I want to provide a working definition. In its simplest terms, conspiracy theory refers to a narrative that has been constructed in an attempt to explain an event or series of events to be the result of a group of people working in secret to a nefarious end. Though we often associate the signifier 'conspiracy theory' with apparently 'crazy' Internet rants, it is important to keep in mind the truism, 'Just because you're paranoid, doesn't mean they're not after you.' In other words, conspiracies *do* happen – sometimes the theories prove correct. This relationship between conspiracy theory and, say, investigative journalism – between conspiracy theory and theories of conspiracies – must be thought together, for any distinction I might set up at this point will later prove unsustainable. But in keeping with the wider concern with popular knowledges in general in this book, I also want to position conspiracy theory as a knowledge-producing discourse – characterized by a collection of statements and texts shaped within and by different (para)institutional contexts which promote a particular knowledge about the world.

Conspiratorial acts and theories about them have, as I've already said, often been a part (overtly or covertly) of many societies. So while I will limit myself to a contemporaneous configuration of conspiracy theory I want to also acknowledge the arbitrary nature of this choice. I should also make it clear at the outset that it is impossible to provide a definitive account of conspiracy theory's development.

Indeed, writing an account of conspiracy theory is fraught with problems. (These problems are worth meditating on because they point us towards what is unsettling and distinct about many popular knowledges, particularly when we try to chart them in the same way as more legitimated, established knowledges.) Ironically, conspiracy theory is itself a practice based upon the distrust of official histories even if it does not question the basic linear premise of historical narratives. A methodological problem arises from a parallel irony: that many of the 'underground' zines and publishers are sceptical of the usual outlets for distribution. For example, one conspiracy zine, *Steamshovel Press*, makes a virtue out of the fact that it is hard to obtain (its website reassures its prospective readers that it is 'not available in bookstores where the conspiracy prevails').[2] And the slogan for the website, *Conspiracy Planet*, reads 'Your antidote to media cartel propaganda'.[3] This resistant strand to mainstreaming makes any plotting of a conspiracy milieu a difficult endeavour. But there are other problems with such an undertaking. First, any claim of an origin can be usurped by previous examples because the boundaries of where this history begins are never secure.[4] Second, the many influences that fed into what can contemporarily be thought of as conspiracy theory – such as cyberpunk, hacking, UFOlogy and the legacy of the counter-culture,[5] as well as reactionary, survivalist Militia rhetoric – also problematize a genealogical endeavour because of the taxonomic challenges such disparate threads pose. While plotting a subcultural 'history' of conspiracy theory would be bound to leave important gaps, I will, however, aim to present a series of cultural markers that will help to identify the accumulative character of a subcultural concern, stance, or practice, and later, the emergence of a distinct but disparate commercial conspiracy industry. It is, of course, important to note that these two strands are not in any way exclusive realms, but are interrelated in complex ways.

ZINE AND NOT HEARD

In the late 1980s and early 1990s, the production of zines[6] – small-scale publications devoted to esoteric topics and counter-hegemonic sentiments – were facilitated by technological developments that made personal computers, laser printers, and desktop publishing software more readily available.[7] While zines are a particular form of print media, we should note, as Mark Fenster does, that 'the history of the distribution of conspiracy theory in America through broadsides, pamphlets, periodicals, [and] books ... stretches back to the earliest years of the United States' (1999: 183). Fenster posits the publications by the anticommunist,

McCarthyite John Birch Society and the left-wing publication, *The Realist*, run
by Paul Krassner, as important influences on the conspiracy community. Kenn
Thomas, editor of *Steamshovel Press*, one of the first conspiracy theory zines,
cites other, counter-cultural publications as the precursor to his own:

> *Steamshovel* began in 1988 as a small book review newsletter. In 1992 it
> became a news-stand magazine. Previous to '88 I had been a consumer of
> conspiracy literature and sometime contributor/correspondent with pub-
> lishers like Jim Keith, who did the old zine *Dharma Combat*, and Bob
> Banner's old journal, *Critique*. I turned *Steamshovel* into a conspiracy
> magazine after Mae Brussell (mother of all conspiracy 'theorists') died and
> Banner joined a self-help cult and renamed his zine *Sacred Fire* and stopped
> doing conspiracy writing. It seemed important to keep the whole conspiracy
> research movement together.[8]

Al Hidell of *Paranoia*, established slightly later in 1993, describes his influences
as being those of established conspiracy researchers John Judge[9] and, like Kenn
Thomas, Mae Brussell,[10] as well as established conspiracy theory networks:

> Our influences were researchers like John Judge, who in turn had been
> influenced by Mae Brussell, a short-lived conspiracy publication by Larry Flynt
> (of the porn magazine *Hustler*), an organization known as a-Albionic,[11] and an
> organization known as Prevailing Winds.[12] Also, we had our own conspiracy
> discussion group, the Providence Conspiracy League.[13]

In a similar vein, publisher Ron Bonds provides background information to
account for the success of his specialist press, IllumiNet, explaining the move
from bulletin board to publishing:

> IllumiNet was originally a computer BBS system (computer bulletin board)
> started in approximately 1982. I wanted to provide an on-line source for
> Conspiracy information. It featured message bases on several subject areas:
> Conspiracy; Occultism; UFO's (of course!); Paranormal phenom [sic] ... etc.
> We were the first to offer conspiracy discussions, files and information of
> this type online in the US and I believe in the world. We decided to begin
> publishing so that we could reach a wider audience. My relationship with
> Jim Keith[14] and John Keel stimulated the process and we have experienced a
> decent amount of success since.[15]

Crucially, Bonds, writing at the turn of the millennium goes on to claim that
'conspiracy theory came into its own in the last six years or so', positing 1993/94
as a turning point in conspiracy theory's appeal. He also claims that IllumiNet was
'perfectly positioned to take advantage of the new-found interest'. He appears to
acknowledge the misleading or problematical nature of classifications based on

ideas of marginal interests – how specialist publishing, that is, can still be highly profitable – when he writes, 'we have always been a "small" publisher,' adding, 'but that's all relative today.' Al Hidell provides his own view on why 1993 was ripe for the publication of *Paranoia*. He claims that not only did the energized zine and publishing scene provide a cultural and economic context, but that 1993 was the 30th anniversary of the assassination of Kennedy, renewing interest in this area. He also cites the Waco siege as coinciding with *Paranoia*'s first issue, generating conspiracy theories in the public sphere.

Conspiracy theory is still disseminated through 'alternative' media: small-scale zines are produced and distributed via traditional postal networks and news-stand outlets but this cottage industry production also includes the creation of websites and maintenance of discussion boards on the Internet (see Duncombe (1997: 197) on the emergence of electronic zines or Fenster (1999: 185–8) discussing conspiracy newsgroups in relation to a conspiracy community). This enables even ideas expressed through small-scale production (with low overheads) to be widely disseminated, albeit in limited circles (access to a computer being an obvious prerequisite in the example of the Internet conspiracy sites). Indeed, conspiracy theory commentator Jonathan Vankin suggests that, 'one effect of the Internet boom has been the dismantling of the conspiracy-theory star system... Now everyone with a modem's an information conduit' (1996: xvii). As well as providing the means for investigators in the style of Mae Brussell and John Judge, the Internet has increased knowledge of and aided subscription to magazines such as *Paranoia, Steamshovel Press, The Skeptical Inquirer* and the Australian *Nexus* and made books from specialist presses such as IllumiNet, Feral House and Prometheus Books more widely available. But it would be a mistake to consider this 'alternatively' mediated conspiracy theory as entirely in opposition to its mainstream counterpart. Many fanzines of Fox's *The X-Files*, for example, have been produced beyond the control of the Network. A phenomenally successful and prolific strand of this includes 'slash' fiction – fan erotica – which flourishes on the Internet. Additionally, commercial products often generate an Internet interest in conspiracy theory. Moreover, the mainstreaming of conspiracy theory has undoubtedly increased interest in small publications, talk radio and independent bookshops.

CONSPIRACY A GO-GO

In his commentary on the commercialization of conspiracy theory, Al Hidell considers Richard Linklater's *Slacker* (1991),[16] Oliver Stone's *JFK*, and *The X-Files* as major factors in bringing conspiracy theory to the attention of the wider public. This mainstream guise inspired other forays into conspiracy TV and film later in the 1990s such as the short-lived television series *Dark Skies* and *Roswell High* (1999–2002), the film *Roswell* (Kagan 1994), and the bigger budget *Men in*

Black (Sonnenfeld 1997) and *Enemy of the State* (Scott 1998).[17] At the same time when cultural products like *The X-Files* were widening knowledge of a conspiracy theory discourse, numerous business ventures capitalized on this interest, making a loosely identifiable conspiracy industry more prominent. Displaying a timely marketing move, a mainstream summer of 1997 Hollywood blockbuster, starring Mel Gibson and Julia Roberts, appropriated the very signifier – *Conspiracy Theory* (Donner 1997) – for its title, in an attempt to attract audiences through generic appeal. Mainstream book distributors such as the Internet traders Amazon.com have acknowledged conspiracy theory and the paranormal as a distinct and profitable category.[18]

Conspiracy theory also provides a televisual theme, which has become manifested in a wide spectrum of guises. Countless documentaries detail individual conspiracy theories as wide-ranging as those concerning September 11, Princess Diana's death, various aviation disasters, Bible codes (indeed, all kinds of codes, particularly since the success of Dan Brown's bestseller, *The Da Vinci Code* (2003)), and the moon landings. Magazine format conspiracy shows have been attempted, two of the most prominent in the UK being *Fortean Times* (C4) and *Disinfo Nation* (C4). As well as spawning imitators, *The X-Files* itself has generated its own wide array of merchandise, including clothes, watches, videos, DVDs, games, CD-ROM, books, calendars, mugs, mouse-pads and lunch boxes.[19] Conspiracy theory is, as I have already suggested, a profitable filmic genre. *Men in Black* (1997) for example, grossed US$84 million at the box office in five days, making it the biggest non-sequel opening to that date. Conspiracy theory also provides less conspicuous revenue in the form of tourist attractions such as Dealey Plaza's Sixth Floor Museum or Roswell's International UFO Museum and Research Center. Additionally, it is the rallying banner behind conferences such as the annual November in Dallas Conference held by JFK Lancer, and events like the UFO convention held in Roswell to commemorate the fiftieth anniversary of the alleged crash of a UFO there in 1947, which have substantially increased local revenue.[20]

Though the high pop-cultural moment of conspiracy theory may have passed, it has ensured conspiracy theory a stable presence on the cultural scene. And so a plethora of conspiracy books continue to be published, television production companies continue to make documentaries, and the conspiracy theory presence on the Internet seems undiminished. It is debatable whether a film like Michael Moore's *Fahrenheit 9/11* (2004) can be considered on the spectrum of conspiracy theory (and this is something I will return to in my case study of September 11) but it certainly shares features common to other conspiracy theory products. What is certain is that traces of conspiracy theory's previous, and sometimes contradictory, cultural identities and roles continue to inform its current, multifaceted form. That is, its identity as highly political paranoia, as counter-cultural practice, as cool, hacker/slacker aesthetic and as highly commercial, mainstream product, continue to shape conspiracy theory's cultural role, though it is difficult to reduce it to any one of these. It is, then, a highly versatile and resilient knowledge.

BUYING (INTO) CONSPIRACY

The commodification of conspiracy theory has established a common, popular vocabulary. The 'fringe' ideas ('fringe' because of low circulation before Internet and television interest) expressed in zines and small publisher's titles that have formed the core of UFOlogy folklore (*Roswell, Area 51, The Majestic Twelve*), JFK conspiracy theories (the grassy knoll, the magic bullet), and Militia anti-New World Order rhetoric, are now common currency for a wider audience. More significantly, texts that have helped popularize conspiracy theory can be considered as cultural texts which circulated and still circulate not only the individual hypotheses presented through their narratives, but a particular knowledge-producing discourse that determines those hypotheses.

Arjun Appadurai convincingly argues that commodities should be thought of not in the purely Marxist sense but as 'things with a particular type of social potential, that ... are distinguishable from "products", "objects", "goods", "artefacts," and other sorts of things – but only in certain respects and from a certain point of view' (1986: 6). This risks positing commodification not only as a factor in the process of fetishization, but as itself fetishized – divorced from its conditions of production to emphasize exchange – but it usefully focuses on the 'commodity potential of all things' and extends the focus from just production to the commodity's '*total* trajectory from production, through exchange/ distribution, to consumption' (Appadurai 1986: 13). Appadurai's emphasis on the 'commodity situation in the social life of any "thing"' (1986: 13) being defined by the dominance of its exchangeability is helpful in our discussion of conspiracy theory that, as a knowledge, has only been dominated and defined by the exchange value of its textual manifestations relatively recently. Additionally, Appadurai's configuration of a commodity as 'not one kind of thing rather than another, but one phase in the life of some things' (1986: 17) can help us to think through the disparate group of texts and communities that can be identified with conspiracy theory.[21] Yet understanding that commodification is just one stage in the social life of things should not render us indifferent to the specificity of this stage, or what is at stake in the increased commodification of conspiracy theory – the aestheticization of accusation and the production of an ironic-sceptical stance.

A commodified conspiracy theory is one that invites knowledge without belief or commitment. When conspiracy theory is commodified, I want to suggest, we are invited to consider it as a knowledge that can be bought (into) when others seem insufficient. In an interview about his work, Don DeLillo comments:

I think I tried to get at the slickness connected to the word *paranoia*. It was becoming a kind of commodity. It used to mean one thing and after a while it began to mean everything. It became something you bought into, like Club Med. (DeLillo in conversation with Begley 1993: 287)

DeLillo succinctly captures the generalization of paranoia and its escalating play as a signifier. As I have pointed out above, conspiracy theory, connected to but not synonymous with paranoia, has undergone a similar process of commodification since the early 1990s. The way in which the film *Conspiracy Theory* enlists the signifier, for instance, assumes that audiences can be attracted through generic appeal. 'Conspiracy theory' thus starts to signify a marketable category rather than a subterranean activity. In *The X-Files*, Agent Mulder has a poster in his office that resonates ironically in light of the depleted investment consumers of conspiracy display; it reads 'I want to believe', in reference to the existence of extra-terrestrials. The way in which desire to believe displaces belief as the object of the sentence indicates the ever-receding or deferred position of belief if we are to think of it as an unobtainable desired object (or stance from which a subject might speak). The audience, in fact, is being asked to suspend its *dis*belief, rather than to believe. Our investment in the narrative is always negatively defined. Like Mulder's scientifically grounded partner, Agent Scully, the audience does not have to wholly relinquish its dominant discourse in order to align itself with Mulder. Mark Fenster reads such a situation as allowing an aestheticized relationship between conspiracy theorists and theory to dominate the scene (1999: xxi). All of which suggests that we can employ a kind of knowledge as just another fashion accessory, for the sub- or popular-cultural capital it might bestow upon us.

Taking 'belief' out of the equation means that conspiracy theory can be marketed to, and parodically adopted by, those concerned with a generalized, rather than specific, conspiracy or injustice. On a potentially positive note, conspiracy theory can come to signal a healthy scepticism towards official accounts and encourage active readers without requiring an investment in each conspiracy narrative. Because of the way in which power is organized, this ironic stance suggests, these stories might as well be true, or it might serve us well to act *as if* they are. This logic recalls a remark by one of Don DeLillo's characters in his conspiracy saturated novel, *Underworld*: 'Believe everything. Everything is true' (1997: 801); or another's: '[a conspiracy theory is] easy to believe. We'd be stupid not to believe it. Knowing what we know' (1997: 289). According to this rationale, the redundancy of belief has not led to its eradication, but generalization. If we believe everything it will be because certain covert acts of aggression that have subsequently come to light (like those conducted under America's infamous Counterintelligence Program) will have meant that the possibility of conspiracy has been irrevocably posited. Douglas Kellner echoes this position when he writes: 'distrust in the face of science, technology, government, and conventional attitudes forces an individual to penetrate beneath the lies and illusions, to seek the truth' (1999: 170). He thinks that this quest might take the form of a search for new modes of representation and enquiry. A pragmatic cynicism towards official narratives might result from a commercially mediated conspiracy theory, and this could prompt a deeper questioning of epistemological apparatuses, but such optimism is usually quelled in the face of assumptions about conspiracy theory's lack of political resonance.[22]

There is a risk that the aestheticization of conspiracy theory only serves to depoliticize any challenging or radical potential it might have had (we could, however, think this is a good thing in relation to right wing Militia groups). A commodified version of conspiracy theory must be seen to highlight the way in which conspiracy theory provides us with no line of action, or renders impotent its disruptive potential. Such criticisms have been lodged against conspiracy theory by many cultural commentators. For example, Mark Fenster recognizes that 'conspiracy as play may at its best represent a productive and challenging cultural and political practice', but feels that it is more often 'a cynical abandonment of profound political realities that merely reaffirms the dominant political order' and 'substitutes fears of all-powerful conspiratorial groups for political activism and hope' (1999: 219). However, what I will go on to suggest in the next chapter is that the way in which conspiracy theory exceeds or complicates a (whether positive or negative) narrowly defined political invest- ment is far more informative. For conspiracy theory appears (to varying degrees in different contexts) *both* politically engaged *and* deeply ineffectual in the realm of democratic politics. Knight (2001) helpfully relates this apparently contradictory status to the way in which conspiracy theory is employed in both an ironic and earnest fashion. In this way, conspiracy theory is characterized by a continual oscillation between the figural and the literal. For example, because the effects of institutionalized racism, make it look *as if* there has been a conspiracy, exactly how these theories are being invoked by African American communities becomes undecidable. Do such conspiracy theories refer to an actual conspiracy or merely something *like* conspiracy?

As I go on to look at my two case studies, I want to keep the ambivalences identified above in mind – the ambivalent status of both conspiracist belief, and conspiracy theory's claims. For I think ambivalence accounts for the anxiety which attends conspiracy theories in the public realm and an attitude that sees conspiracist ideas as a rational reaction to the current political climate. Ultimately, however, as I will go on to consider in the next chapter, the inability of the 'official' accounts of each event to contain interpretation and prevent a turn to popular knowledge, will challenge any optimistic or pessimistic reading of these conspiracy theories.

TWO EVENTS, COUNTLESS THEORIES

The first case-study I want to consider might at first seem outdated. And yet, in the year I started writing this book (2004), new developments in the case concerning the death of her ex-Royal Highness, Diana Princess of Wales in Paris, 1997, were still coming to light, further fuelling the conspiracy mill. In fact, the British inquest was only opened in January 2004 some seven years after the car crash in which Diana and her lover, Dodi al-Fayed, were killed; and it was only in 2003 that Diana's butler, Paul Burrell, made public a letter she had sent to him in which Diana made the startling claim that someone was planning a car 'accident' in order to 'make the path clear for Charles to marry' (see Kerr 2003). In addition, the belief of some wrongdoing seems to have increased, not lessened, in the years since her death. For example, a front-page headline in the UK's *Daily Express* in 2005 claimed: '94% of You Believe Diana Was Murdered' (Palmer 2005: 1). It is true to say, however, that as the conspiracy theory event *du jour*, it has been surpassed by my second case study – the theories that accompanied September 11. Yet, it is the persistence of Diana conspiracy theories and the ongoing distrust of any official line on her death that should testify to conspiracy theory's enduring status as an important cultural phenomenon. Just when you thought it was safe to retreat back into the world of contingency and happenstance, another Diana conspiracy theory documentary airs, raising more questions.

My two case studies share some similarities. Both events that prompted the theories were accompanied by national mourning; both were seen to be of enough national significance to interrupt normal television scheduling (and given that the television industry in both the US and Britain is big business, this is no small matter); both required heads of state to make public announcements; both created physical, and virtual, sites of public mourning (the physical sites being, of course, Ground Zero for New York, the Point de L'alma in Paris and Kensington Palace Gardens for Diana); both events became part of the way a nation understood itself; both were opportunities (whether they were taken up or not) for national self-reflexivity; both happened in an Internet-literate age; both continue to be a source of much speculation. The differences, however, are perhaps even more significant. The human death toll for September 11 is incomparable to the events in Paris. The different geographical location of the events is, of course, notable (although the clear distinction between an American and European event is far from clear-cut given the multitude of nationalities that perished in the World Trade Center, and that the effects of mourning were felt far beyond the geographical location in both cases). The ramifications for global stability and loss of human lives in military reprisals is only relevant to the case of September 11. Both the similarities and differences make these events and the conspiracist responses to them important. They enable us to see conspiracy theory as an identifiable knowledge, but force us to take on board the singularity of each response.

DIANAGATE [23]

The Paparazzi/British Intelligence/Knights of the Templar/the Yakuza/international arms cartels/the CIA/the Trilateral Commission/aliens (delete as applicable) killed Diana, Princess of Wales. All of these factions have been cited as responsible on a website, blog, or discussion board 'near' you (which, providing you have access to the Internet, means all of them). Not all posters, bloggers and writers put forth theories as such. Soon after the crash, many simply pointed out the contradictions in media reportage:'a CNN eyewitness report that a blonde woman stumbled out of the car ... differs widely from the report depicting [an] unconscious blonde at the scene of the incident.'[24] Others concentrated on the possible motives behind a planned killing:'How convenient it would be if Diana was out of the way. Her millions would go back to the royal family... Her sons would be the sole custody of Prince Charles where he could mould them into the unfeeling world of a royal';[25] 'I understand that the English Secret Services and Buckingham Palace could not have this ... the mother of the future king a Moslem!!! No way ... so they killed them both.'[26] A number of theorists simply point towards the appearance of a cover-up:'Don't you think that the surviving man's injuries are a little too convenient? His jaw and tongue were apparently ripped off and mangled so he will never be able to speak.'[27] Indeed, suspicious circumstances and incongruities form the basis of many conspiracist sentiments:

> The driver was drunk three times [over] the limit and the bodyguard, Trevor Reese-Jones, who was sitting in the front seat did not warn the Princess... Mopeds or motorbikes are favoured vehicles for assassination as they are very manoeuvrable. A car cannot outrun or evade a motorbike ... It has been rumoured that Diana's seat belt was left undone even though Reese-Jones would have told her to do it up in the event of a high speed chase ... Some sources (unknown) report high radio activity from British Authorities around that time. What was the nature of this radio activity, detonation via electronic means?[28]

Latterly, attention has focused on the incongruities between what the conspiracy theorists believe and what the official French Inquiry has come up with: that it was an accident caused by a drunken driver. And, of course, that letter, already cited, from Diana to her butler in which she predicted the circumstances of her own death, remains a sticking point for many conspiracy theorists unwilling to accept such a strange revelation as an uncanny co-incidence.

Ian Jack and Peter Marlow note that Diana's death prompted the national memory to be awoken, that memory being 'the story that the nation tells about itself' (1997: 10). If conspiracy theories are to be acknowledged as part of the discourse that surrounded the death of Diana, that story needs to be renegotiated to include a questioning and reinterpretation of the way in which a nation tells, and is told, the story of itself (such discussion of national storytelling will be important for the September 11 conspiracy theories too). The numerous conspiracy theories that are still being exchanged display an attempt to become involved in the continued construction of this story. However, the treatment of conspiracy theories by some accepted 'rational' discourses of enquiry highlights a preference at work for only certain knowledges and their strategies of legitimation, prompting the question: what causes the selective acceptance of the 'acceptable'? The way in which the official media reported the Internet Diana conspiracy theories highlights a concern over who is interpreting and how. Several attempts to limit interpretation, and regulate the knowledge that produces it, have been made – Tony Blair's plea to end speculation on Diana's death (see Wintour 1998: 1) or Reverend Ian Cundy's release of Diana's burial certificate to quash rumours of a more private burial site (see Harding 1998: 4) come to mind. Such appeals to decorum and decency are obviously intended to endorse a tasteful and respectful response to a very public death. But the conspiracy theories that proliferated and which persist to this day show how this prescriptive approach to mourning and tragedy – and to official stories – does not answer to or reflect the experience of people and the kind of knowledges they employ when making sense of events.

My aim therefore is to examine a narrative construct that allows readers to rewrite or re-cognize events, and perhaps more importantly, to reconfigure context (by bringing apparently peripheral narrative threads to bear on the death of Diana and the attacks on the World Trade Center) and the boundaries of contextualization (when the knowledge employed to interpret and cognize a story becomes an integral part of that story).

alt.conspiracy.princess-diana

The death of Princess Diana only becomes suspicious if an excess that the official story or history cannot explain is acknowledged. To many, her death was simply the outcome of a fatal car accident and the climax of a 'tragic' life, but others, many of whom found an audience on the Internet, were not satisfied with this account. When Diana died, unlike at the time of JFK's assassination, the apparatus for the widespread production, exchange and circulation of 'unofficial' theories was already in place. Indeed, the lone dissenting voice of say, Jim Garrison (the New Orleans district attorney who attempted to expose a conspiracy concerning the assassination of JFK) can today only be a romantic model for the regular contributor to one of the many conspiracy newsgroups on the Internet (of course, since Garrison, JFK conspiracy theories and theorists have proliferated beyond count, but it was not an immediately mediated phenomenon).[29] *The First Diana Conspiracy Site* was set up in Australia within hours of the event and many were to follow.[30] *Sun Tzu's Newswire* service claimed on their

Internet site that ninety-three new or updated documents were found by the Alta Vista search engine early the day after Diana's death (1 September 1997) and was distributing a story under the headline 'Diana conspiracy talk spreading fast' (Rongstad and St John-Smith 1997). A subsection of the newsgroup *alt. conspiracy* was devoted entirely to Diana conspiracy theories – *alt.conspiracy. princess-diana* – by February of 1998 it was reported that 7,673 websites concerning Diana conspiracies could be found on the Internet (Ellis 1998: 15–16), and by 2001 that number was estimated to be at 36,000 (Parsons 2001). The Diana theories (along with the responses to September 11, as I shall later show) reveal contemporary conspiracy theory to be an instantaneous response reliant upon an already established knowledge network.

The conspiracy theories posted on the Internet range from Francophobic sentiments to papal conspiracies against the British royal family spanning hundreds of years. The way in which these theories become predictable is particularly notable. Although set up as 'alternative' theories, they soon become the accepted and expected product of conspiracy theory's own brand of logic. Consider the following excerpt from an Internet website:

> Princess Diana's new found independent financial power through her rich boyfriend became a political hazard. Diana was becoming more and more political in her visits to promote peace efforts in Bosnia, etc. This became a threat to The New World Order objective of a destabilized Soviet Union and a threat to the lucrative arms exporting business; England is the world's largest exporter of mines. The Royal Family had motive, resources, and opportunity and is a key member of the New World Order organization; anything affecting the Royal Family is seldom an accident but rather meticulously planned and orchestrated. Operations such as this one are most likely carried out by an Intelligence Organization, with the prime suspect being British Intelligence. (New World Network)

Once 'The New World Order' (a supposedly secret organization fronted by the UN, seeking to take control of all nations) is invoked, and the royal family connected to it, threats to a preordained political status quo can become a motive for murder. Once you believe in an alien government, The New World Order, or any secret cabal having ultimate power over world events, there is nothing beyond their realm of influence. All events can be connected to whichever organization is your chosen conspirator. The advantage of believing in The New World Order is that it is not one of many conspiratorial groups, but *the* conspiratorial force: the umbrella under which many factions operate. The citation characterizes the royal family as a near omnipotent force through its connections to The New World Order. The conspiracy theorist assumes that an organization that plans and orchestrates does not let accidents happen to it. Random events (accidents, love interests) are translated into components of far-reaching schemes. The website continues by insisting that 'the odds of all of these things happening is beyond random chance.' It is not necessarily the narrative details of these theories that are significant to the enquiry at hand, but how they display a particular method of analysing events and arriving at knowledge; how contingency is dismissed in favour of conspiracy.

Other Diana conspiracy theories centre on the recurring trope of 'un-answered questions' contradictions in reportage of the event, and a motive for murder. In this way, the conspiracy theories attempt to question the official narratives presented by the mainstream press and television coverage. One conspiracist commented: 'I was awake until 5:30 am (in the UK) and there wasn't a word about [Diana's death] on the BBC (even though the news reader became visibly upset at around 5:15 am).'[31] A writer for the online version of *Conspiracy Nation* claims that journalists have anonymously revealed to him proof that Diana was assassinated by British Intelligence. He foregrounds the information by mistakenly claiming that the UK's Official Secrets Act is a mechanism that prevents the media from discussing any possible foul play in the Diana case. Moreover, he adds, 'any discussion is forbidden about how the Official Secrets Act exactly works' (Skolnick 1997). Suspicion of the mainstream British press and its perceived failure to reveal the truth legitimates the presence of Internet conspiracy theories for subscribers (to the Internet and theories both). *New World Network* states that 'corporate funding and Government regulations have successfully insured that the media reports only superficial stories meant to entertain and not analyse or expose the truth' (New World Network). These sentiments are only confirmed when *dietrologia* – an Italian term that Don DeLillo employs to denote 'the science of what is behind something' (1997: 280) – is employed: when 'news' is divided into surface and depth, or in front and behind, the media not reporting the latter type of news is read to be part of the conspiracy. The notion of a cover-up, here associated with the press, can always be suspected under the logic of conspiracy, which demands conclusions that the mainstream press is not generally interested in providing. For a conspiracy theorist, the 'cover-up' acts as an homogenizing agent to present the image of a corrupted 'them' and romanticized and radical 'us', as well as a lived socio-political reality. In this type of oppositional scheme, events are inevitably attributed to 'them' rather than put down to chance or coincidence.

The Internet is particularly suited to the presentation and endorsement of this romanticized image of the radical theorist for several reasons. First, although initially a military and academic mechanism, the Internet has also been fashioned by early bulletin boards. These bulletin boards are part of hacker mythology: used by maverick computer users to disseminate information about phreaking (telephone fraud) and hacking (database exploration). As such, the Internet has increasingly become characterized (and I am making no claims for what *actually* is the case) as a relatively unregulated and non-corporate sphere for the exchange of 'underground' ideas.[32] Second, the immediacy of the Internet as a medium aids the fast circulation and response to ideas. In newsgroups (online discussion forums), users are invited to post their own theories and others can reply to them. The idea of a collective enemy can therefore be rapidly endorsed and mythologized. Third, while a particular newsgroup may unofficially establish its own standards of discussion and initiate self-regulation in the form of derision,[33] participants can post entries which have few, if any, verifiable sources. This provides the perfect forum for hyperbolic and rousing accusations against a conspiring other.

DIANA: WHOSE STORY?

With the death of Diana, a public outpouring of grief sat alongside widespread distrust of the official account and frustration with the main narratives. The story of a modern and poignant tragedy; an ethical and political discussion centring on privacy laws and the conduct of the paparazzi; a debate concerning royal etiquette and the future of the monarchy: these were all official narratives which couldn't seem to fill the gap left by 'unanswered questions'. In this section, I want to consider the gulf that emerged between the very different stories about and responses to Diana's death.

Compared to the activity online, there were relatively few articles charting the interest in Diana conspiracy theories in the mainstream press. This absence did not go unnoticed by the Internet conspiracy theorists themselves. The mainstream press's understandable inability to allow for the possibility of a different type of reportage left a gap for the hypotheses generated by other knowledges. One contributor expressed dismay at what s/he perceived to be the total absence of alternative stories: 'I find it unusual that the mere mention of the possibility of foul play is totally non-existent in media coverage.'[34] This absence did not, as I have already noted, quell conspiracy theories but prompted more. The existence of a whole area of speculation not monopolized by the broadsheet press, or even the more speculative tabloids, opened the way for a popular knowledge to take hold.

One contributor questioned the status of 'stories', acknowledging that when an official body endorses a claim, the question of credibility can be suspended:

'The driver was drunk' story was released by French police, after blood samples. The 'anti-depressant' story was credited to supposed 'sources'. No official status, but it is reported with the same amount of credibility as a real NEWS STORY. The whole thing might have been made up by someone on this BOARD. But there have been heaps of great stories on this board, and not ONE has been reported. [Capitals are the author's own.][35]

I want to note the surprising faith placed in a 'real news story', and the claim that conspiracy theories are 'just' good stories. However, once these apparently conservative reactions are sifted through, what is striking is the questioning of why some speculations were reported and some were not, when at that point *all* hypotheses regarding the crash were equally unsubstantiated. The contributor's remarks imply that all stories or possibilities should be reported if one is.

Conspiracy theories were, then, conspicuous by their absence. The absence may have been more notable to a conspiracy theorist scouring the press for reports but a lack of speculation must also have been evident to a wider public. When conspiracy theories did begin to materialize in the broadsheet press they were framed in significantly different ways from other speculations (such as the uncorroborated claims made regarding the role of the paparazzi in the crash). Indeed, when a newspaper shares the ideological concerns of what it is reporting, 'the reported discourse is not generally demarcated from the report itself, and there is generally a focus upon the ideational meaning (the "content") of the reported discourse and a neglect of its interpersonal meanings and its context' (Fairclough 1995: 25). If, however, the discourse being reported is at odds with the logic upon which the reporting mechanism is based, the report must create a distance between the primary and secondary discourse. Two journalistic approaches to conspiracy theory that do create this distance include a focus on the spread of conspiracy theories (an infection which apparently hasn't affected the journalist him/herself), and a humorous engagement with conspiracy theory.

To give an example of the former, the extension of conspiracy theory beyond the Internet into less virtual (and stigmatized) spaces, such as dinner tables and pubs, became the focus of an article in the *Independent on Sunday* by Chris Blackhurst. To begin with, Blackhurst situates the death of Diana within a conspiracy discourse: 'The [Fiat] Uno is Diana's grassy knoll (the site of Kennedy's alleged second assassin)' (1997: 1). The direct reference to the Kennedy assassination and the proliferating theories about it acknowledges not only that the Diana theories are produced within a discursive history of conspiracy theory, but also hints at the way in which official stories (such as the one expressed in *The Warren Report*) offer little chance of closure. (I will consider this non-depletable opening that produces hypotheses in detail at the end of this chapter and throughout the next.) Blackhurst continues by making explicit this simple but crucial breach into which a conspiracy theory can take up residence: 'We think Diana was killed through drunken driving. We think Henri Paul was so tanked up when he drove her away from the Ritz hotel that he wanted to show the paparazzi what for, with terrible results. We think. I think. But we do not know. I do not know' (1997: 1). The collective 'we' and individual 'I' cannot 'know' while 'unanswered questions' continue to plague the investigation. But there will always be 'unanswered questions' because new questions can always be asked when old ones are answered. Even when a question is answered, a conspiracy theorist does not have to accept that it is the 'right' answer (for conspiracy theorists, questions are rarely answered by the official story – only by themselves). A discourse is precisely that which enables us to think we know: a mechanism that allows knowledges to be produced and answers to be arrived at. If I choose to read an event through the discourse of conspiracy theory, this will determine my agenda: I will find a sinister rather than structural reason for unanswered questions.

Blackhurst's *Independent on Sunday* article initially contrasts the Internet conspiracy theories, written by 'students in anoraks – desperate like the fund-amentalist Muslims, to pin something on the Satans of the Western security services,' to the conjectures made by 'people who read serious newspapers and watch serious television programmes' (1997: 1). He lists a range of 'acceptable' professions – 'a public relations advisor, an academic, a City banker' (Blackhurst 1997: 2) – as a way into discussing the 'democratization' of conspiracy theory after Diana. He wants to know why the anoraked students and fundamentalists have been joined by the white-collar workers in questioning the 'official' version, even though they belong to 'official' professions and are aligned with 'rational' belief systems. The initial oppositional gesture situating Muslims and Internet 'geeks' on the one side and 'serious' people on the other, demonstrates the ways in which conspiracy theory is given pejorative connotations. Similarly, the first references by the BBC to an alternative reading of events were in reference to Colonel Gaddafi's claims of an assassination. As Ian Hamilton in the *London Review of Books* points out, the presentation of this viewpoint through Gaddafi, who holds a 'crackpot' status in the Western media, instantly positions conspiracy theories against the mainstream (1998: 16).

Hamilton rightly, in my opinion, observes this type of condemnation to be racist in its implications. Even Tony Blair had to address this connotation after denouncing the Diana death industry and conspiracy theorists. Downing Street issued a statement denying that 'its criticisms of conspiracy theorists are a coded attack on Mr Fayed' (Wintour 1998: 1), who was reported in the *Mirror* to have claimed he was 99.9 per cent sure that the deaths were not an accident. In a UK Channel 4 documentary, *You're Fayed* (2005), Mohammed al-Fayed was not shy to express his views on the royal family, calling Prince Phillip a 'gangster' responsible for the 'murder' of his son, Dodi, and Diana. On a visit to Egypt soon after the Paris deaths, Hamilton was exposed to a wholly different way of approaching the news. He reports that, in Egypt, conspiracy theories concerning the deaths of Dodi and Diana are mainstream ideas (voiced by the press and state officials) and that proponents of such ideas in public are greeted with respect. While British shops placed tributes to Diana in their windows – a photograph, a commemorative mug, flowers – a travel agency in Alexandria displayed a doctored wedding photograph of Diana and Dodi and a sign asking 'Who Killed Diana?' Hamilton comments that 'far from being thought of as spooky or sensational, the [display] merely summarized a general, and wholly settled, conviction in the Middle East: that accident was no accident' (1998: 16). The 'acceptable', 'accepted', 'tasteful' and 'tactful' are revealed to Hamilton as arbitrary and culturally specific.

While the broadsheet press appeared comfortable devoting large amounts of column inches to Diana in the week of her death, it seemed uneasy with the same amount of space being devoted to the possibility of a conspiracy that was entertained on the Internet. If this situation is read through the terms set out by Stuart Hall in his seminal essay 'Encoding/ Decoding', the press's concerns reveal a tension over a reader's failure to pick up, or deliberately overlook, intended meanings: 'what they really mean to say', Hall writes, 'is that viewers are not operating within the "dominant" or "preferred" code' ([1980] 1993: 100). The press, in the case of Diana, initially appeared to have little time for readers who interpreted the events that led to her death in an oppositional way. Humour was used as a framing device for pointing out the differences between the way in which the Internet and the print press have responded to Diana's death. And while humour is very much a part of conspiracy theory's discourse, it is one point on an oscillation between the playful and serious. Articles in the mainstream press that took a humorous approach did nothing to acknowledge this ambivalence.

An article in the *London Evening Standard Magazine*, for example, introduced a lengthy list of conspiracy theories as follows:

> For the nerdish, nervous and plain nutty around the world, Diana's death has been the JFK assassination to the power of infinity. In Kennedy's case, of course, the rumour milling and conspiracy hatching were done underground. But today, lucky us, we have the Internet, and the conspiracy machinations all take place in public. (Ellis 1998: 15)

The article – a double spread – is laid out as a mock-up of a website, complete with tool bar and Internet address: http:www.es.magazine/page.16-17~issue.6.2.98. The conspiracy theories are literally framed by a specific context. Coupled with the use of words such as 'nerds', 'nervous' and 'nutty' to indicate the type of people who endorse these ideas, this framing invites readers to distance themselves from conspiracy theorists. Clear boundary maintenance operating between primary and secondary discourses can be detected here. This encourages readers to consider their speculations as unconnected to those found on the Internet. Setting is clearly all important: this, as Norman Fairclough tells us, 'is concerned with the extent to which and ways in which reader/ listener interpretation of secondary discourse is controlled by placing it in particular textual context' (1995: 60). The *Evening Standard* article provides just one example of how conspiracy theorists' speculations were framed as entertainment and presented at a distance from the event of Diana's death. The light-hearted presentation of these theories allowed unsubstantiated stories to be relayed without the risk of libel. It gave 'reputable' newspapers the chance to continue writing about Diana when all the 'news', as such, had been told. This type of complicity has been noted by *News of the World* editor, Patsy Chapman:

> There is a veritable growth industry of so-called quality newspapers re-gurgitating sensational stories by reporting what the tabloids did with them. 'In-depth recycling' I call it. (Quoted in Snoddy 1992: 187)

If a story has been subjected to a certain standard of critique, the broadsheet press will repeat it; if it has not, they will often attempt to subject it to one. This is, of course, an important difference. However, it displays the double standard that Chapman emphasizes: it is acceptable for the broadsheets to remove a story from one context and place it into another, but they criticize genres such as conspiracy theory and the tabloids for initially decontextualizing facts and stories.

Almost one year after the crash, John Litchfield, writing in the *Independent*, observed that 'No road accident has been the subject of so much speculation, distortion and outright invention.' He asks why 'so many of the facts of the case [are] still disputed or confused by the world's press', adding 'let alone the dottier theorists on the Internet' (Litchfield 1998: 9). Litchfield goes on to acknowledge the complicity of the press in the process of speculation – admitting that speculation may spring from the same structural combination of factors – but distances the conclusions they come to from those of the 'dottier theorists on the Internet'. He blames the combination of the French judicial system – 'exhaustive but secretive, and yet riddled with selective leaks – and the impatient Anglo Saxon press, used to official co-operation and more reliable channels of information' (Litchfield 1998: 9). Litchfield considers speed to be of paramount importance to the British press. Lack of information, or secrecy, encourages speculation in this equation. While Internet conspiracy theorists self-reflexively discuss this state of secrecy using the trope of the cover-up and by pointing out contradictions in reportage, the broadsheet press showed no interest in such reflections unless they were presented through editorial pieces such as Litchfield's.

Litchfield does acknowledge a lack of closure but only so that he can position conspiracy: he writes, 'What is less likely [than a conspiracy] is that the full truth of what happened in the approach to the Tunnel de l'Alma will ever be known' (1998: 9). Litchfield cites the dominance of speculation surrounding the case as the reason for closure being 'less likely' than conspiracy. For Litchfield, then, one possible conclusion – that there was a conspiracy – left open by the lack of closure inherent in the investigation is compared to the structure of that closure. That is to say, Litchfield tries to delegitimize one conclusion in comparison with others by invoking the very structure that ensures its possibility.

Mark Lawson attributes the belief in conspiracy theories to the 'collapse in editorial authority' (1998: 21). He elaborates:

> Increased commercial competition has brought pressure for rapid printing or transmission and the resultant spreading of information – half-fact, no fact, innuendo, gossip – which has nothing to commend it as journalism other than the fact that no other news outlet has got it. (Lawson 1998: 21)

Again, speed is considered to be all-important. If speed and a resultant exclusivity are privileged over verification, Lawson fears a decline in journalistic standards. As a result, he considers the gap between the broadsheet press and the tabloids to be closing. Evidence of this is to be seen, according to Lawson (1998: 21), in the serialization of sensationalist books by both the *Daily Mirror* and *The Times*, showing an affinity with the 'low-fact culture' of which conspiracy theories are a product. Lawson sees this as the 'most tawdry form of mourning' in an attempt to keep Diana alive. While the paparazzi are 'unable to disguise her absence', editors and writers can, Lawson remarks wryly, 'just fake it' (1998: 21). Again, it is uncertain how Lawson's commentary distances itself from this situation when it clearly enters into a debate concerning the way in which Diana is represented.

Lawson wants his observation – that the gap between the broadsheet and tabloid newspapers is reducing – to support his call for a restoration of reporting 'standards'. However, it inadvertently shows that gossip and speculation are a part of all press and that a call to 'standards' may be exposed as nostalgia, failing to reflect the public interest in iterative reports (which can repeat statements from another context while acknowledging the difference inherent in that endeavour) rather than repetitive news. The serialization in *The Times* is not an aberration in an otherwise 'respectable' press, but the continuation of a trend, the possibility of which has perhaps always resided within a notion of journalism as a storytelling occupation. It would, in this way, be hard to trace exactly when reportage becomes speculation and how we are to judge the reportage of speculation itself. The practice of reporting statements made in certain contexts is not deemed to be good journalism under Lawson's logic. Whereas the conditions of an enunciation are the focus when reporting conspiracy theories by al Fayed or from the Internet, it is the content that is of importance when an 'official' statement is released.

READINGS: IN EXCESS

I want to return to Blackhurst marvelling at the infiltration of conspiracy theory into 'serious' circles. It is a gesture repeated elsewhere, such as in Frank Furedi's *Independent* commentary in which he writes: 'There was a time when only eccentrics were interested in conspiracy theories. However, in recent times conspiracy has gone mainstream' (2004). There is here a concern over 'reality'. It is expected of those who are derided by our mainstream press (Blackhurst's anoraked Internet users and the Muslim fundamentalists) to haggle over 'reality' in the form of conspiracy theory, but it is less acceptable for those involved in the production and maintenance of 'reality' (the PR advisor, the City banker, the academic) to do so. Indeed, to 'keep a grip on reality' is to subscribe to a certain performance or production of 'reality'. Blackhurst is concerned (following the logic of violence and media debates) that due to a constant diet of films and novels that depict the secret services as capable of anything, 'when something happens in real life, we turn to a plot from fiction. Occasionally, fiction becomes reality' (Blackhurst 1997: 2). Blackhurst's acknowledgement of how the oppositions he sets up – fiction/reality, conspiracy theories/serious conjecture – become obscured, points towards the crux of the Diana theories.

Diana conspiracy theories have arisen because the official story cannot achieve closure: it is necessarily subject to breaches in the narrative that can only be bridged temporarily. The paradigmatic 'official report' – *The Warren Report* – contains fifteen volumes of testimony and eleven of exhibits all detailing 'evidence' pertaining to the assassination of John F. Kennedy. DeLillo points to the Joycean quality of *The Warren Report*: he describes it as 'a masterwork of trivia ranging from Jack Ruby's mother's dental records to photographs of knotted string' (quoted in DeCurtis 1991: 54). 'Evidence' in the form of testimony and exhibits prompts, rather than prevents, more conjecture. Each narrative detail is the springboard for further speculation. Ambitions to be comprehensive seem to lead a report further from its goal of closure. The attempt to finalize an account, to forge an ending (the lone gunman theory in the case of JFK, for example) is a move that can prompt suspicion and endless questioning. The French report on the Paris deaths of Diana and Dodi did little to alleviate suspicions. And while the new British Inquest promises to investigate every thread, it will be interesting to note which conspiracy theories are investigated and which are not (those accusing the late Queen Mother of being an alien will presumably not find their way into the final report).

The Diana conspiracy theories are excessive in that they highlight the excess produced by any reading that claims full knowledge or attempts closure. In this way, conspiracy theory challenges context: returning upon the discourse or 'official story' that attempts to exclude it, forcing it to widen its scope. Newspapers eventually acknowledged this contextual challenge. They began to report Internet conspiracy theories and have continued to do so. Thus, the mainstream press report the Internet Diana theories while the Internet comments on the press coverage. In this way, media reportage becomes part of the Diana story. Knowledge and interpretation become narrative elements, guaranteeing that the nation's story – 'the story that the nation tells about itself' – will never be subject to closure.

It would not be sound to suggest that conspiracy theory itself is a discourse free from reliance upon certain exclusions. Conspiracy theories may challenge one totalizing narrative, only to propose another. Indeed, I wouldn't want to overstate the subversive potential of Diana conspiracy theories or any others, only to recognize the challenges they present to an implicit regulation of knowledge and interpretation. The Diana theories display a re-negotiation of interpretative prerogatives. Despite resistance, interpretation of Diana's death is shown by conspiracy theories to exceed issues of authority as the nation's conjectures become part of the official history. If the nation's story is an economy of the *'langue* of the law and the *parole* of the people' (Bhabba 1990: 2), the Diana theories, as counter-narratives, to some extent, will eventually affect the general structure and meanings of that story. Though clearly not in reference to conspiracy theories, the potentially progressive implications of this process of challenge and change are succinctly worded by Homi K. Bhabba: 'Counter-narratives of the nation that continually evoke and erase its totalizing boundaries – both actual and conceptual – disturb those ideological manoeuvres through which "imagined communities" are given essentialist identities' (1990: 300).

The Diana theories certainly 'evoke and erase' totalizing boundaries: they evoke and attack 'Britain' as if it were a coherent notion and yet erase this totality by suggesting that it is always already infiltrated by subversive elements. Britain's boundaries are at once invoked and complicated by this model. The possible 'disturbance' produced by counter-narratives is a subtle seismic movement: the shift remains unperceived until the landscape has been recognizably transformed. Conspiracy theories are, then, not just an instance of Fredric Jameson's 'cognitive mapping' – 'an unconscious, collective effort at trying to figure out where we are and what landscapes and forces confront us in [the] late twentieth century' (1992: 3) – but, also, an active element in the alteration of that landscape they are said to map. Writing and interpreting in this case are not exclusive activities. The Diana theories cannot be thought of as one concrete alternative to the official story, or to one articulation of the nation's story, because what is official and what constitutes the nation is always already being redefined and recontextualized by them and other narratives.

One newsgroup posting states: 'I suspect that the Diana assassination is big, but it's a cover for something even bigger.'[36] The deferral of closure implied by this statement – the idea that even the revelation of a conspiracy is suspected to be part of a wider conspiracy – demonstrates the necessary possibility of a conspiracist reading, even when the subject is conspiracy. I will go on, in the next chapter, to show how theories that claim Diana was abducted by aliens and substituted by a replica; that the car's passengers were killed in advance and later planted in an already crushed Mercedes by arms dealers angered by Diana's anti-landmine campaign; or that Henri Paul was brainwashed by British Agents on behalf of the monarchy and force-fed sacs of pure alcohol that slowly disintegrated, are necessary possibilities. This is not to say that they are possibly 'true'. These theories are necessary possibilities of interpretation in the same way that Derrida ([1972c] 1993) deems a letter going astray – the chance that it might not arrive – to be a necessary possibility and structuring element of what is thought of as an 'arrival'. Geoffrey Bennington describes this economy: 'what makes possible immediately makes impossible the purity of the phenomenon made possible' (1993: 277). After looking at September 11, this economy will lead me to suggest that academic discourses perhaps revile conspiracy theories because these conjectures make explicit an implicit structuring element of traditional interpretation and cognition. Conspiracy theories put on display a possibility of reading, or rather, a perceived 'impurity' of reading. This can place into question the production of statements and procedures of interpretation associated with 'accepted' knowledge. We may well choose not to take on board the individual hypotheses of what 'really' happened at the Pont de l'Alma, but cannot afford to ignore the contemporary epistemology that produces them.

'WHAT AN ABSOLUTE CROCK OF HORSE PUCKY!' AFTER SEPTEMBER 11

The anxiety that Diana conspiracy theories were met with in the public sphere is also evident in the reception of September 11 conspiracy theories. However, I want to argue in this section that they were produced by, and within, a significantly different climate to that within which the Diana theories were produced. This different climate has affected the reception of conspiracy as an explanation.

September 11 has understandably been posited as an epochal event by many commentators (although Derrida (2003), in an essay I will turn to at the close of this chapter, has challenged such assumptions). It has initiated heightened feelings of insecurity in America; articulated a split between the Middle East and the 'West' along cultural and religious lines, and shaped US and British foreign policy, as well as that of other nation states (whether in support or defiance of the US-British stance). The scale of both the event and the political-military ramifications mean that it is difficult not to see it as a defining moment. Given that it was the first attack on home territory for America since Pearl Harbour in 1941 (or the War of 1812 if Hawaii doesn't quite count as 'home territory'), one apparently concocted through Arabic conspiratorial networks, one might reasonably think that it would quell rather than prompt domestic conspiracy theories (conspiracy theories that cite the US government as the conspirators). But even a cursory look at the Internet conspiracy theory sites and message boards concerning September 11 reveals an ongoing (if not heightened) distrust of government agencies undiminished by September 11 in conspiracy theory 'circles' despite a reported rise in trust in government immediately afterwards (see Morin and Dean 2001). Indeed, some conspiracy theorists refer to the official explanation of September 11 as the 'conspiracy theory' itself, in an attempt to appropriate the pejorative connotations of the phrase (see Dowbenko 2003).

That is not to say that September 11 hasn't affected the register and concerns of conspiracy theorists. Of note, rather, is the persistence of conspiracy rhetoric in the face of potentially paradigm-shifting events. In this way, September 11, rather than instigating great domestic change, becomes part of an already established logic: people find familiar ways of knowing to understand and discuss it perhaps *because* not *in spite* of its potentially disruptive nature. (One could think about this not only in terms of the employment of conspiracy theory, but the rhetoric of patriotism or sentiment that also took hold in the days and months following September 11.) September 11, then, must be thought about as much in terms of continuity as disruption.

The proliferation of conspiracy theories after September 11 becomes less surprising in these terms. They range, as with the Diana theories, from playful ideas to inflammatory sentiments. Some do not attempt to substantiate their theories, while others elaborately source and contextualize their claims. Despite these differences in approach and commitment, many of the conspiracy theories suggest some level of US government complicity in the events of September 11, ranging from forewarnings of a terrorist attack, to outright orchestration of it to justify any number of actions (war against Afghanistan and Iraq; control of the oil market; the implementation of the Patriot Act and its infringement on civil liberties). The energy for such theories can be found in the absence, more than the presence, of evidence or answers: the lack of a published photograph of Flight 77 after having crashed into the Pentagon arouses suspicion; the late mobilization of scrambler planes raises eyebrows; the President's lack of reaction to the news that America was under attack during a low-key visit to a school suggests to some that this news was 'no news' to him. Alternatively, conspiracy theories abound that consider the available evidence 'too present', or to put it another way, implausibly convenient: like finding the passport of suspected hijacker Mohammed Atta (reported as Satam Al-Suqami by some reports) at the bottom of the World Trade Center[37] or the discovery of Arabic flight manuals and a copy of the Qur'an in Atta's hire car.

The focus of one conspiracist film distributed free of charge over the Internet – Darren Williams' *9/11: Pentagon Strike* (www.pentagonstrike.co.uk) – is precisely the lack of answers and dearth of public evidence surrounding the Pentagon strike in Washington, DC. The film suggests that rather than Flight 77, it was a small military plane or missile that struck the Pentagon. The implications of this alternative version of events are far reaching. Was the flight intercepted by scrambler planes? Was there a Flight 77 at all? An article by Carol Morello in the *Washington Post* picked up on the astonishingly fast circulation of Williams' film: 'Now urban legends have become cyberlegends, and suspicions speed their way globally not over months and weeks but within days and hours on the Web' (2004: B01). When Williams' site crashed from the number of visitors attempting to view the film, others who had downloaded it provided access. 'Demand for the video was so great', Morello reports, 'that some webmasters solicited donations to pay for the extra bandwidth.'

Having reported the popularity of these ideas, Morello goes on to present the problems conspiracy theories posed for the bipartisan 9/11 Commission. She quotes the commission's executive director, Philip Zelikow:

> When we wrote the report, we were ... careful not to answer all the theories. It's like playing Whack a Mole. You're never going to whack them all ... What we tried to do instead was to affirmatively tell what was true and tell it adding a lot of critical details that we knew would help dispel concerns.

Morello follows her interview with Zelikow by one with a political scientist, and then an 'expert' on cults, in order to explain the social function of conspiracy theories. Morello also gives space to some of the conspiracy theorists themselves. And although the article gives the last word to Zelikow dismissing conspiracy on the grounds that the government simply isn't organized enough, its tone is surprisingly neutral, particularly in comparison to some of the reports I have already looked at with regards to Diana. Without the framing and distancing devices noted in most of the mainstream press responses to the Diana conspiracy theories, it was left to the *Washington Post*'s own Internet discussion board to restate the critical distance and express distaste and disgust for the conspiracy theories reported in the paper.

Interestingly, the online community associated with Williams' film (www. Cassiopaea.org and their website *Signs of the Times*) reproduced the *Washington Post*'s discussion forum and the disparaging comments about the conspiracy community's beliefs. The *Signs of the Times* editorial responded thus:

> By reaching a large audience, the *Post* story will give those people who have doubts about the 'official version' of 9/11, an opportunity to examine many of the unknown or suppressed facts surrounding the 'alleged' terrorist attacks at the Pentagon and the WTC.
>
> On the other hand, it will also galvanize those who have a vested interest in keeping these facts hidden from public view, to begin a deliberate campaign of ridicule, name-calling and debunking in order to marginalize our efforts as 'conspiracy' or 'fringe'.
>
> A good example of this comes from the Washington Post discussion forum, that in less than 24 hours after printing the story, has already collected over 130 posts.
>
> Seems we have touched a nerve.
>
> Here are some samples of comments posted...

> – The Internet just gives every NUT a larger voice. Ordinarily you would never hear from these nutjobs. There will always be fruitcakes that think

the government did this to itself. These folks should start their day with 0.5 mg of Haldol.
- The Post isn't under any obligation to investigate every fruitcake's conspiracy theory.
- Even goof balls with a computer and time on their hands can act like they are contributing something.
- The conspiracy theory story and pentagon 9/11 theory is pure trash.
- What an absolute crock of horse pucky!
- Hey, the Post runs an article and all the nuts coming running. I think they might have given a furlough at the asylum today.
- Shame on you (and the other conspiracy theorists) for making a mockery out of their loss.
- You truly are a dolt. Don't you have to be back at the institution???
- I want GWB out of the White House badly, but I'm not about to result to tomfoolery to do so, and I advise you to consider the same. This is just foolishness.
- Virtually everything you think or believe could be garbage. You must be very very insecure.
- Back in pre-history before the Dawn of the Internet, these Ten Percenters were scattered and dispersed. Forced to wear tall pointy caps, objects of village ridicule, wandering the streets muttering to themselves in self-deluded mania, we all knew them for what they were – KOOKS! [...] Moreover, cleverly constructed Internet sites give the air of legitimacy to the unadulterated conspiracy lunacy disseminated by these Ten Percenters.
- Well duh! It's obvious the plane was sucked up by the Bermuda Triangle, where the passengers were kidnapped by aliens. This was all organized by the Israelis. (*Sign of the Times* Editorial 2004)

The *Washington Post* readers' Internet postings quoted here – whether through allusion to psychological normalcy, appeals to reason, the use of denigrating and disparaging remarks, or the employment of humour – resemble the discursive formations employed by the press in relation to the Diana theories. While the response of *Signs of the Times* to the aggressive postings is too simplistic (the editorial claims that these posters are unwilling to face the truth and are threatened by the potential disruption to their understanding of the world) it nevertheless picks up on an anxiety the postings express regarding the symbolic order of acceptable acts of cognition and their close relationship with codes of 'taste'. Despite these attempts by *Washington Post* readers to maintain the boundaries between knowledge and popular knowledge, it is important to recognize a shift in attitude towards conspiracy to be found in (at least *some*) sectors of the press.

An article by Jonathan Raban in the *Guardian* goes further than the neutrality of the *Washington Post* article. Raban actually calls for the reasonableness of, if not the conspiracy theories outlined above, then certainly a widespread paranoia concerning the conduct of the government in response to the secrecy of the Bush administration and its peddling of 'generalised, promiscuous anxiety through the American populace' (2004: 7). Raban writes, 'Conspiracy theorising is fast becoming a legitimate means of reporting on a government so secretive ...' (2004: 6). He fashions secrecy as responsible for conspiracy theory: a mode he sees on the rise in American journalism, citing an article in the *New York Times*, which, while distancing itself from a theory by labelling it 'far-fetched', nevertheless 'went on to expend 40 serious column inches to the far-fetched story' (Raban 2004: 7). Conspiracy theories are being reported this time around because the political climate characterized by secrecy and security alerts makes conspiracy seems more 'reasonable' and less 'fringe'. Conspiracy theory becomes popular across the board rather than just populist. In an article sceptical of the evidence produced by the US government after September 11, Anne Karpf, again in the *Guardian*, echoes the thoughts and doubts expressed on websites such as *Signs of the Times* outlined above. Karpf writes:

> You could detect in [the convenient discoveries of evidence concerning al-Qaeda] the clear hand of American propaganda. This isn't, of course, to claim a dirty tricks department somewhere in the heart of Washington. That would have you immediately accused of peddling conspiracy theories, though I'm coming to think that conspiracy theories have had a bad press. What are they, after all, but 'joined-up government' by another name? (2000)

The concern at being branded a conspiracy theorist lingers, but the links between different practices, between the methodology of conspiracy theory and other, more 'legitimate' strategies, is recognized.

Michael Moore's film *Fahrenheit 9/11* (2004) entered this scene, drawing on the mood of distrust and exacerbating it. The documentary finds links between the Bush family and the Saudi royals including the bin Ladens, and concentrates on positioning George W. Bush as the villain. As with the Diana conspiracy theories, a decisive negotiation of national and global identity can be seen in evidence in *Fahrenheit 9/11*. In a move that oddly reflects a trend found in right-wing American Militia rhetoric, Moore tries to reclaim the meaning of American patriotism for the left. Rather than it being unpatriotic to question the government, for example, Moore's documentary posits such challenges as precisely the most American thing to do (in line with an ideal of free speech and revolutionary beginnings). If Bush *et al.* position themselves as patriotic, those in opposition have to find new spaces and inventive ways of being 'patriotic'. Moore carefully avoids condemning the troops that have found themselves in Iraq; rather, he exposes army recruitment procedures that heavily target the economically underprivileged and undereducated, and more generally, an exploitative military industrial complex. In making these links, Moore presents an entertaining and persuasive (if factually problematic) conspiracy theory.

I do not mean to imply that conspiracy theory has suddenly become 'acceptable' (Moore's film was met with anything but consensus regarding its merits, for example). A review by Mark Lawson of a television programme on UK's Channel 4 detailing a number of September 11 conspiracy theories again expresses the pervasive concern that conspiracy theories are in poor taste (in fact, Lawson is often wheeled out to air this view): 'The alternative hypotheses for September 11...have more in common with Holocaust denial: you gasp that people can be so dismissive of body-counts and substantial documentation' (Lawson 2004). Additionally, 'conspiracy theory' still seems to function as a term of denigration for many prominent figures. For example, a report in the *Guardian* tells us that 'Tony Blair today derided as "conspiracy theories" accusations that a war on Iraq would be in pursuit of oil, as he faced down growing discontent in parliament at a meeting of Labour backbenchers and at [Prime Minister's Questions]' (Tempest 2003). Nevertheless, the notable shift in the discursive positioning within certain sectors of the media is an indicator, I think, of how the status of knowledge changes according to political climate and other factors. There are climates of 'crisis' that make an otherwise 'irrational' mode of cognition more 'rational'. The popular-cultural moment of conspiracy may have passed, but its socio-political formations are still with us, perhaps increasingly so. What we see here is a dialectical movement whereby conspiracy theory shifts more to the centre while other kinds of cognition (such as telepathy, say, or 'new' ways of knowing that haven't yet been identified) remain firmly on the margins or even out of sight. The structure doesn't change in this scenario, only the players.

THE WORST IS YET TO COME

How might we think outside this dialectical movement? Well, I want to reach this point via an essay on September 11 by Derrida in which he reformulates the temporal configuration of trauma in a way that holds back any promise of synthesis. Such ideas might go some way towards accounting for the abundance of conspiracy theories in response to September 11 and the attendant tolerance of these theories in some cultural sectors, while not relying on the dialectical logic outlined above.

In his discussion of September 11 with Giovanna Borradori, Derrida says, 'what is terrible about "September 11", what remains "infinite" in this wound, is that we do not *know* what it is and so do not know how to describe, identify, or even name it' (2003: 94). The trauma is not just played out through the repetition of a past event but is experienced as a proleptic paralysis. Derrida says, 'the wound remains open by our terror before the *future* and not only the past' (2003: 96). Trauma, in its psychoanalytic guise, is generally understood to be, as

Jean Laplanche and Jean-Bertrand Pontalis describe it, '[a]n event in the subject's life defined by its intensity, by the subject's incapacity to respond adequately to it, and by the upheaval and long-lasting effects that it brings about in the psychical organisation' (1988: 465). In other words, the reference point for trauma is in the past, however subsequently psychically repressed and deferred that past 'event' is. But Derrida suggests, in relation to September 11, that what is traumatic about this trauma (it should be clear that Derrida is talking about trauma in a philosophical, as well as psychoanalytic, register) is the way in which it opens up and keeps open the possibility of unknowable, future (perhaps worse) traumas. Trauma comes about when we cannot tolerate or master an influx of excitations. However these excitations might come not only from the 'experience' of what has happened, manifested as a repetition compulsion of this past experience, but as the anticipation of what is still yet to 'happen'. September 11 inflicts a more radical trauma because, unlike during the Cold War when the threat came from two superpowers poised for and capable of mutual annihilation, this threat comes from 'anonymous forces that are absolutely unforeseeable and incalculable' (Derrida 2003: 98). A disrupted balance of world power means that we cannot locate the source of (nor contain) our fear. Indeed, 'It is the future that determines the unappropriability of the event, not the present or the past' (Derrida 2003: 97).

The open wound makes mourning impossible: closure evades; conscious working through, or *durcharbeiten* as Freud called it,[38] will not be effective. Derrida explains:

> Imagine that the Americans, and through them, the entire world, had been told: what has just happened, the spectacular destruction of two towers, the theatrical but invisible deaths of thousands of people in just a few second [sic], is an awful thing, a terrible crime, a pain without measure, but it's all over, it won't happen again, there will never again be anything as awful as or more awful than that. I assume that mourning would have been possible in a relatively short period of time. Whether to our chagrin or our delight, things would have quite quickly returned to their normal course in ordinary history. One would have spoken of the work of mourning and turned the page, as is so often done, and done so much more easily when it comes to things that happen elsewhere... But this is not at all what happened. There is traumatism with no possible work of mourning when the evil comes from the possibility to come of the worst, from the repetition to come – though worse. Traumatism is produced by the *future*, by the *to come*, by the threat of the worst *to come*, rather than by an aggression that is 'over and done with' (2003: 97).

This structure of trauma is perhaps played out in some of the discourses that surrounded September 11, including conspiracy theory. For conspiracy theory, it seems to me, at least attempts to articulate this 'threat of the worst'. Conspiracy theories flood in to fill the void of a nebulous, dispersed terror or fear. Of course, in Derrida's terms, such imaginings would fail to deplete or manage this traumatic anteriority because the trauma lies in the fact that the 'worst' will never arrive and we cannot but fail to predict 'it' completely. Nevertheless, conspiracy theories, as well as trying to make sense of an event, draw a line from that event into the future: if the government/the CIA/the New World Order can do this, imagine what they can do in the future! Equally, the centralized conspiracy rhetoric from the White House uses a similar logic with respect to the generalized enemy in the figure of the terrorist. Events like September 11 are usually seen by conspiracy theorists as just one element in an ongoing, much larger plot that will only fully come to light in the future. Unlike the rhetoric of patriotism and emphasis on individual and collective acts of heroism that were apparent in the aftermath of September 11, conspiracy theories (including the rhetoric of terror that emanated from the White House) addressed this fear of, and threat from, the 'worst to come'. The centralized, governmental conspiracy rhetoric focused on the future threat of terrorism became a mechanism for sanctioning all kinds of repressive and aggressive measures (ranging from infringements of civil liberties for US citizens, and loss of life for those deemed to be the closest representatives of such a threat, like al-Qaeda, Afghans or Iraqis).

The future threat, when it is spoken for, when it is translated into something tangible, when it is brought into a knowable horizon, can act as a licence to exert control and menace. But for those without access to power, the articulation of the threat to come in conspiracist terms represents something of a check against the governmental monopoly on fear. That is to say, in meeting the structure of trauma evidenced in the centralized, governmental rhetoric of threat and conspiracy, conspiracy theory *at least* does not give the government a monopoly on how the symptoms of trauma should be acted upon and dealt with. While conspiracy theorists suspicious of government actions risk becoming locked in a game of accusation and counter-accusation, they do provide alternative (if equally apocalyptic) futures: futures in which America itself is called upon to re-examine its place and conduct in the world – futures of self-reflexivity, no matter how redundantly expressed. If nothing else, these conspiracy theories go some way to creating a level playing field: attempting to prevent the government from being the only faction translating the radical future threat into knowable targets. There is 'violence' in these ideological acts of translation or materialization (performed by either 'side') – there is 'violence', as I will explore further in relation to gossip, whenever what is indeterminable is forced into the realm of the determinable – but a greater 'violence' would be apparent if the White House were the only faction able to perform this 'violence' on meaning.

While conspiracy theory's 'fourth estate' and levelling roles are important, I want to move on in the next chapter to concentrate more on the conditions that generate theories. Rather than analyse the content of the conspiracy theories that flood in to fill this radically open, traumatic, 'future', I want to think more about the structure that makes conspiracy theories necessary possibilities. In Chapter 3, I will still be concerned with the cultural politics of conspiracy theory, but I will do so by looking closer to home: considering the ambivalent relationship between academic interpretation and conspiracy theory rather than competing national narratives. Obviously, it is common for knowledges to be mutually hostile because one meta-narrative claim is threatened by the presence of another; yet what I want to consider is the specific treatment of the knowledge-producing discourse of conspiracy theory by more traditional, established and 'rational' discourses. Through such an enquiry, I will explore further what I have already detected in this chapter (whether in the response of the press to Diana conspiracy theories or the *Washington Post* readers' disgust at September 11 theories): that is, the ideological anxiety that attends knowledge production and access to it. For through closer attention to this relationship I can begin to learn what conspiracy theory has to teach me as a cultural theorist. From there I can look towards a cultural studies able to take on board adequately, rather than dismiss, conspiracy theory. But, as I hope the detail of this chapter has shown, conspiracy theory is not merely a convenient trope in this book, not just a stepping-stone on my way to saying something about cultural studies. I am very much interested in both cultural studies and popular knowledges. In order to consider the singularity of a popular knowledge, I think it is necessary to look to cultural manifestations of it. In the process, some general qualities have been revealed: qualities that have implications both for an idea of 'knowledge proper', and therefore a cultural analysis still invested in that idea.

CHAPTER 3

Cultural Studies on/as Conspiracy Theory

In an online plea to save Birmingham University's Centre for Contemporary Cultural Studies (the first cultural studies centre of its kind), Paul Gilroy wrote:

> Conspiracy theorists may present the Birmingham closure as a matter of settling scores by colleagues envious of the reputation of its cultural-studies brand; or it may be seen as belated punishment for radicalism. Indeed, earlier incarnations of the unit had a history of conflict with administrators who found its innovations hard to accept and its political positions unpalatable.[1]

Having raised the spectre of conspiracy Gilroy hastily goes on to stress that the closure has less to do with a plot against cultural studies and more with the 'immediate pressures on higher education in Britain'. Despite this denial, I think it is worth investigating the layers of paranoia hinted at a little further (the paranoia of those working 'in' cultural studies about their own position, the paranoia of those from other disciplines about student interest in cultural studies, and an institutional or managerial paranoia about the politics and aims of cultural studies). To do this, I want to look at the relationship between conspiracy theory and cultural studies: not just, as I keep stressing, to learn what cultural studies has to teach us about conspiracy theory; but also to consider what conspiracy theory might have to teach us about cultural studies – a field that can itself be seen to be subject to, and structured by, the possibility of a number of (internal and external) conspiratorial narratives.

At issue here is the problem of approach. Doesn't conspiracy theory, as a form of (albeit popular) interpretation and knowledge, have implications for how we interpret and produce knowledge about it? Perhaps this is nothing new; after all, at one time or another in the history of cultural studies various cultural forms and practices (for example, subcultures, fans, the 'everyday') have been presented as requiring a unique frame of reference or analysis. To give a recent example, Jeremy Gilbert (2004) has identified music as 'exceeding' a notion of culture as a set of signifying practices. But although I think that there are certainly cultural practices and texts that present *more* problems to the way in which we approach them than others, they may reveal a difficulty at the heart of cultural analysis in general. Consequently, although I have been

emphasizing the specificity of conspiracy theory, I also want to consider how
it highlights a general problem with the position from which cultural analysis
occurs. In this way, we can appreciate conspiracy theory as a unique form of
popular knowledge or interpretation, *and* address what this might mean for any
knowledge we produce about it or how we interpret it.

Ultimately, I want to propose: first, that as a mode of interpretation or knowing
itself, conspiracy theory might raise questions about cultural analysis, about
interpretation and knowing *per se*; and second, that as a mode of interpretation
or knowing accused of being 'illegitimate' or marginal in some way, and as a
synthetic, interdisciplinary knowledge, conspiracy theory might have much in
common with cultural studies (at least in terms of the perception of cultural
studies by others, or cultural studies' own internalized paranoia about how it
is perceived). I want to argue that what might be unusual about conspiracy
theory (why it is such an interesting, 'singular' case study when it comes to
thinking about popular knowledge) – namely, the way it is regarded as excessive
or paranoid interpretation – is also precisely that which makes it significant for
other discourses or disciplines including (and, I will suggest, especially) cultural
studies.

As a way of thinking through these issues I will draw on another mode
of thought that occupies a precarious position with regards to legitimacy:
deconstruction. Deconstruction is particularly interesting and useful in this
context, not least because it has explicitly and rigorously turned its attention to
the aporias that lie at the heart of legitimacy, knowledge and interpretation.

CULTURAL STUDIES ON CONSPIRACY THEORY

My intention in the rest of this chapter is to demonstrate how the analysis
of conspiracy theory hitherto practised by cultural and literary studies can
be seen as an indicator of a more general weakness – one that I will suggest
could be a productive 'weakness' if such analyses are seen, not so much as the
end point of cultural analysis, but as more of a beginning. I'm going to start by
mapping out some of these various analyses, before going on to think about
conspiracy theory, and from there cultural studies, in a different, what we might
call 'deconstructive', way.

The academic approaches to conspiracy theory broadly fall into three camps:
those that claim conspiracy theory to be a form of latent insurrection; those that
deplore it for its lack of political seriousness; and those that wish to monitor
and correct its 'worst' ('irrational', 'illegitimate') excesses. Each is problematic.
The first is a form of 'cultural populism'. Without aligning myself with those
critics, like Jim McGuigan, who characterize some work in cultural studies as an
uncritical celebration of culture, it is important to question the analysis of culture
that relies on measuring a practice like conspiracy theory (whether positively *or*

in fact negatively) against a pre-given ideal of political intervention. John Fiske, the usual suspect when it comes to castigating cultural studies for producing overly optimistic readings of popular culture, claims that popular knowledges like conspiracy theories allow disenfranchised subjects an opportunity to narrate their place within a system that renders them powerless. Fiske asserts that 'skepticism is a way of coping with the inescapable contradictions between top-down and bottom-up power and the ways of understanding social experience which each produces' (1993: 199). He looks towards conspiracist or sceptical narratives and finds a method by which the negative experience of capitalism can be, if not rectified, then at least articulated.

The other side of the analytical coin would be to chastise conspiracy theory for being a poor or inadequate engagement with politics. Karl Popper's denouncements of 'the conspiracy theory of society' (1966: 94–9) as a naive way of accounting for history is a common sentiment in academic discourses. Frederic Jameson picks up on this tradition when he describes conspiracy theory as 'a poor person's cognitive mapping' (1988: 356). More recently, Daniel Pipes and Hilal Khashan prove that this sentiment is still strong:

Arabs must leave behind a worldview dominated by conspiracy theories. This means distinguishing between serious analysis and fantasy, fact and rumor, reality and wishful thinking. But this change may be slow in coming, for insecure and repressive regimes have nurtured conspiracy thinking through their media and by suppressing basic liberties, especially freedom of expression. Worrying about possible schemes to overthrow their illegit-imate regimes, the rulers have created an atmosphere of perpetual fear that has helped to institutionalize conspiratorial thinking. Moving on to a more responsible and mature form of politics means leaving behind the conspiratorial mindset. (1997)

The academic distaste for conspiracy theory is not a recent trend but the unease at being associated with this apparent 'para-scholarship' is perhaps more acute since the form itself has become more commodified in ways recounted in the previous chapter.

In the mid-twentieth century, historians could be concerned that their work, via Karl Popper, might be accused of being a conspiracy theory, signalling a weak and monolithic form of analysis; just as public speakers wanted to avoid the label for fear of being associated with populist politics. But today the term 'conspiracy theory' has many more connotations. Now that the term refers to a wide-reaching, commodified culture, the fear of being associated with con-spiracism today could be exacerbated by the proximity with commodified popular culture.

To be sure, the academic texts that express unease about conspiracy theory often focus on its widespread appeal. Concerns like Elaine Showalter's (from a study that I will place into a category of its own below) highlight an anxiety over epistemology and the public sphere. How can intellectuals appeal to a public that processes information through a different epistemological model? Showalter seems to fear a *mass* epidemic. Configured as a mass, conspiracy culture is presented as an obstruction to the rule of reason. Showalter comes from a very different political identification but this kind of argument is a staple of reactionary rhetoric. For example, Gustave Le Bon conceived of the masses in a similar manner in order to frame his theories of anti-mass based democracy. Le Bon posited the individual against the crowd, seeing the latter as less rational and sophisticated than the former: 'In the collective mind the intellectual aptitudes of the individuals, and in consequence their individuality, are weakened. The heterogeneous is swamped by the homogenous' ([1895] 1977: 29). The 'homogenous' crowd accumulates 'stupidity', operating, he thought, according to the lowest common denominator. The crowd, in contrast to the individual, is irresponsible (Le Bon [1895] 1977: 30), impetuous (Le Bon [1895] 1977: 31), and irrational (Le Bon [1895] 1977: 112). As we shall see, Showalter's study suggests that public narratives obstruct the 'real' truths – truths that, if given precedence, would reconfigure the mass as a series of individuals. The influx of conspiracy theory related Internet sites, television drama serials such as *The X-Files* and chat shows, as well as talk radio, have transformed concerns like Showalter's into an anxiety over the way in which knowledges are circulated and established outside, or on the margins of, the traditional site for knowledge-production: the academy. The commodification of conspiracy theory makes the way in which academics and the press deal with conspiracy theory a more pressing issue for those concerned with how popular cultural texts and practices come to be configured.

Although Fenster usefully details many contemporary manifestations of conspiracy theory and considers some of its semiological and rhetorical characteristics (1999: xvii), he eventually criticizes conspiracy theory for not being a politically viable outlet. Fenster writes, 'totalizing conspiracy theories suffer from a lack of substantive proof, dizzying leaps of logic, and oversimplification of the political and economic structures and power' (1999: xvii). For Fiske, of course, this act of simplification is precisely the point – it allows those unversed in the sophisticated rhetoric of politics to engage with issues of power and their experience of subjugation. But for Fenster, the inequalities conspiracy theorists read as proof of conspiracy are, rather, the defining characteristics of capitalism and would be more fruitfully addressed as such. Fenster claims that while apparently showing increased public participation in political spheres, 'conspiracy theory ultimately fails as a political and cultural practice' because it does not constitute or encourage political action in democratic terms (1999: 225). Fenster is concerned at how studies like Fiske's (1993) praise the empowering effects of conspiracy theory without pushing the logic of this far enough to acknowledge who is *dis*-empowered by it. While a diagnosis such as

Fenster's assumes a model of a political cultural text that conspiracy theory fails to live up to, Fiske's praises the resistance conspiracy theory can provide for historically disenfranchised groups such as African Americans, while overlooking (as Fenster in fact himself points out) the racist tracts that can also be termed conspiracy theory.

In his book *Conspiracy Culture* (2000), Knight helpfully resists the pull to make political judgements about conspiracy theory. He summarizes the problem with such approaches thus: these studies 'end up insisting that other (usually less sophisticated) people's everyday cultural practices fulfil one's own political agenda – and then chastising them for failing at what they never intended in the first place' (Knight 2000: 21). Like conspiracy theory itself and accusations of conspiracy theory, the academic study of conspiracy theory has been employed to various political ends. While these analyses have much to offer in the way of situating a practice like conspiracy theory within its socio-political context, the idea of politics itself is never addressed. Gary Hall, drawing on the work of Geoffrey Bennington, explains:

> Politics here is the one thing it is vital to understand, as politics is that by which everything else is judged ... politics is at the same time the one thing that *cannot* be understood; for the one thing that cannot be judged by the transcendentally raised criteria of politics is politics itself. Consequently, the last question these 'political' discourses *can* raise is *the question of politics*. (2002: 66)

As a transcendental signifier, 'politics' organizes and limits the kinds of questions that can be asked of conspiracy theory and even of politics itself. If made to respond only to this agenda, if mobilized only within this discourse, many aspects of conspiracy theory remain unthought.

Outside of this issue of the directly political, Showalter gives a different spin to the second more pessimistic account of conspiracy theory in a way that exacerbates the problem of addressing one discourse according to the concerns of another. On first impressions, it might seem that Showalter does justice to the idea of conspiracy theories and other alternative ways of knowing in *Hystories: Hysterical Epidemics and Modern Culture*. She claims, for instance that, 'Modern forms of individual and mass hysteria have much to tell us about the anxieties and fantasies of western culture' (Showalter 1997: 12). Indeed, Showalter takes on board the complaints and struggles within the 'hysteric' narratives that she considers, and even acknowledges the sometimes ambiguous position these discourses of complaint assume in relation to scientific, political and medical discourses. Showalter postulates that classical hysteria can be seen collectively re-emerging as recent phenomena like Gulf War syndrome, chronic fatigue syndrome (ME), or alien abduction narratives, which she calls 'psychogenic syndromes' (Showalter 1997: 12). Far from using this to delegitimize the symptoms such 'epidemics' produce, Showalter is commenting on how psychological problems are denigrated and denied in modern culture. The resistance of sufferers, support groups and some therapists to acknowledge the neurological origin of such complaints derives from the negative connotations ascribed to hysteria, not least because of its association with the feminine. From within the discourse of psychoanalysis, Showalter asks us to explore what 'symptoms' such as conspiracy theory can tell us about the 'real' psycho-social demands of the turn of the century.

Throughout the book, Showalter positions conspiracy theory as a symptom of contemporary hysteria that should be dealt with in private as individual psychological ailment rather than in public as social narrative 'reality'. Her compassion should not distract us from her explicit objective: to get her readers to 'interrupt or halt these epidemics' (Showalter 1997: 12). Any understanding of these so-called 'epidemics' is to be only a step towards the strategic erasure of them. We can secure this, she suggests, with the very media – television and the press – that have helped create them: she writes 'We can ... use the media to fight rumors as well as to spread them' (Showalter 1997: 12).

Showalter's quest to counter the message of conspiracy theories is a familiar trope. In their *Times Higher Education Supplement* book review, Peter Knight and Alasdair Spark describe how the authors of a spate of studies concerned with conspiracy and conspiracy theory, including Showalter, present their sense of duty as alarmism about popular paranoia (Knight and Spark 1998: 22). The authors cited by Knight and Spark perhaps unsurprisingly 'identify paranoia as pseudo-scholarship' but, more significantly, they 'feel they have to correct [paranoia's] inaccuracies' (1998: 22). Knight and Spark explain the general tone of these works:

> It is not enough to examine and interpret conspiracy theories, these writers seem to suggest. Responsible writers must also take a stand, push back the tide of increasing gullibility by presenting What Is Really Going On in simplified form; in short, they must correct and instruct. (1998: 22)

Very much within this vein, Showalter claims that:

> the hysterical epidemics of the 1990s have already gone on too long, and they continue to do damage: in distracting us from the real problems and crises of modern society, in undermining a respect for evidence and truth, and in helping to support an atmosphere of conspiracy and suspicion. They prevent us from claiming our full humanity as free and responsible beings. (1997: 206)

Showalter's text obfuscates social conditions in favour of psychological explanations. Or rather, social narratives and practices are valuable only for what they can tell us about how hysteria manifests itself, rather than as objects of study that might problematize the way in which Showalter mobilizes one knowledge system (based on an Enlightenment ideal) to curb another. She tries to draw paranoia back into the specific, as it were, away from its generalized, mass appearance. Paranoid discourses and conspiracy theory are reduced to a logic of psychological symptomatology. This pathologizing of conspiracy theory has a long history in the literature on paranoia. It has been reinforced relatively recently by a number of studies including Daniel Pipes' *Conspiracy: How the Paranoid Style Flourishes and Where It Comes From* (1997) and Robert S. Robins and Jerrold Post's *Political Paranoia: The Psychopolitics of Hatred* (1998). Ironically, as Jodi Dean points out, in

> trying to demonstrate the abnormality of political paranoia ... those who view conspiracy as pathology have to concede that sometimes there really are conspiracies afoot and sometimes paranoia in politics makes good sense ... Were they to follow through with this concession, their diagnoses would be premised on establishing whether or not a conspiracy exists, thereby trans-forming the critics themselves into conspiracy theorists. (2002: 51)

At a conference concerned with conspiracy cultures, Showalter fell into just such a trap when she ridiculed the discourse of Gulf War syndrome and its associated fears of government conspiracy, set out to counter the claims with hard evidence, and appealed to fellow academics to be 'guardians of reason'.[2] Though reason is placed in the transcendental position rather than politics, it is to a political end. 'Reason', here, is more a shibboleth for authority or academic prudence. (I should say that it is the way the idea of reason is mobilized as a redeeming academic ideal that is questionable, rather than the complex concept of reason itself, of course.) I would suggest that it is more productive for cultural theorists to question why this configuration of reason needs to be guarded than to guard it themselves. With Showalter's 'call to arms', she grounds her work in the assumption that academics share a notion of 'reason' never questioned in her study. For example, some people, as we have seen in relation to post-September 11 feelings about conspiracy theory, do not necessarily feel that paranoia is always unreasonable: sometimes paranoia is the most reasonable response to a political situation (see Marcus 1999).

Showalter's thesis implies that not only should academics 'know better' (as Knight and Spark point out), but that they should guard the organizing signifiers that secure this 'better knowing or knowledge'. By translating the conspiracist experiences described in her study into a knowable and appar-ently comprehensive scientific discourse, and in claiming this to be the work of academics, there is no place to consider what the experiences she wants to explain away can tell us about the very academic discourses she wants to do this explaining away. Showalter does not entertain the possibility that to ask these narratives to prove themselves 'legitimate' by the very criteria that root her discourse rather than theirs might constitute a Lyotardian *differend*:

> As distinguished from a litigation, a differend would be a case of conflict
> between (at least) two parties, that cannot be equitably resolved for lack of a
> rule of judgement applicable to both arguments. One side's legitimacy does
> not imply the other's lack of legitimacy. However, applying a single rule of
> judgement to both in order to settle their differend as though it were a mere
> litigation would wrong (at least) one of them (and both if neither side admits
> this rule). (Lyotard [1983] 1988: xi)

Lyotard asserts that each genre of discourse supplies a set of possible phrases
following its last (so that conspiracy theory might link the Roswell incident
to a government cover-up of alien life, whereas a historian might look to
military weapons testing). That conspiracy theory prescribes a different phrase
regimen to that of an academic discourse should not *ipso facto* delegitimize it.
A *differend* occurs when there are no procedures to present the different in the
contemporary sphere of discourse. Rather than judge the individual hypotheses
that are produced under the name of conspiracy theory from within a discourse
by which it has already been deemed illegitimate, might it not be more helpful
to consider conspiracy theory as a 'genre of discourse' that does not play by
the same rules as the one from which I am writing? Especially if I do not want
my very address to silence that which I hope to observe, question, and self-
reflexively consider.

CULTURAL STUDIES AS CONSPIRACY THEORY

While I think that the issues raised by the approaches outlined above – the way
in which we experience and articulate politics in apolitical or non-traditional
ways; alternative attempts at 'cognitive mapping'; and the legitimation of
psychological problems – are important, they leave open a number of questions
about the act of analysis or interpretation, and the mobilization of knowledge
itself. Instead of being disappointed in conspiracy theory's failure to formalize
discontent, critique its reactionary tendencies, celebrate its disruptive potential,
or correct its inaccuracies, I want to explore, as Lyotard terms it, the 'wrong'
([1983] 1988: 9) that occurs when attempts are made in academia to denounce
or distance themselves from conspiracy theory, or when conspiracy theory is
written about as if it had nothing to do with what founds being able to know
or interpret in the first place.[3] In addition, I will look for ways of addressing the
apparent opposition between 'legitimate' and 'illegitimate' knowledges, between
Showalter's discourse, for example, and the one she critiques.
    What we quickly discover on doing so is that it becomes impossible to map
conspiracy theory and academic discourse onto a clear illegitimate/legitimate
divide. For not only does the *differend* expose the way in which difference is
'violently' reduced to something within an already knowable horizon that can

then be judged; but we begin to see how there could be illegitimate legitimacies (such as Showalter's combative response to conspiracy theory), legitimate illegitimacies (such as justified paranoia), and also illegitimate illegitimacies that do not simply become legitimate. Any simplistic distinction between legitimate and illegitimate is thus dislodged. And with this the possibility is opened up of beginning to read cultural studies itself as an illegitimate illegitimacy (as an unacknowledged conspiracy theory). This is a helpful gesture if we want, as I will towards the end of this chapter, to take on board something that is very much at stake within cultural studies when it comes to its analysis of conspiracy theories – namely, cultural studies' own unstable, ambiguous and sometimes 'paranoid' relationship with 'legitimacy'.

HYPERREAL KNOWLEDGE

First, however, a theoretical detour is needed in order to explore the relationship between legitimized and non-legitimized knowledges further. Though somewhat dated now, I want to (selectively) employ Jean Baudrillard's formulation of the hyperreal because it will help to conceptualize legitimized and non-legitimized knowledges on what I described earlier as a continuum. Following Baudrillard's contention that hyperreal images become 'more real than the real' (1987: 28), we might say that conspiracy theory is 'more knowledge than knowledge'. For instance, Baudrillard describes how: 'Cinema plagiarises and copies itself, remakes its classics, retroactivates its original myths, remakes silent films more perfect than the originals, etc.' (1987: 28). Post-modern cinema thus becomes more cinema than cinema, obsessed with producing the perfect replica of itself. With this model in mind, we could think of conspiracy theory's difference from and similarities to other (more legitimated) knowledges as a heightening of the latter's narrative concerns, an acceleration of their mode of signification and semiosis, and as putting on display their conditions of possibility. This hyperreal operation is, like all simulation, subversive in its implicit suggestion that all knowledges 'might be nothing more than simulation' (Baudrillard 1983: 38). In other words, conspiracy *theory* can suggest that all knowledge is only ever 'theory'; that the relationship between a sign and its referent is necessarily inflected by imaginary processes; and that any transcendental truth claims rely on contingent strategies of legitimation.

I should make it clear that I am citing Baudrillard's term in an isolated sense. With regards to the way in which the hyperreal puts on display the workings of the 'real', such a formulation is only helpful if we complicate the apparent privileged status given to the 'real'. In order to avoid the undue nostalgia that can be seen to permeate Baudrillard's thought, we must think of the 'real' as having retained the possibility of the hyperreal, and as being in some ways constituted by it. Baudrillard's theory of the sign is best viewed on a representational level:

certain socio-economic and aesthetic contexts, that is, may make it *seem* as if the symbol is emancipated from its referential obligation, yet, it is a freedom that was always already there, enabling it to function as a symbol.

To a certain degree, Baudrillard invites such an understanding. He writes that his 'design of classification' with regards to modes of representation 'leading' to the hyperreal is:

> certainly formal, but it is a little like the situation among physicists who each month invent a new particle. One does not dispel the other: they succeed one another and increase in number in a hypothetical trajectory. (Baudrillard 1990: 13, translated by and quoted in Genosko 1994: 44)

Gary Genosko comments on this passage and how it encourages us to read the orders of simulation as an 'abstract problematic'; he thinks that this should deter us from a 'strictly phasal and subsumptive reading' (Genosko 1994: 44). Upsetting a logic of identity or causal temporality by this idea of simultaneity at least hints at the mutual contamination of the real and hyperreal proposed above. Rather than resulting in a lack of meaning, the hyperreal can expose a condition of the 'real' – that it must be able to be simulated, to be iterated in a different context – that allows for its exaggerated 'other'. Herein lies the tension. And a similar tension, I want to suggest, can be located in the relation between academic discourses (such as, but not exclusively, cultural studies) and conspiracy theory. For what we see is that conspiracy theory puts on display a possibility of reading, the invisibility of which (achieved through processes of non-recognition or delegitimization) other knowledge-producing discourses rely upon. The conditions that enable knowledge-producing discourses to function can also be used to question their very foundations; and the close proximity between academic discourses and conspiracy theory places this risk in a public context.

However, while I think this is true for academic discourses in general, there is something specific that cultural studies can learn from conspiracy theory, not least because cultural studies is probably the discourse or knowledge most suited to analysing contemporary phenomena of this sort. We could, for example, see conspiracy theory's self-legitimating structure (the 'truth' is in the telling, and the telling is often claimed to be 'dangerous') as similar to what physicist Alan Sokal, who submitted a hoax to the cultural studies journal *Social Text*, finds so distasteful about cultural studies. Sokal finds the apparent 'epistemic relativism' (2000: 51) he sees at work in much cultural theory highly problematic. He thinks the argument of his 'fake' cultural studies paper (that quantum gravity has progressive political implications) was accepted precisely because it affirmed the attitude of the editors towards social (and scientific) constructionism and an uncritical populism. His essay slipped through the net not only because *Social Text* was sympathetic to the apparent politics of Sokal's essay but also because, unusually for a cultural studies journal, it is not peer-reviewed (see Robbins and Ross 2000: 55). In other words, the journal could be seen as self-legitimating. Quoting Larry Laudan, Sokal claims that his hoax revealed the misguided nature of modern critical and cultural theory that 'appropriate[s] conclusions from the philosophy of science and put[s] them to work in aid of a variety of social cum political causes for which those conclusions are ill adapted' (Larry Laudan quoted in Sokal 1996: 93). However, the focus of the emergent anxiety evident in Sokal's hoax and response (to which I will return below) extends beyond a concern over the borrowing and decontextualization of terms, to the systematic questioning via critical and cultural theory of the boundaries between science and other kinds of knowledge.[4]

ECONOMIC INTERPRETATION

To assess fully the implications of a close, perhaps hyperreal relationship between conspiracy theory, knowledge in general, and cultural studies in particular, we must recognize that as part of its work as a popular knowledge, conspiracy theory is a form of interpretation; and that as such it raises important questions about this aspect of knowledge production itself: about interpretation *per se*.

The novelist and semiotician Umberto Eco may not at first appear like an obvious person to turn to in order to think these issues through at this stage. Yet his work on interpretation can be illuminating here, not only because he indirectly discusses conspiracy theory but because he provides another example of the anxiety already displayed by Showalter and Sokal. Addressing this anxiety adequately will take us closer to deconstruction and a 'deconstructive' cultural studies.

Concerned, as he is, with establishing the limits of interpretation, Eco wants to claim that some interpretations can be classed as 'overinterpretation'. He is never fully able to define the difference between interpretation and over-interpretation but relies on the idea that overinterpretation cannot be checked against the coherence of a text as a whole and is not supported by community consensus. He claims that a community provides a 'factual guarantee' (Eco 1992: 144). In the end, he resorts to claiming that although it is often difficult to recognize a good interpretation; one simply *knows* when one encounters bad or over interpretation. Eco is focusing on interpretations of literary texts rather than historical events so he does not use the name 'conspiracy theory'. But from his novel, *Foucault's Pendulum* (1988), the link between overinterpretation and conspiracy theory is clear – his novel is the dramatic exposition of what it means to overinterpret as the protagonist/narrator creates and lives by a conspiracy theory he and his friends construct. In *Foucault's Pendulum*, overinterpretation takes the guise of a Hermetic reading or what we would contemporaneously think of as conspiracy theory. In Eco's theoretical writings, overinterpretation includes deconstruction.

Eco would have us believe that the link between Hermeticism/conspiracy theory and deconstruction is one that discredits deconstruction. In order to do this, Eco (in a gesture similar to that of Sokal's reductive characterization of cultural theory) has to soften deconstruction and refashion it as a reader-oriented relativism that seeks to validate any and every interpretation. Eco considers deconstruction to be a continuation of the Hermetic project – one that is informed by principles of:

> universal analogy and sympathy, according to which every item of the furn-iture of the world is linked to every other element (or to many) of this sublunar world and to every element (or to many) of the superior world by means of similitudes or resemblances. (1990: 24)

The objection to Hermetic drift and deconstruction as interpretative methodologies focuses on the logic of resemblance that supposedly guides them both. Eco points out that conclusions cannot be made from a set of circumstances just because those circumstances might remind us of others and their corresponding results: he insists that 'one must distinguish between a relationship of causality and a relationship of similarity' (1990: 29). Eco also criticizes deconstruction for encouraging the idea that 'every expression is a secret, or an enigma that evokes a further enigma' (1990: 27). This, Eco writes, results in there being 'no way to test the reliability of an interpretation' (1990: 27). He fears the subsequent translation of the whole world into a 'mere linguistic phenomenon ... [that] devoids language of any communicative power' (Eco 1990: 27).

Eco's disagreement with deconstruction hinges on what he considers to be Derrida's misreading of Peircean 'unlimited semiosis' (the process by which an interpretant's reading of a sign can always be taken up by another interpretant *ad infinitum*). Eco insists that the difference between 'unlimited semiosis' and Hermetic/deconstructive drift (which he reads as being equivalent) is that the former still allows for some readings to be discounted, whereas the latter has to allow for every interpretation to be valid. Such a logic, his theoretical and creative writings suggest, is dangerous in the extreme.

For example, in *Foucault's Pendulum*, the opinions of Lia are set up as the yardstick of common sense against which other interpretations can be measured. When the protagonist/narrator, Casaubon, approaches Lia with a supposedly encrypted text, she takes a few days to reach her own interpretation. She claims that the message is a merchant's delivery list, a kind of 'laundry list' (Eco 1988: 534). She berates Casaubon for overlooking quotidian explanations in order to translate the text into what he wants it to say. In his theoretical writings, Eco refers to this behaviour as 'using' rather than critically 'interpreting' the text.

Eco claims: 'To critically interpret a text means to read it in order to discover ... something about its nature. To use a text means to start from it in order to get something else' (1990: 57). Lia is commended for 'just knowing' what is right in a way that Eco, in an essentialist gesture, suggests is tied to her active experience of life through the body, as opposed to Casaubon's which appears mediated by the mind. The difference arises in a number of situations: for instance, when trying to explain why Hermetic interpretation is wrong, Lia says: 'people with a brain in their head, if they're shown an alchemist's oven, all shut up and warm inside, think of the belly of the mama making a baby, and only your Diabolicals think that the Madonna about to have the Child is a reference to the alchemist's oven' (Eco 1988: 364-5).

Lia is concerned with the function of metaphor, indicating that only one trajectory works, leading to a reproductive/religious image that is central, she believes, to human experience. At the end of the signifying chain stand a Madonna and child. She considers it wrong to 'use' them as a means to get to 'something else'.

The target of Lia's derision is essentially the logic of conspiracy and Hermetic analogy – forms of overinterpretation that are guided by the assumption that 'tout se tient' (Eco 1988: 179), which translates as 'everything is connected'. While Casaubon aims to expose the arbitrary nature of the connections between events that form a conspiracy theory through a parody of his own, Eco dramatizes the seductive power of a discourse disregarding whether or not one 'really believes'. Once connections have been made, and a context established to support them, they cease to appear arbitrary. At this point, a particular logic has 'seduced' and been subscribed to. Casaubon describes this seduction as a decreasing distinction between the object of parody and the parodist: 'Among the Diabolicals, I moved with the ease of a psychiatrist who becomes fond of his patients ... After a while, he begins to write pages on delirium, then pages of delirium, unaware that his sick people have seduced him' (Eco 1988: 370).

Casaubon tells us how 'wanting connections, we found connections – always, everywhere, and between everything' (Eco 1988: 463). Casaubon has produced such a convincing account of history that he becomes lodged in its methodology and can now see no alternative: what began as fiction has become truth, even if truth is a fiction which has very 'real' effects.

Eco fashions deconstruction as similarly seductive but the characterization of deconstruction as Hermeticism stumbles early on. Hermeticism leads us on an identifiable (if maddeningly plotted) journey of connections whereas deconstruction radically upsets how that journey can be perceived (we might, for example, be encouraged to think about that which separates as well as joins in a chain of meaning). Indeed, it is not on a promise (which can be fulfilled) of knowledge or meaning that deferment works. Cognition is not simply present in and of itself; processes of knowledge are, rather, deferred or differentiated by a non-coincidence of the subject. In his well-known explication of Husserl, Derrida explains how the 'I' that speaks or writes 'I am mortal' is never purely present to itself as it relies on the possibility of being repeated in the radical absence – death – of that 'I': an absence which will complicate the idea of a thinking subject based on ideals of presence (see Derrida [1967b] 1973). Meaning does not come 'nearer', it has not slipped through our fingers, but is structurally differentiated. It cannot be thought of as an object to be discovered.

Mirroring Lia's derision in *Foucault's Pendulum*, Eco reduces the question of interpretation to one of 'common sense', claiming that much deconstructive theory 'disregards very obvious truths that nobody can reasonably pass over in silence' (1990: 36). Peirce may have endorsed a semiotics which emphasizes how signs refer to other signs rather than to 'a presence' or 'the thing itself' (Eco 1990: 37), and one in which 'the transcendental meaning is not at the origins of the process,' but this meaning 'must be postulated as a possible and transitory end of every process' (Eco 1990: 41). This agreed privileged meaning, as Eco points out, sits uncomfortably with the approach of deconstruction but not because of a relativism lacking in rigour as he suspects, but because for Derrida meaning is always subject to deferral and differentiation. Derrida formulates meaning as indefinitely deferred by *différance* and dispersed by 'dissemination'. The more radical implications of Derrida's thought are obscured in Eco's misrepresentation of these quasi-concepts. 'Dissemination', for example, suggests an unlimited dispersal, or scattering of meaning: indeterminable, and impossible to predict or anticipate. A play on the arbitrary etymological link between semen and semantics, dissemination can be seen to disperse meaning like 'the seed that neither inseminates nor is recovered by the father, but is scattered abroad' (Spivak 1976: xi). Meaning is always already lost to an imaginary moment of production, never to lead to insemination and fertilization. Writing does not end in the unproblematic conception of meaning, or find its meaning in a united bond, but is left to fend for itself, always already orphaned by this radical reformulation of the authorial role.

In Eco's configuration, dissemination is confused with polysemia. What Eco fails to acknowledge is that deconstruction does not encourage or lead to a countable number of readings – even if this is an infinite multiplication of 'one' – but fundamentally problematizes numerical imaginings of this sort and how they privilege the idea of an 'original work', which is seen to have endless resources for interpretation. Derrida clearly states: 'It is [the] hermeneutic concept of *polysemy* that must be replaced by *dissemination*' ([1972b] 1981: 262). Dissemination does not exclude the possibility of determinate meanings being produced in context. Indeed, what Eco misses out of his account of Derrida is the aporetic tension between determinacy and indeterminacy. Meanings can be posited, drawn towards specificity, but this specificity is enabled or structured by indeterminacy.

I will consider this double bind (what makes meaning possible, also makes it impossible) at several junctures in this book but what should be clear at this stage is that Eco's characterization of deconstruction as a form of nihilism is misleading. Eco's critique of deconstruction will only work along the lines of a crude comparison with Hermeticism. I would suggest, as with cultural studies above, that the link between deconstruction and Hermeticism/conspiracy theory exists, but not to the ends that Eco assumes. The link does not delegitimize both conspiracy theory and deconstruction, but rather shows deconstruction to be the mode of thought that (like conspiracy theory and potentially cultural studies) highlights an aporia of legitimacy, knowledge and interpretation. We will return to this shortly after questioning the safeguards Eco claims protect us from overinterpretation and unsound knowledge, for such policing has implications for any demarcation between popular and other kinds of knowledge.

COMMUNITIES OF DISSENSUS

An 'overinterpretation', according to Eco, employs Hermetic association and, by doing so, moves interpretation beyond a boundary of reading that the text itself suggests, and is endorsed by an interpretative community. In other words, a bad interpretation exceeds the boundaries of the community consensus.[5] While Eco suggests that an interpretation can be '[checked] against a text as a coherent whole', the ability to detect bad interpretations is, he implies, instinctive. He writes, for example, that 'it is impossible to say what is the best interpretation of a text, but it is possible to say which ones are wrong' (1990: 148). To the question, 'what kind of guarantee can a community provide?' Eco conjectures, 'I think it provides a factual guarantee' (1992: 144). Eco substantiates this 'factual guarantee' by citing the example of how children learn not to touch fire or play with knives. Identifying a bad interpretation becomes linked to experiential instinct. Such a link is dramatized through the death-bound plot of *Foucault's Pendulum* in which physical danger is the result of overinterpretation.

Eco does not claim that a community should privilege one reading above others, but that it can privilege one *kind* of reading. Some texts are 'open texts' that can support a number of readings, but even in these cases, the community of knowers can agree upon their 'open nature and the strategies that make them work that way' (Eco 1990: 41). Eco supposes that while a community can agree that multiple readings are supported by certain texts, its members must also recognize when an 'unreliable' methodology has been employed to arrive at an interpretation. Consensus provides a way to identify readings that are not contextually legitimate rather than helping to decide 'the best' or 'most accurate' reading. The community polices the limits of interpretation rather than commends or venerates one single interpretation. Knowing which texts support multiple readings introduces problems of arbitration as does the undecidability of what is and what is not contextually legitimate. Where do the boundaries of context lie and what happens when those boundaries are constantly being challenged by interpretations relegated to the 'outside'? The 'overinterpreters' can constitute a community of their own and have interpretative criteria that are at odds with other cognitive-interpretative communities but can also influence and challenge the 'main' interpretative community or rational paradigm. The way in which interpretative communities are not exclusive realms but are constantly being negotiated by challenges to them serves as the basis of Lyotard's refutation of Habermasian consensus as the ultimate goal of discourse. A consideration of this will problematize Eco's reliance upon 'community consensus' as a check upon interpretation.

Lyotard claims that 'the principle of consensus as a criterion of validation' is 'inadequate' ([1979] 1994: 60). He sees consensus as assuming two forms. First, the Habermasian ideal: 'an agreement between men, defined as knowing intellects and free wills [...] obtained through dialogue' (Lyotard [1979] 1994: 60). Consensus, then, is a concept tied to a narrative of emancipation. This becomes problematic when the possibility of emancipatory rhetoric being employed to nefarious ends becomes apparent (the rhetoric of National Socialism being the most obvious example). Second, consensus is seen as a politico-economic instrument: Lyotard states that the system 'manipulates [consensus] in order to maintain and improve its performance' ([1979] 1994: 60). Lyotard's second model fashions consensus as an ideological tool that can be 'used toward achieving the real goal, which is what legitimates the system – power' ([1979] 1994: 61). Lyotard therefore sees the disruptive potential of paralogic 'moves' to be beneficial to the interpretative community. Paralogic moves, that is, are seen to be helpful for the very reason that the community rejects them. He explains how

> Countless scientists have seen their 'move' ignored or repressed, sometimes for decades, because it too abruptly destabilized the accepted positions, not only in the university and scientific hierarchy, but also in the problematic. The stronger the 'move,' the more likely it is to be denied the minimum consensus, precisely because it changes the rules of the game upon which consensus had been based. (Lyotard [1979] 1994: 63)

Those readings or findings that upset the system in which consensus is privileged are not granted consensual acceptance. This kind of regulation, however, merely observes science behaving like any other 'power center whose behaviour is governed by a principle of homeostasis' (Lyotard [1979] 1994: 63). Lyotard calls this behaviour 'terrorist' in the sense that the system gains efficiency by the threatened elimination of a 'player from the language game' ([1979] 1994: 63). Individual aspirations need to fall in line with the needs of the system.

According to Lyotard, accepting Habermas's idea of consensus would entail making two assumptions. First, that 'it is possible for speakers to come to agreement on which rules or metaprescriptions are universally valid for language games, when it is clear that language games are heteromorphous, subject to heterogeneous sets of pragmatic rules' (Lyotard [1979] 1994: 65). Second, it assumes that consensus is the goal of dialogue whereas it 'is only a particular state of discussion, not its end' (Lyotard [1979] 1994: 65). Lyotard calls for a justice that is not based on consensus. He stresses the heteromorphous rather than isomorphic nature of language games and privileges dissensus and paralogy over consensus, challenging the emphasis Habermas places on a statement's ability to contribute to an emancipatory ideal. When the role of consensus is questioned in this way, Eco's notion of a 'bad' interpretation clearly becomes problematic. While Eco's configuration of consensus indicates that a 'bad' interpretation can injure the community in some way, I would want to consider what 'injury' or 'violence' is done when an interpretation or way of knowing – a 'move' in the language game – is denied a hearing or is not allowed to enter into an arena in which it can generate other ideas and responses.

Eco's formulation, like Habermas's notion of the public sphere, assumes that there is a common goal in interpretative and cognitive endeavours. Eco's recognition of the lure of knowledges other than those rooted in scientific rationalism should suggest to him the difficulty of such an assumption. What role, for example, can desire or pleasure play in interpretative practice? What needs are fulfilled by creating 'alternative' interpretative communities?[6] Eco fails to recognize either the three editor cum conspiracy theorists in *Foucault's Pendulum*, or those other conspiracy theorists the editors name the Diabolicals, as communities. Rather, these factions are characterized as exceeding a community. Explicating Eco's theories, Peter Bondanella states that 'overinterpretations or paranoid interpretations will eventually be refused by the community' (1997: 289). Yet, if those 'overinterpreters' can be recognized as constituting interpretative communities of their own, they in turn develop their own 'refusals' and contextual criteria. The co-existence of a number of communities, the internal consensus of each being constituted by dissensus, complicates the employment of community consensus as an anchor of interpretation.

Eco's texts obscure the way in which overinterpretation inheres in the very principle of interpretation: that for there to be an idea of what interpretation is, there must be overinterpretation. Overinterpretation is a constitutive factor in interpretation before an exclusionary gesture can then be made. Overinterpretation, in other words, is already 'there'. In the following citation, Derrida complicates the relationship between thought, speech and writing, but his formulation can help critique any simple notion of interiority and exteriority implicit in a notion of the boundary, including Eco's distinction between interpretation and overinterpretation: 'The outside bears with the inside a relationship that is, as usual, anything but simple exteriority. The meaning of the outside was already present within the inside, imprisoned outside the outside, and vice versa' (Derrida [1967a] 1984: 35).

Reading this figuratively, as soon as a line is drawn – a boundary designated – there is no 'pure' interior because the same line that delineates this also demarcates the outside. The inside has to 'get outside itself' for the outer edge of the boundary to be drawn and this is what lets the outside in or the inside out.[7] The boundary is a border to both interpretation and overinterpretation and as such implicates each in the constitution of the other. This complex economy must cause us to question any simple notion of Eco's interpretative community. It must be asked how exclusions will be arbitrated. The idea of community consensus implies that a community of knowers will have to exclude not only those interpretations that exceed their criteria, but also the interpreters that produce them. It becomes a question of plural 'communities' rather than a singular 'community'. Once communities are defined against each other, the boundary joins as well as separates.

There is nothing unusual about Eco's desire to make judgements about interpretations. Cultural theorists have to measure the soundness of an interpretation every time they look for information on the Internet, every time they read the newspaper or listen to someone speak on television, whenever they review the research of peers or examine student work. But Eco's attempt to devise a system to demarcate the limits of interpretation is unsustainable. Because of iterability, an interpretation free from the possibility of misinterpretation or overinterpretation is impossible. Separating interpretation from overinterpretation ignores how all interpretation is fuelled, and made possible by, the repetition, grafting, quoting of the text to be interpreted in the radical absence of its author. Derrida writes: 'This citationality, duplication, or duplicity, this iterability of the mark is not an accident or an anomaly, but is that ... without which a mark could no longer even have a so-called "normal" functioning' ([1972a] 1982: 320–1). This radical absence, this quasi-metaphorical 'death', means that while one can appeal to authorial intention and historical context, they provide no final determination nor end to interpretation. Iterability means that an interpretation can never be saturated, complete; it can never preclude the need for other interpretations. Bennington explains that 'the unity of the act of writing and/or reading is divided':

> the gap thus introduced between the agencies of 'sender' and 'addressee' (but also within each of these agencies) implies, at the least, that writing can never fully 'express' a thought or realize an intention... The necessary possibility of the death of the writer ... opens writing to the general alterity of its destination, but simultaneously forbids any sure or total arrival at such a destination: the presumed unity of a text, marked in principle by its author's signature, thus has to wait on the other's countersignature... But every determinate addressee, and thus every act of reading is affected by the same 'death', it therefore follows that every countersignature has to wait on others, indefinitely, that reading has no end, but is always to-come as work of

the other (and never of the Other) – a text never comes to rest in a unity or meaning finally revealed or discovered. (1993: 55–6)

If we accept what Eco says about overinterpretations being excessive failures, this is only useful if (rather than marginalize, ridicule, dismiss or demonize them as he does) it allows us to see them on a continuum with other failures (of communication) in Derrida's thought (like unhappy performatives, or letters gone astray). These 'failures' of course are not failures in the strict sense, because without them there could be no possibility of 'success', rendering the success, in our case, interpretation, contaminated in advance. With reference to performatives, Derrida observes how J. L. Austin recognizes that

the possibility of the negative ... is certainly a structural possibility, that failure is an essential risk in the operations under consideration; and then, with an almost *immediately simultaneous* gesture made in the name of a kind of ideal regulation, an exclusion of this risk as an accidental, exterior one that teaches us nothing about the language phenomenon under consideration. ([1972a] 1982: 323)

In a similar vein, Eco and Showalter exteriorize overinterpretation as though it has nothing to do with what allows them to interpret overinterpretation at all. Derrida asks, 'What is a success when the possibility of failure continues to constitute its structure?' ([1972a] 1982: 324). What, we might ask, is an interpretation when 'overinterpretation' constitutes its structure?

How exactly does deconstruction problematize interpretation that idealizes the text, object or event to be interpreted? Derrida has shown how such idealization is flawed because no text, no event to be interpreted, is fully present to itself. There will always be a hidden, occluded 'element' that cannot be revealed and resolved within a text because it is its undepletable, inexhaustible condition of possibility. This element, for want of a better word, is not a mysterious secret that a hermeneutic approach could reveal; it is a conditioning absence. Paradoxically, the implications of this absence – namely that interpretation is impossible – does not stop us from interpreting. In fact it enables anything called interpretation to take place again and again. Interpretation is never complete because of a profound absence in the text being interpreted, and because that same absence conditions any subsequent interpretative text.

Here, I have to face the implications of failing to take into account that overinterpretation, rather than subtending or deviating from interpretation, actually conditions it. For me to be able to interpret anything – analyse it away from its original context – and to enjoy the freedom that interpretation brings with it, I must in principle be able to enjoy that freedom indefinitely in a radical de- and re-contextualization. Therefore, overinterpretation is a vehicle of interpretation's freedom. What limits interpretation is not any natural principle of interpretation but only those institutions that have the authority to rule interpretations in or out of court.

To dismiss or disqualify these readings is to overlook the way they already reside within and make possible other more 'acceptable' readings. If interpretation finds itself inhabited and conditioned by this 'excess', it can be limited only by secondary legislative, positive, empirical acts. This regulation raises important issues for interpretation in general, and cultural studies in particular. First, it puts on display an aporia of legitimacy (what founds the discursive authority to regulate interpretation in the first place?). Second, it enables us to find a prior 'politics' that comes 'before' any cultural studies reading of a practice or text that deems it politically successful or unsuccessful. In this way, cultural studies might come to look more, I would argue (rather than less), like the radically open 'discipline' it began as and has the potential to become.

CULTURAL STUDIES ON/AS CONSPIRACY THEORY

Though cultural studies professes to ask questions of a self-reflexive nature – indeed is in some ways predicated on the desire to examine the political implications of university disciplinarity, canonization, and processes of legit- imation – the kind of fundamental self-reflexive questions that are revealed by a deconstructive reading of conspiracy theory seem to have been largely overlooked by the majority of previous studies. What I am talking about here is not the familiar gesture of placing oneself within the interpretative field, to acknowledge how our agenda and prejudices shape interpretation (though this is of course important) but rather a self-reflexivity about the very possibility of interpretation, of being able to say anything about one's positionality, agenda, prejudices. The apparent reluctance within some cultural studies approaches to conspiracy theory to take on board fundamental questions of this sort (about the conditions of possibility for interpretation and for politics, about the logic of supplementarity, about the kinds of issues raised in different ways by not just deconstruction but also conspiracy theory) suggests a blind spot. I am using this term 'blind spot' carefully here. Unlike something that only needs to be revealed once, a blind spot requires attention every time we drive. What it hides at one moment will not be the same the next. All this can suggest a response to a strain of cultural studies that feels that we've been down the deconstruction or theory 'road' in the 1980s and 1990s, been there, done that and don't need to 'go there' or 'do it' again, and which I'm aware may be the response of many in cultural studies to my engagement with Derrida in this chapter and elsewhere. Equally, this ever-shifting blind spot affects every countersignature: We can provide a theoretically challenging framework within which cultural practices and texts can be read, but must accept that they will always exceed this framework in ways we should not be able to anticipate.

Such a blind spot may stem from a certain paranoia within cultural studies about its own legitimacy; but it may also arise because, as I will explain below, to take on board these questions – to perform a cultural studies thought through the work of Jacques Derrida (and thus able to acknowledge its ambivalent relationship to conspiracy theory, for example) – might put at risk any hard won legitimacy; might even risk cultural studies no longer being recognizable *as cultural studies* (see Hall 2002). It might mean, for example, not being able to say that a conspiracy theory (or any other strange, crazy, odd, paranoid or just plain stupid text) is outside the cultural studies' 'canon', because these judgements themselves are inhabited and made possible by overinterpretation, paranoia, and conspiracy theory. The decision itself would be unstable.

In general, cultural studies is unable to acknowledge any possible resemblance on its part to conspiracy theory. Instead, cultural studies has to maintain its 'critical distance' from the conspiracist text that nevertheless interests it as a form of culture. One possible reason for this could be that having begun as a marginal discipline of somewhat uncertain status, its subsequent institutionalized legitimacy can't bear much scrutiny within that discipline because, let's face it, cultural studies receives enough attacks of this kind from elsewhere.[8] To take just one example: the 'Sokal affair' I referred to above obviously represented a direct attack against the legitimacy of cultural studies as a mode of enquiry (see the editors of *Lingua Franca* 2000). As we have seen, Sokal's concern stemmed from the way in which cultural theory had appropriated terms from science and used them out of context; or, put a different way, Sokal was concerned that scientific terms were being used by people without the authority to do so.[9] But rather than being purely negative, I want to suggest that such an incident can also be seen as *affirming* the cultural studies 'project' – as being endemic of cultural studies' openness to the question of what legitimate knowledge is (an openness that constantly gets rehearsed as a challenge to 'canonized' histories or knowledges and to disciplinarity, but rarely in terms of legitimacy *per se*). Instead of excusing the Sokal incident, then, and fashioning it as an aberration in an otherwise functional discipline, cultural studies should own it. By doing this, the Sokal affair could reinforce the capability of cultural studies to be, after Derrida's use of the term, a discipline 'under erasure', if you like; because it represents a moment of undecidability around the issue of legitimacy which is central to what cultural studies in many ways is. Cultural studies can force us to question what knowledge is and therefore what cultural studies is. And because the answers to such questions and the rules according to which answers can be arrived at are unstable, the risk of being deemed an illegitimate discipline is definitive.

From this point of view, the Sokal affair represents something of a missed opportunity for cultural studies. For Sokal's forgery, in common with conspiracy theory (which is a kind of forgery in its own way – a forged form of knowledge about the world perhaps), demands questions to be asked concerning the status of knowledge, including the knowledge that cultural theorists draw on. The Sokal affair doesn't show up the inadequacy of cultural studies; rather, like conspiracy theory, it suggests that the legitimacy of knowledge cannot be decided in advance of any reading. Too often cultural studies leaves little room for questions of this kind to be asked. Instead, cultural studies has a tendency to keep such questions at bay, associating them understandably with attacks against its validity. To acknowledge the close relationship that cultural studies has with 'illegitimate' forms of knowledge such as conspiracy theory (both are synthetic discourses made from an indefinite amount of sources; both raise questions of legitimacy and institutionalized knowledge) would, in this view, risk undermining cultural studies. But, as I will explore below, cultural studies is vulnerable to attacks on its legitimacy, not because there is something dubious about its project but rather because all knowledge, all interpretation relies on an aporia of legitimacy. As a 'discipline' (or inter- or post-discipline) conceived on the margins of the university, cultural studies just has a greater capacity for opening itself up to questions of legitimacy than others. But to open itself to these questions, it would need to make a revelation.

TOP SECRET

Cultural studies would have to break a 'conspiracy of silence' to reveal a secret: that cultural studies could well be a con, a scam, a swindle. Cultural theorists may be a bunch of charlatans. Others certainly suspect that this is the case and say as much. The suspicion others unleash upon cultural studies is that we all just arrange data to suit our own purposes, to arrive at a conclusion we've already decided upon in advance. When cultural studies gets lambasted for being too 'speculative' (as we will see Alec McHoul and Toby Miller do in Chapter 4), or too post-structuralist (recall Bruno Latour's question in *Critical Inquiry*, 'Is it really the task of the humanities to add decon- struction to destructions?' (2004: 225)) or when Alan Sokal or Jim McGuigan (albeit in very different ways) critique cultural populism, this seems to me precisely a concern over the legitimacy or proper representation of cultural 'intelligence', of how we are going to present information gathered in the field. Are we agents who have dirtied our own hands, who have hard-and- fast data to back up our claims? Or have we been sitting in our 'ivory tower' reading second hand accounts of events? What have we risked in order to bring this particular 'intelligence' to light? These are the suspicions of those out to attack cultural studies: they suspect that cultural studies *is* illegitimate because of the way it gathers intelligence. The secret I think cultural studies has to divulge sounds only slightly different for these detractors, but has radically different implications: what I think we need to reveal is that it is a structural possibility that cultural studies is indeed illegitimate.

Traditional ways of getting around the possibility of illegitimacy (of keeping the secret *secret*) entail claims to metanarratives like Marxism or Humanism; or rooting one's statements in ethnographic observation or hard political economy. We try to assert the legitimacy of cultural studies by appealing to its political project, for example, or by having it resemble a science as closely as possible, hoping that the more respectable discipline's credibility will rub off on ours. But I don't want to patch up this risk of illegitimacy or to keep it secret. Before I am branded a traitor or informer for breaching the cultural studies' version of the Official Secrets Act, I should defend my 'experimental' revelation. In the real British Official Secrets Act, a disclosure is deemed damaging if it (and I'm going to substitute the references to the Crown and State here with cultural studies to make my point):

> (a) it damages the capability of ... the armed forces of [cultural studies] to carry out their tasks or leads to loss of life or injury to members of those forces or serious damage to the equipment or installations of those forces; or
> (b) ... it endangers the interests of [cultural studies] abroad, seriously obstructs the promotion or protection by [cultural studies] of those interests or endangers the safety of [cultural theorists] abroad ... [10]

Rather than damaging the capability of cultural studies to function as cultural studies, to carry out the important political and cultural work we often feel that we are here to do, or putting at risk the reputation or professional life of any cultural theorist at home ('within' cultural studies) or abroad (in other disciplinary contexts), my disclosure of this secret is intended to support and develop the interests of cultural studies.

The frequent attacks against cultural studies show up a risk of illegitimacy that is never far away. But cultural studies doesn't need to keep the secret of its possible illegitimacy because, as should be clear by the end of this book, it is not just our secret: it pertains to everybody who works with knowledge. But too often cultural studies keeps the secret, associating disclosure with a threat against our validity, funding and furtherance (threats that we are usually busy fielding from elsewhere). To acknowledge an aporia of legitimacy and authority would, in this view, risk undermining cultural studies. But what I have been suggesting is that cultural studies is vulnerable to attacks on its legitimacy, not because there is something dubious about its project but rather because there is an aporia of legitimacy and authority conditioning *all* knowledge. This is something that I will return to in my discussion of gossip.

The secret, then, despite my earlier call to break the conspiracy of silence, remains undepleted. The secret is not that which has been hidden, later to be revealed, and is in principle, fully knowable. Nor is it an enigma that remains unknowable (like God). It is not the object of knowable or unknowable knowledge at all. Rather, we are faced with the more radical 'Derridean' secret:

that which remains outside the phenomenal event as it happens but which nevertheless conditions that event. The irreducible, non-present secret (or in fact 'non-presence') in this sense structures presence. I can name this secret 'undecidable legitimacy' or something like that but this is really only akin to saying the secret is that no-one knows the secret. The secret remains irreducible even while we try to reveal it, keeping the future open: keeping, to pick up Derrida's thoughts on September 11 that I closed the previous chapter with, the trauma traumatic. I will not have revealed anything that will help us to decide in advance about any future encounter with knowledge. All I can say is that illegitimacy is neither present, nor unpresent in cultural studies, its presence is undecidable, the risk, irreducible. Illegitimacy is a necessary possibility that enables us to say anything that has validity and force, enables us to say anything outside an already calculable realm of set responses.

This second version of the secret is, then, the first without the lure of final revelation. The first version pointed towards an aporia of legitimacy at the heart of knowledge-claims and 'disciplinary' authority; the second makes it clear that the secret can only ever be that no-body knows the secret. Cultural studies is well placed to 'expose' rather than 'keep' the secret of undecidable legitimacy: a secret that conditions any knowledge statement, and anything that we could recognize as cultural studies. Cultural studies could be *the* mode able to question the very nature of legitimacy (once it has stopped trying to keep the secret that legitimacy is always in question). We are not breaching the cultural studies' version of the Official Secrets Act because nothing I have said can harm the existence of cultural studies but it might make it more robust, more able to show that it understands the status of the knowledge or 'intelligence' it gathers and presents in various dossiers for public consumption. How, then, can we produce a cultural studies that would be able to take on board the possibility of its own illegitimacy?

Cultural studies theorists (such as Fenster and Fiske) have not explicitly tried to draw a clear line between interpretation and overinterpretation, between knowledge and non-knowledge, between rational concerns and hysteria as their contemporaries in literary studies (such as Eco and Showalter) and political science (such as Pipes) have done. Nevertheless, in writing about conspiracy theory primarily in terms of a politically successful or unsuccessful object, they too often fail to take into account their own positionality (their own discursive legitimacy) to any radical degree. And if what I have suggested above is true – that it becomes harder for us to decide what counts as cultural studies when we follow through the implications of questioning discursive authority – it is understandable. How – to rephrase the question I posed above – can we produce a cultural studies that would be able to take on board some elements of its mistaken, paranoid, conspiracy theory-like nature rather than trying to control, limit, marginalize or repress them? Does risk – or radical openness to the possibility of overinterpretation and conspiracy theory (and other 'aberrant' elements) – lead to a 'cultural studies' that looks more or less like cultural studies? Or more *and* less: after all, this is the 'same' cultural studies that Stuart Hall is referring to when he discusses the necessity of inclusivity as a way for cultural studies to remain open-ended (see Hall 1996: 150 and 263). While I am sure Hall is envisaging interdisciplinarity rather than acknowledging paranoid tendencies in this scenario of inclusion, the idea of open-endedness cannot be advocated in a limited sense. What would an open-endedness that had to be regulated, that had to 'end' somewhere, be worth? Significantly, Hall has also called for cultural studies to go towards, rather than away from, 'dangers' (1992: 285), which is precisely what I am trying to do in this book.

In a typically provocative manner, Slavoj Žižek claims that cultural studies has *already* subsumed these conspiratorial elements, suggesting that, in fact, cultural studies reads like a conspiracy theory:

> If standard Cultural Studies criticize capitalism, they do so in the coded way that exemplifies Hollywood liberal paranoia: the enemy is 'the system', the hidden 'organization', the anti-democratic 'conspiracy', not simply capitalism and state apparatuses. The problem with this critical stance is not only that it replaces concrete social analysis with a struggle against abstract paranoiac fantasies, but that – in a typical paranoiac gesture – it unnecessarily redoubles social reality, as if there were a secret Organization behind the 'visible' cap-italist and state organs. What we should accept is that there is no need for a secret 'organization-within-an-organization': the 'conspiracy' is already in the 'visible' organization as such, in the capitalist system, in the way the political space and state apparatuses work. (2002: 170-1)

And I would have to agree that in its least rigorous and effective guise, cultural studies can fall back upon the simplification of power to be found in paranoid rhetoric. In many ways, what is worrying about certain strands of conspiracy theory – the way in which it enables someone to produce knee-jerk reactions to anything that threatens their belief system – is true also for cultural studies. Witness, for example, the kind of unreflexive liberal response Wendy Brown received when she questioned the premise of women's studies (see Brown 2001, and my discussion of it in Chapter 1). Yet, this near paranoid defensiveness is not what I have in mind when calling for cultural studies to take on board 'marginal' elements like conspiracy theory (and other popular knowledges). The kind of inclusion I'm thinking of does not manifest itself as vague allusions to an evil system instead of close readings of particular politico-economic conjunctures. The idea is not to replicate the failures of conspiracy theory but to take on board the lessons to be learnt from conspiracy theory regarding authority, legitimacy, and how to approach cultural phenomena without silencing it, in order to re-imagine cultural studies and what it is capable of becoming.

I will revisit these issues in different terms as I come to look at my second popular knowledge - that of gossip. Indeed, in turning to gossip, all that we have said here about how conspiracy theory functions is relevant. The relationship that we have considered between conspiracy theories and other more legitimated knowledges, including our own, will have implications for considering gossip too. In fact, as I increasingly learn the lessons of popular knowledge, it will become less possible to maintain my distance from it. I say all this by way of a welcoming: as I write this book, as I attempt to take on board what the form and content of popular knowledge has to tell me, I am trying to open myself to ways that might better reflect this close relationship. By the time I come to my next case study in Chapter 5, I will try, at least for part of it, to produce a more 'gossipy' discussion of gossip. Similarly, it remains a necessary possibility that I might, in discussing conspiracy theory, have here constructed a conspiracy theory of conspiracy theory. That is as it should be.

CHAPTER 4

Hot Gossip: The Cultural Politics of Speculation

TEST YOUR GOSSIP-OMETER

- Which member of the British Royal family has refused calls to take a blood test to settle the issue of his/her paternity?
- Which of your friends is having an affair?
- Which supermodel attends Narcotics Anonymous?
- Which member of your family is most likely to be heavily in debt?
- Which A-List movie star hunk wears a hairpiece to disguise his baldness?
- Who is just about to get the sack in your workplace?
- Which international tennis star was formerly a high-class call girl/rent boy?

Obviously, I can't tell you the answers – not even the ones about people in the public domain. For a start, I don't know if the gossip I've encountered is true. And you're probably not sure either. But if you answered most of these confidently the likelihood is that you are already well aware of the way in which we receive and use gossip. You may think, therefore, that this chapter is not for you. Yet the fact that we are all so familiar with gossip – celebrity or otherwise – testifies to the importance of understanding exactly what is at stake when we encounter it. For the time being, I won't be divulging any more gossip, but in the next chapter, I will consider some early twenty-first century encounters with gossip. First, I want to explore the cultural politics of gossip.

Hollywood gossip columnist Hedda Hopper famously defended her work by saying 'Nobody's interested in sweetness and light.' But such appeals to human nature only get us so far when trying to understand the ubiquitous appearance of gossip (and its avatars) not only within popular culture, but even realms traditionally associated with 'hard' knowledge, like the university, government, and the economy. The cultural politics of gossip, therefore, *includes* a self-reflexive consideration of the position from which cultural politics can even be considered. In this way, I will attempt to scrutinize the implications of gossip's multiple contexts, focusing in the latter half of this chapter and the next on the way in which they challenge the status of knowledge and claims to legitimacy and authority. To begin a broader discussion about the places in which we encounter gossip and its many guises, I want to look at gossip as a cultural phenomenon before moving on to think about how it has been positioned as an academic 'object'.

THE SCENE OF GOSSIP

Within the remit of gossip, I am thinking not only of the face-to-face practice of speaking about an absent third party, say among friends or colleagues, but also the speculations and revelations that fill the pages of tabloids and magazines. On this continuum countless variations lie - workmates discuss who is next in line for promotion; talk of a teacher's affair with her pupil spreads around the playground; speculation about a rock star's sexuality filters into a tabloid's gossip column. All trade in a tension between the public and private - whether the 'public' is local or global. When an unsavoury political scandal emerges, a familiar defence proposed by those who played an instrumental role in the exposé is that it is in the public's interest to know the moral character of those involved (making the personal political in a way never intended by feminism when it coined the phrase). In the Bill Clinton–Monica Lewinsky affair, for example, the trustworthiness of Clinton was very much at the heart of the case, especially as Clinton initially denied having relations with 'that woman'. The question of Clinton's moral character (not only did he have extra-marital relations, but he *lied* about them) was seen to justify, for many, the prurient publishing of explicit details about their affair. The private in this case, is seen to be very much an issue of public concern. Justifiable or not, this making public - of the ('real' or invented) private lives of celebrities, politicians, colleagues, or peers - ensures that we can encounter gossip every day of the week even if we don't engage in the practice within our immediate community.

Gossip Industry

The gossip industry involves not only individual celebrities but also, as Jack Levin and Arnold Arluke (1987) point out, his or her agent and any publicists and gossip columnists - encompassing cultural intermediaries. The contemporary celebrity industry is almost unthinkable without gossip - the production, generation, and cultivation of it. Gossip has long been recognized as supporting various entertainment industries such as film or music. Though highly reliant on these industries for story content, celebrity gossip is now widely acknowledged to be a highly profitable industry in its own right. Though much of the British tabloids' content could be said to be lead by gossip already, they also include extremely popular columns or supplements devoted to reporting gossip. While this is a tradition that reaches back through the history of print - at least as far, Roger Wilkes wagers, as the news sheets of Restoration Grub Street and even satirical Tudor pamphlets such as Thomas Nashe's *Pierce Penilesse* of 1592 (Wilkes 2002: 18) – the British *Daily Mirror*'s '3 AM girls', the 'Bizarre' column in the *Sun*, or 'The Goss' in the *Star* reflect a more forceful gossip industry influenced by 'pioneering' journalists like Louella Parsons and Hedder Hopper who reported from behind the scenes of the Hollywood film industry in the first half of the twentieth century.

With the rise of the Internet, the history of gossip enters a new phase. The Internet both exacerbates the popularity and consumption of political spec- ulation and celebrity gossip (through sponsored, profit-making online gossip/ speculation sites) and challenges their protocol (the relatively unregulated Internet allows mediated gossip to have an interactive element, making it more like everyday gossip). For example, the UK based Popbitch.com offers a free weekly email bulletin collated from gossip posted on the message boards by real (or feigned) media workers. Started as a chatroom for music industry insiders to share their knowledge, Popbitch deliberately avoids mainstream brand sponsors or back scratching relationships with celebrity publicists. Journalist Kate Burt quotes Popbitch's anonymous creator as saying: 'the minute you go down the business route ... you play into the hands of PRs' (2001). Popbitch attempts to avoid libel (not always successfully – the site was closed down for three weeks after a tale involving an innocent TV presenter and some extremely unpleasant allegations of illegal sexual preferences) by disclaiming responsibility for any third party contributions, which of course, is what the site consists of. The site's reputation for finding stories before the press and for printing ironic and entertaining stories that blur fact and fiction sustains its popularity among subscribers.

The interactivity and speed of the Internet has obviously shaped contemp- orary gossip practices. Wilkes cites the Clinton-Lewinsky affair as one that displays the role of the Internet in contemporary gossip. The scoop was due to be published by the American magazine *Newsweek*, but the Office of the Independent Council intervened as they were conducting an investigation and the publication date was postponed. Cybereporter, Matt Drudge, found out about the story and published it first on his homemade website (see Wilkes 2002: 316).

Indeed, it is possible to go so far as to claim that any history of gossip needs to be thought in tandem with the history of different modes of mass com- munication and their effects. The telephone, for example, has been studied as a medium that influenced social interaction including gossip (see Fischer 1995), while Marshall McLuhan claimed that radio 'contracts the world to village size, and creates insatiable village tastes for gossip, rumor and personal malice' (1965: 306). Others have argued that mass communication can both intensify and arrest gossip: so that while the proliferation of television and print media has obviously contributed to the conditions of celebrity culture that fuels a 'gossip industry', and provides a medium through which gossip can be relayed to millions at a time, Ralph Rosnow and Gary Alan Fine point out that technologies such as the telegraph also had the opposite effect, quelling rumours quickly before they could spin out of control (1976: 94). The mobile phone, which has been compared with the old 'garden fence' (see Fox 2001), and the Internet are just the latest communication devices to feature in the continuance of, and investment in, gossip.

The New Gossip Economy

We therefore encounter and manage a great deal of gossipy knowledge every day, coming at us in both public and private realms, from the media and our acquaintances (of course these distinctions are anything but clear cut). Yet this glut of popular knowledge is not what Tony Blair primarily has in mind when he talks about the rise of the 'knowledge economy' and the importance of 'knowledge workers'.[1] The knowledge economy is often described as the logical next phase of capitalism after industrialization: one that places a premium upon invention and innovation.

Knowledge in this recently identified economic phase is hailed as the most important asset in many enterprises (from mining to venture capital) rather than – as in previous eras – land, non-renewable raw materials or traditional products. While knowledge in the knowledge economy is primarily thought of in terms of codified technical know-how (such as that information which can be communicated through, and learnt from, a manual), it is also the tacit, non-codified, contextual knowledge embodied in humans (such as how to make that manual successful and useful). In other words, what is valuable in the knowledge economy is knowing how best to work with the knowledge we have. Which is where gossip comes in. Far from being excluded from the economy, it might play a central role in it – helping people to understand the knowledge around them and how best to use the power it engenders. If so, formal and informal knowledge networks can be given equal credence (the economy, unlike gossip's critics, does not care how valuable knowledge is ascertained). This has certainly been recognized in knowledge management circles. Earl Mardle, for example, a freelance consultant, entitles his article 'Gossip – the Original Knowledge Economy' (2004). He states that it is futile for an organization to try to limit gossip in the way that some management teams desire 'when the magazine stands and most of TV is predicated on salacious gossip and unsubstantiated rumour, including business columns and especially politics' (Mardle 2004). But he also advocates recognizing 'gossip [as] an economics of information' that can be harnessed for the health of the organization.

I will consider more carefully this relation between gossip and the knowledge economy at the end of this chapter; for now, we simply need to recognize that gossip, far from being a property of the 'gutter', arises in the most respected and 'rational' domains. Not only is it a key commodity or currency within the current economic mode (in the way described above) but it can be seen to influence the financial markets. Therefore, gossip about which stocks or currencies will rise or fall is not merely a comment upon financial markets from the outside. This kind of gossip can also have a direct (and indirect) influence on the health of those stocks and currencies. Equally, gossip about world events can affect the market. In February 2005, for example, a rumour that American spy planes had caused an explosion near an Iranian nuclear plant caused the financial markets to wobble.[2] Studies in behavioural finance have long suggested that markets are influenced by emotional criteria rather than just rationalized predictions (see Shleifer 2000).

GOSSIP IS...

When gossip arises in such wide-ranging contexts, it becomes harder to find an adequate description. Scholars in the field have put forward many definitions. Sissela Bok describes gossip as 'informal personal communication about other people who are absent or treated as absent' (1982: 91). Ayim includes a long list of qualifications:

> 1) gossip is informal talk, 2) conducted within a very small group of parti-cipants, 3) who know each other fairly well, and 4) trust one another not to violate each others' confidence. 5) The subject matter is highly personal, focused on knowledge of other people, and 6) the person or people who form the subject matter are not among those doing the discussing. Another set of features, though not necessary, is frequently associated with gossip: 1) There is a sense of illicitness connected with the activity of gossip, and, hence, participants often engage in it covertly; 2) gossip is conversational... depending upon real interchange among participants. Other characteristics of gossip are subject to much debate: 1) whether gossip endorses or under-mines social norms, 2) whether its content is trivial or highly significant, 3) whether it is limited to women or extends to men as well, 4) whether it occurs only in private domiciles, or extends to shop talk as well, and 5) whether it is unreliable and unsubstantiated or highly accurate and worthy of belief. (1994: 86)

In this apparently exhaustive list, however, the possibility of a gossip industry or economy does not seem to figure. This is where Jan B. Gordon's open definition comes in useful (though it too introduces a problematic dimension). He suggests that gossip is 'a discourse which enacts informational transfer while disclaiming (or being prohibited) from any foundational responsibility or representational share in its effects' (Gordon 1996: 57). This definition moves beyond a concern with context (professional or private), gender, mode (conversational, trivial, significant), medium (face-to-face or mediated encounters), meaning, or worth; to focus on the role of responsibility in any instance of gossip emission or production. Gossip, in this guise, is information or knowledge with a disclaimer clause: whereas information and knowledge are traditionally thought to be traceable to a source if they are to be considered information or knowledge at all, gossip puts on display the difficulty of such a pose. Illustrating this point, Homer Obed Brown writes, 'If [gossip] is groundless and self-constituting it is because communities are so. It establishes an authority without an author. This ambiguity of gossip is emblematic of its riddle of narrative voice (and perhaps of language itself): who (or what) speaks (writes)?' (1977: 579). While other modes of knowledge transmission are busy checking their sources, as Gordon would have it, gossip is enjoying itself. Hedonist gossip is largely unconcerned with its past (where the content comes from) and its future (what will happen as a result of the content being shared). I will return to this issue of inheritance and responsibility in the next chapter, by which point I will have revised (or re-inscribed the meaning of) the terms of Gordon's definition. But at this juncture I want to note that Gordon's fear is widespread and taps into a deep-seated cultural antipathy towards gossip. And, although that antipathy might precede today's gossip industry, it is perhaps exacerbated by that commercial context due to popular culture's negative moral connotations.

I want to draw on these definitions but add a crucial dimension. I think we should also think about gossip as a highly speculative endeavour. In this way, the status of the information it communicates is ambiguous in terms not only of its verity, but also of whether it is claiming any veritable status at all. It could simply be about putting an idea into circulation that may or may not prove to be a good investment.

In the next few sections I will outline the academic treatment of gossip in order to pave the way for my own intervention. The treatment and positioning of gossip has been dictated by two opposing trends. The more established approach – drawing inspiration from a range of discourses – saw gossip as a negative and destructive social force. After Max Gluckman's seminal 1963 essay, 'Gossip and Scandal', an ethnography of gossip among Makah Native Americans, the other, more recent approach positioned gossip as an essential and effective part of group maintenance and management. I want to provide examples of these two approaches as a way to begin thinking about what gets lost between them.

EVIL TONGUES

The mayor of a small Columbian town recently outlawed gossip. He said, 'Human beings must recognise that having a tongue and using it to do bad is the same as having dynamite in their mouths' (see Flett 2005: 4). Offenders could be sentenced to four years in jail. Extreme as this example is, the sentiments behind it are commonplace. Many commentators and critics at various points in history in a variety of geographical contexts have presented the consumption and production of gossip as a negative force. For these critics, gossip is a form of contamination that needs to be eradicated. For example, Sissela Bok claims: 'gossip can be an intoxicating surrogate for genuine efforts to understand... It turns easily into habit, and for some a necessity. They may then become unable to think of other human beings in other than trivial ways' (1982: 100). Bok's warning fashions gossip as a narcotic that encourages addiction. There is no room, in this scenario, for both 'genuine efforts to understand' and gossip – gossip colonizes the cognitive field but can only ever be a surrogate, rather than a mode of knowledge in its own right. Gossip is dangerous because it is bad practice, excessive, unfixed in truth, unsecured by the presence of those discussed, and presents information out of context. Nicholas Emler, when exploring why gossip has received such bad press, suggests that criticisms arise from the idea that 'gossip is not merely a sin of omission – one should have been using one's time more productively – but also a sin of commission. It is deliberate mischief making' (1994: 119). According to a Protestant work ethic and equivalent concerns with productivity and utility, gossip is not productive enough (it wastes time that could be spent in labour) *and* overly productive (of distractions from work). It produces too much labour and talk of the 'wrong' kind.

A history of the word's usage suggests a reason why the practice of gossip has gained negative connotations. The etymological root of gossip simply means 'God-related' (God's sib). The word evolved from the description of a godparent to include a close friend. Before the nineteenth century, gossip could be used to refer to fellowship and fraternity between men, but it was its other meaning – which referred to a woman's friends invited to be at a birth – that led to its latterly female gendered identity. By the time of Dr Johnson's dictionary of 1755, a gossip is defined as 'one who runs about tattling like women at a lying-in' (quoted in Wilkes 2002: 7); and in the nineteenth century, 'the term gossip referred specifically to "idle talk" and "tattling"' (Levin and Arluke 1987: 5). This gradual feminization consolidated gossip's negative cultural status.

Below, I'm going to briefly focus on several realms in which gossip becomes an object of critique. I have chosen these discourses as examples because it seems to me that though distinct, each can be considered an important and influential form of societal regulation (ranging from explicit prohibition to subtle influence).

Religion

The injunction against gossip and its equivalents in a range of religious texts is striking. The Christian commandment – 'You shall not bear false witness against

your neighbour' (Exod. 20: 16) is echoed throughout later Books.[3] Sylvia Schein
(1994: 140) hones in on a few of these echoes including: 'You shall not go
around as a slanderer among your people' (Lev. 19: 16); 'A gossip goes about telling secrets' (Prov. 11: 13); 'Like a gold ring in a pig's snout is a beautiful woman
without good sense' (in earlier versions, 'good sense' is given as 'discretion') (Prov.
11: 22); and 'A gossip reveals secrets; therefore do not associate with a babbler'
(Prov. 20: 19). Peter Fenves finds in Amos a clear instance of this prejudice: 'the
price of associating with those who engage in empty conversation is spelled
out' (1993: 256, fn. 15). Schein and Fenves also detect an avid concern with
gossip and attempts to regulate speech in general in the New Testament. Schein
points out that 'gossip appears among such serious transgressions as malice,
envy, murder, and deceit' in Romans 1: 29 and Corinthians II 12: 19 (1994: 140).
Fenves (1993: 256) cites the example of Paul admonishing the Ephesians: 'Let
no evil talk come out of your mouth' (Eph. 4: 29); and James's description of the
tongue as a flame (James 3: 6). In his 'letter', James goes on to encourage purity at
the source of language, asking Christians not to bless and curse out of the same
mouth: 'Does a spring pour forth from the same opening both fresh and brackish
water?' (James 3: 11). Ultimately, the tongue – speech, communication – is at risk
of betraying its owner at every step and must be kept in check: 'but no one can
tame the tongue – restless evil, full of deadly poison' (James 3:8). Vigilance and
restraint must be practiced as gossip (along with boastfulness, curses, blasphemy
and so forth) is fashioned as a poison waiting to contaminate the tongue and
impair the moral or spiritual 'health' and even (if we give credence to the use of
'deadly') *existence* of the speaker. In line with this, great attention is given to the
distinction between appropriate and inappropriate speech in general in Sirach
(20: 1–8, 18–20).

Fenves casts his net wider for other scriptural injunctions against gossip:

> Talmudic and rabbinic literature … often denounces *loshon hora* (evil tongue,
> hearsay, gossip) … The justification against the injunction against *loshon
> hora* remains constant: once God entered into human language, he
> sanctified it, and so its only altogether legitimate use lies in the preservation,
> remembrance, and study of divinely sanctioned speech. Every other use, even
> those that are not blasphemous or otherwise *ra* (evil, wicked), amounts to
> illegitimate intrusions into a domain made holy by the divine presence. (1993:
> 256–7)

Editors of *The Encyclopedia of the Jewish Religion* explain that the rabbis of
classical Judaism in late antiquity warned against gossip in the most heightened
terms. For example, the rabbis claimed that slander, talebearing, and evil talk
were worse than the three cardinal sins of murder, immorality, and idolatry.
Indulging in *lashon ha-ra* is seen to be akin to denying the existence of God
(see the entry for 'Lashon Ha-ra' in Zwi Werblowsky and Wigoder 1986). Of note

for our discussion later concerning the unstable verity of content transmitted through gossip is that while Judaism distinguishes between slander (*lashon ha-ra*), which refers specifically to true talebearing, and *motsi' shem ra'* (causing a bad name), which applies to untrue stories, 'both are totally forbidden by Jewish Law' (Zwi Werblowsky and Wigoder 1997: 648). Here, then, the verity of the gossip is not at issue, but rather the very act of passing potentially damaging information on whether true or false.

Islam too warns of gossip's adverse effects on the community. *Al-Gibah*, the translator of a short book by Husayn al-Awayishah on the subject tells us, is not an easy concept to translate, but 'it may be loosely covered by the term "gossip"' (Khattab in al-Awayishah 2000: 5). al-Awayishah cites many indictments against gossip for Muslims and offers an Islamic code to live by that strictly excludes it. One vivid deterrent can be found in *Sunan Abu-Dawud*, a collection of sayings and deeds of Prophet Muhammad recorded by Abu-Dawud (see translation by Hassan 1983). The following *hadeeth* describes the fate of gossipers: 'The Prophet said: When I was taken up to heaven I passed by people who had nails of copper and were scratching their faces and their breasts. I said: Who are these people, Gabriel? He replied: They are those who were given to back biting and who aspersed people's honour' (Book 41, No. 4860).

Not only is producing gossip prohibited but listening to it is seen as a lapse in the conduct of a good Muslim: for Allah, according to the Qur'an, said, 'Every act of hearing, or of seeing, or of (feeling in) the heart will be enquired into (on the Day of Reckoning)' (al-Isra 17: 36).[4] Another *hadeeth*, this time from Sahir Bukari, tells us that Allah's Apostle said, 'Whoever believes in Allah and the Last Day should talk what is good or keep quiet, and whoever believes in Allah and the Last Day should not hurt (or insult) his neighbor' (Volume 8, Book 76, No. 482). Correcting any indulgence in *Al-Gibah* is advised in the first instance, and failing that, walking away - the words of Allah are clear on this point: 'turn away from [men engaged in vain discourse] ... unless they turn to a different theme ... do not sit in the company of those who do wrong' (al-An`am 6: 68). To avoid being blameworthy in the sight of Allah for even just overhearing gossip, a Muslim should go to the person being spoken about to confront them with what has been observed (al-Awayishah 2000: 56-7). Gossip about a lapse in faith is itself seen as a lapse. Focus on other people's faults - which forms a good deal of gossip's content - is an unquestionable distraction from faith.

Etiquette and Ethics

As Spacks (1985) and Gordon (1996) show, the moral ramifications of gossip have concerned many essayists and novelists. Anxiety about the moral code that gossip apparently challenges and the spiritual corruption of those who indulge in gossip, seem to be leftovers from religious guidance regarding conduct that

I have just looked at. Spacks writes, 'Moralists did not abandon the language of Christian reference, but their increasing shrillness suggests that readers could no longer automatically be expected to assume the primacy of their Christian obligations' (1985: 28). But on certain occasions, as Spacks points out, moralists focus less on the one who is gossiping, and more on the damage inflicted upon the one gossiped about: 'The three aspects of gossip condemned by the moralists ... - its circulation of slander, its betrayal of secrets, its penetration of privacy - all embody threats to those made the objects of gossip's discourse' (1985: 33). Gossip's tendency to objectify becomes a matter for concern for those objectified.

The necessity of protection against the adverse effects of gossip can also be detected in earlier literature with a slightly more amorous focus. Literature concerned with courtly love, for example, fashioned gossip as 'most "uncourtly"' (Schein 1994: 140): a force against which love and lovers must protect themselves. To illustrate, Sylvia Schein quotes Andreas Capellanus' *Art of Courtly Love* ('a sort of summary of the rules or the doctrine of courtly love' from the twelfth century): 'love decrees that if the lady finds that her lover is foolish and indiscreet...or if she says that he has no regard for her modesty, she will not forgive his bashfulness' (quoted in Schein 1994: 140). Gossip in this guise threatens the success of love. Of course, gossip may be un*courtly* in one sense (ungentlemanly, unwise, ungracious), but what is not acknowledged in this configuration is the way in which gossip could be said to be at the heart of the court - the court, that is, was only made up of reputation making or breaking, and the circulation of political gossip, which would not have excluded love gossip. In this blindness, as Schein goes on to show, gossip is personified in the courtly literature 'as the enemy of love': 'Guillaume de Lorris in his *Romance of the Rose* (ca. 1237), an allegoric epic about ideal love, includes among the allegoric figures ... [one] he calls "Evil Tongue"...' (Schein 1994: 140).

Love figures here as a bond that keeps the secret of intimacy between lovers. Real love, true love, will not abide disclosure or indiscretion. It becomes aligned with a trust between only two. Any third person is considered an evil tongue waiting to expose the details only contextual within the trust of love, or able to threaten the bond with incitements to jealousy. 'Besides being condemned by Scripture, then', Schein points out, 'gossip was considered "uncourtly", an initiator of jealousy and therefore a foe of love and of lovers' (1994: 141). Keeping clear of gossip becomes less out of fear of sullying an unblemished spiritual record than spoiling one's chances of secular happiness (though, of course, to an extent, courtly love functioned as an allegory for divine love).

Though not evident in this early literature or in the religious texts in which gossip is a risk for either gender, etiquette manuals from the seventeenth century onwards often focused exclusively on the behaviour of women. Gordon tells us how conduct books warned against listening to tales and rhymes, including children's stories. For example, John Locke cautioned parents 'not to allow their children to be terrorized by the "prattle" ... of nurses' stories which interfered with the development of a presumably empirical reason' (Gordon 1996: 37). Gordon sees this as one example of a prejudice against an oral folk tradition but what is in evidence here is a whole binary system whereby women, oral tradition, emotionality, and fantasy are stacked up on one side while men, scholarly tradition, scientific rationalism, and factuality are on the other. In terms of protection, the latterly gendered associations of gossip implied that men (and women) needed to protect themselves from the excesses of gender (that gossip supposedly signified).

The Law

If we turn to the treatment and status of hearsay as evidence in courts (particularly courts of common rather than civil law), it becomes clear that the law is another realm which has felt the need to erect safeguards against the effects of gossip.[5] The degree to which this reflects a society's prejudice against 'bastard' orality rather than a desire to ensure justice is debatable and of course varies in different constitutional contexts.

To take the US example, the guidelines in the *Federal Rules of Evidence* for determining what counts as hearsay in court characterizes it as a 'declarative, secondhand statement offered in evidence *as proof of a matter asserted*. In order for a declaration to be deemed hearsay, the statement must be established as *assertive* in *intention*' (Gordon 2001: 204). Equating gossip with hearsay, Gordon claims that gossip 'has been a "suspect" discourse, in the Anglo-American tradition, when brought to court. For, though there is no reason why second-hand utterances are *innately* less likely to be truthful than those of persons present, this sort of talk is imagined to pervert justice' (2001: 203). Gordon goes on to provide a fascinating history of the treatment of this 'unruly orality' within the law, pointing towards some of the contradictions inherent in this exclusion along the way. For example, there are a number of exceptions to the hearsay rule including the reporting of dying words. If 'hearsay [can be] "rationalized" – rendered firsthand and purged of its authorless, originless, traceless character – through a mediate process by the declarant', Gordon tells us, 'it no longer qualifies as fugitive orality and is thus admissible' (2001: 204–5). The irony is clear: though hearsay is kept at bay through the court's appeal to rationality and reason, 'the more 'irrational' utterances (dying declarations, a child's *res gestae* exclamations, "state of mind" descriptions, highly emotive victim impact testimony)', Gordon explains, are 'judged admissible under the assumption that deception is less likely in highly emotional, associational, or reflective narrative' (2001: 214).

Though written affidavits are given precedence over hearsay in court, the philosophical privilege given to speech (as an assurance of truth, self-identity etc.) is kept intact, for an affidavit is seen as being a more accurate record of what someone has *said* than the spontaneous recollections of another witness. The affidavit is only privileged for its apparent proximity to the actual spoken moment under consideration. The written only supersedes speech when the latter recalls other speech: when it is second-hand, and therefore, ironically, closer to the traditional view of writing. Jacques Derrida has repeatedly shown how writing has been fashioned by Western metaphysics as a mode of representation beleaguered by the risk of forgery as it has to function in the absence of its author. Writing, according to this phonocentric logic, is further away from the truth, more susceptible to lies and fabulation, a mere copy in place of an absent original. What is important here is that despite this ideality given to speech in Western thought, 'the procedural exclusion of hearsay evidence would suggest a prejudice against unregulated orality in Western jurisprudence' (Gordon 2001: 210). Speech is privileged unless it is gossip, for gossip is thought to have been 'contaminated' by the same fallibilities that belong to writing. Presence remains dominant. Hearsay or gossip is thus imagined by common law to be on the 'outside', even when it is permitted (because these instances are fashioned as *exceptional*). In practice, this means being cautious about any spoken evidence that cannot be cross-examined, to limit the possibility of a witness speaking about someone who is not there to defend themselves – all admirable and necessary; but in theory (and this, I would argue, has ramifications for 'practice'), this exclusion and the privileging of presence as a surer access to truth is highly fragile.

While Gordon considers the (in)admissibility of gossip into court as evidence within a trial, Patricia Mellencamp, looking primarily at the American example again, is interested in what happens when gossip takes the dock itself. In discussing libel and defamation (accusations that focus on the effects of gossip), Mellencamp finds gossip to be a pivot around which capital, corporate culture and print culture spin (1992: 157). In these cases, several guidelines are put in place to determine slander from libel, once defined as the difference between casting aspersions on someone else by talking to others, and publishing those opinions. But in the televisual and electronic age, the distinction becomes blurred. (TV presenters, for example, are only talking to others – akin to slander; but that talk is broadcast to millions – closer to libel. The case of Ron Atkinson in the UK springs to mind as one that complicates the distinction. Atkinson, an ITV football commentator, made racist comments about the Chelsea FC player Marcel Desailly, thinking he was off air. Unfortunately for him, his comments were broadcast in several places in the Middle East, including Dubai and Egypt. Slander or libel?)

Attempts to make the definition clear in this age include the idea that something can be considered libel if it is read from a written text but only slander if spoken without a script (Mellencamp 1992: 185). The written text makes the statement seem as though it is presenting itself as fact, while the spoken word can always be taken as mere opinion. The rehearsed and composed is held to be more responsible than the spontaneous and disorganized. However, in a further complication, creative writing is virtually immune to accusations of libel – fiction being seen as dealing with opinion rather than fact. As with the criteria for determining admissible from inadmissible hearsay, these divisions could be challenged.

In the US, the issues raised by gossip (as libel or defamation) are caught in a tension between protecting citizens against defamation and the right to freedom of speech. So while much effort is made to demarcate which kind of hearsay is admissible as evidence in a court of law, hearsay in the guise of libellous gossip is very much at the centre of the litigation 'industry' in the US and elsewhere, where lawsuits involve large sums of money for defendants, claimants, and lawyers alike. Much energy is spent defining what is admissible or inadmissible, and malicious or innocent gossip; a great deal of capital is spent keeping gossip in check.

Philosophy

In philosophical terms, gossip and associated forms of communication such as 'chatter' and 'idle talk' have been posited negatively against the pursuit of truth. Robert F. Goodman believes that gossip is lambasted on the grounds that it is the emotional rather than informational content that drives the speaker and draws the listener. If emotions stand in contrast to reason, 'gossip is repugnant to the rationalist conception of knowledge that we have inherited from the Greeks and that has dominated Western thought since the seventeenth century' (Goodman 1994: 6). This distaste can be clearly seen in early texts. Plato's dialogues, for example, are broken up by 'accusations of *lēros* (small talk)' (Fenves 1993: 6). In *Nicomachean Ethics*, Aristotle describes the desirable conduct of the 'great-souled man' (*megalopsuchos*): 'Nor is he a gossip; for he will speak neither about himself nor about another, since he cares not to be praised nor for others to be blamed' (Aristotle 1984: 1775). As Jorg R. Bergmann reminds us, gossips were seen as stock characters within Greek drama: 'Theophrastus, Aristotle's student ... in his famous "Characters" describes the "backbiter" with the remark, "He is prone to malign one of the company who has gone out; and give him but one the opportunity, he will not forbear to revile his own kin, nay he will often speak ill of his friends and kinsfolk, and of the dead"' (Bergmann 1987: 21–2 quoting from Theophrastus 1953: 117).

The ethico-rationalist grounds for castigating gossip are idiosyncratically appealed to by later philosophers. Chatter for Kierkegaard disrupts the difference between silence and speech. Chatter is not speech with content, it is speech that says nothing but is not silent. Those who indulge in chatter cannot speak or act 'essentially'; rather chatter moves 'ahead of essential speaking, and giving

utterance to reflection has a weakening effect on action by getting ahead of it'
(Kierkegaard [1846] 1978: 97). Chatter is in excess of essential speaking; it
dilutes action. 'Talkativeness' gets one further from what is important, practised
as it is by people who 'are not turned inward in quiet contentment, in inner
satisfaction, in religious sensitiveness' (Kierkegaard [1846] 1978: 97). With
decreasing ideality and increasing externality, Kierkegaard warns, 'conversation
will tend to become a trivial rattling and name-dropping, referenced to persons
with "absolutely reliable" private information on what this one and that one,
mentioned by name, have said etc., a garrulous confiding of what he himself
wants or does not want' ([1846] 1978: 99). It is only by avoiding such a state of
affairs, by attaining 'the inward orientation of silence' that 'cultured conversation' can be achieved (Kierkegaard [1846] 1978: 99). Kierkegaard realizes that
most everyday conversation is based on chatter – gossip about their daily affairs
– and that 'all those garrulous people' would be 'miserable' should it be banned.
He amusingly proposes that a law be passed demanding everyone speak about
things as if they had happened fifty years ago (Kierkegaard [1846] 1978: 100). In
other words, only the essential essence of an event would be reported, gossipy
trivia would fall by the way.

A particular kind of silence is respected by Heidegger too: 'In talking with
one another, the person who keeps silent can "make one understand" (that is,
he can develop an understanding), and he can do so more authentically than
the person who is never short of words' ([1927] 1962: 208). The opposite of
silence is 'idle talk' (*Gerede)* which communicates by '*gossiping* and *passing
the word along*' (Heidegger [1927] 1962: 212**)**. This occurs when the speaker
is more interested in the claim made about an object than understanding the
essential nature of the object itself. The object becomes lost to interpretation
of it. That which is spoken about in this mode accumulates authority simply
through circulation – 'Things are so because one says so' – rather than authentic
discourse which has a 'primary relationship-of-Being towards the entity being
talked about' (Heidegger [1927] 1962: 212). Moreover, Heidegger claims, 'The
average understanding of the reader will *never be able* to decide what has
been drawn from primordial sources with a struggle and how much is mere
gossip' ([1927] 1962: 212). Such a distinction, he indicates, is not an issue for
the average understanding because it thinks it knows everything anyway (it
does not, we could say, know that it does not know). 'Idle talk is the possibility
of understanding everything without previously making the thing one's own'
(Heidegger [1927] 1962: 213). Genuine understanding is positioned against this
repetition of superficial, groundless readings. Rather than disclosure, then, the
effect of idle talk and its accompanying illusion of understanding is to close off
the object and a thorough understanding of it.

Responses to these philosophical charges against gossip will point us towards
a more recent trend of what I want to call 'gossip appropriation' – towards readings that problematize dismissals of gossip to focus on its positive or essential

role in human relations. Having earlier warned about the excesses of gossip himself, Bok responds to the sentiments of Heidegger and Kierkegaard by branding them reductive. These warnings against gossip, Bok claims, 'often fail to consider its extraordinary variety. They ignore the attention it can bring to human complexity, and are unaware of its role in conveying information without which neither groups nor societies could function' (1982: 101). This appeal to societal functionality for gossip's redemption is echoed with a slightly different pitch by Spacks: 'Heidegger's distaste for gossip, and Kierkegaard's, deny the moral possibilities of trivia.' In this way, 'The value of gossip at its highest level', Spacks reasons, 'involves its capacity to create and intensify human connection and to enlarge self-knowledge predicated more on emotion than on thought' (1985: 18-19). Rather than reading gossip as spiritually corrupting, general bad practice, an enemy of love, unsecured by presence, a deviation from the pursuit of truth, harmfully speculative, excessive interpretation, and as an obstruction to genuine efforts to understand, the appropriative readings want to emphasize the social or psychological uses of gossip. In this alternative view, gossip's prevalence in contemporary culture might not be a signal of 'dumbing down' or immorality but a necessary feature of a functioning society.

GOOD GOSSIP

This vindication of gossip might be best exemplified by the premise of an interdisciplinary edited collection of essays entitled *Good Gossip* (Goodman 1994). Though unanimous vindication is not achieved, the collection sets out to counter the traditional moral condemnations of gossip (Goodman 1994: 1-2). As an example of one of the more forthrightly positive accounts in this collection, Nicholas Emler's essay, 'Gossip, Reputation, and Social Adaptation', tells us that 'gossip ... is fundamental to the functioning of all human collectives' particularly 'the successful adaptation of humans to the requirements of group living and the control mechanisms that operate to conserve effectively functioning human groups' (1994: 117). Such an approach takes its cue from anthropological studies like Max Gluckman's 'Gossip and Scandal', which illustrates gossip as group maintenance and management:

> gossip, and even scandal, have important positive virtues. Clearly they main-
> tain the unity, morals and values of social groups. Beyond this, they enable
> these groups to control the competing cliques and aspiring individuals of
> which all groups are composed. And finally, they make possible the selection
> of leaders without embarrassment. (1963: 308)

By bestowing the 'right' to gossip, the Makah Native Americans Gluckman was studying signal when a person has been accepted: 'It is a hallmark of membership'

(Gluckman 1963: 313). Equally, it enables this community to mark its boundary from another as codes of allegiance are drawn.

While anthropologists focus on the socializing processes inherent in gossip – seeing it as an important component of normative group mentality and social functioning – other disciplinary interventions have fashioned gossip as an altogether more subversive object. In the preface to *Gossip*, Spacks is clear about her motives: 'My mission began to define itself as a rescue operation: to restore positive meaning to a word that had once held it, and to celebrate the set of values and assumptions particularly associated with women, as well as with gossip' (1985: x). With this mission in mind, Spacks finds fault with the sociological approach, feeling that it avoids moral judgement. In bypassing 'ancient problems of propriety and of virtue' (1985: 34), Spacks thinks that sociological accounts haven't fully considered the possibility that gossip offers an alternative moral code to that which dominates public life:

> If gossip in its positive aspects indeed reflects moral assumptions different from those of the dominant culture, that fact suggests ... its special usefulness for subordinated classes. It embodies an alternative discourse to that of public life, and a discourse potentially challenging to public assumptions; it provides language for an alternative culture. Gossip's way of telling can project a different understanding of reality from that of society at large, even though gossip may claim to articulate the voice of the community. A rhetoric of inquiry, gossip questions the established. (Spacks 1985: 46)

Gossip, here, is not simply a mode of communication telling us how communities bond or function regardless of the content. Spacks moves beyond form to think about gossip's content – to think, that is, about gossip as a resistant 'way of knowing' (1985: 46). She focuses on gossip's attention to detail, to the particular, and to understanding relationships, finding them to play a vital role for 'alternative culture' or 'subordinate classes'. Here she locates a way for those traditionally disenfranchised by knowledge systems to be able to participate in the construction of 'reality' in a move not dissimilar to John Fiske's in relation to conspiracy theory we have already seen in Chapter 3.

Also to be found in *Good Gossip* are claims to the subversive potential of gossip:

> the theme of resistance or subversion runs powerfully through a number of these chapters. People gossip about the powerful, rich, and famous in order to "cut them down to size." Informal gossip networks flourish in large, bureaucratic organizations as a way of softening, resisting, or subverting their depersonalizing tendencies. Gossip offers passive resistance to many forms of power. (Goodman 1994: 5)

An exemplary essay in this vein is Maryann Ayim's. She considers gossip as an efficient form of knowledge acquisition when other more 'revered' avenues are unavailable: 'Those who remain shut off from the bastions of commonly recognized social and political power will continue to look to gossip as one form of inquiry, knowing, and power available to them as other forms are not' (Ayim 1994: 99). Ayim even goes so far as to say: 'If ... we want to keep the road of inquiry open, we are obliged not just to condone gossip but to encourage it' for gossip is a way of finding things out when more formal modes of inquiry aren't up to the job (1994: 99).

In such positive accounts, however, the aberrant status given to gossip by its detractors is kept largely intact. In positive accounts, gossip is still positioned as an improper or informal knowledge (that holds societies together, say, or that has subversive potential). Gossip is still posited outside of 'official' knowledge. Let me explain through the example of anthropology, for the way in which this discipline configures its relationship with gossip is very telling. At first, it would seem as if anthropology comes closest to collapsing the difference between academic knowledge and gossip. Gluckman, for example, understood the close relationship between the work of the anthropologist and the work of the gossip. Recounting the experiences of a fellow anthropologist, Gluckman wrote, 'When Frankenberg had been in the village for some time, as soon as he went into a shop, the tea-kettle was put on the fire: after all, as *anthropologos*, he was the scandalmonger par excellence' (1963: 315), before commenting on his own time-consuming, gossip-tinged shop transactions during anthropological fieldwork. However, saying that the role of the anthropologist is *like* the role of the gossip – that gossip is an integral part of acquiring information for anthropological study – keeps the identity of gossip and of academic enquiry intact. If gossip is an integral part of the community, the anthropologist can hardly risk paying it no attention. Gossip, in this setup, is employed as a distinct and knowable mode in order to be a part of the community that the anthropologist hopes to observe and understand; but as a research method, it is often imagined to be left at the door of the university on return. Although gossip enters into the world of academics/anthropologists, it doesn't radically upset the categories of knowledge they work with.

Similarly, in Spacks' argument about women's relation to gossip, gossip may temporarily take the place, and therefore challenge the dominance of, 'official' modes of rational thought and communication but it is still configured as outside of official modes of knowing: it is defined against these norms. In these appropriative readings, therefore, the main difference to the injunctions against gossip detailed earlier, is that the 'improper' quality of the knowledge is seen as potentially positive and useful rather than negative and useless. The opposition between knowledge and gossip is kept largely in place. Even when gossip is considered to be a form of knowledge, for example, it is still clear what a 'legitimate' mode of knowledge *is* and therefore how gossip can function *like* it. Though explored, catalogued, and vindicated, gossip itself isn't necessarily interrogated. I want to argue that at one level these appropriative accounts are on the right tracks – that gossip certainly does present a challenge to 'official' forms of knowledge, and that it does have a central role to play in society. But I want to take a step further to show that gossip's identity is challenged as well as challenging. Gossip is not left intact by the encounter with knowledge (as apparently transparent justified true belief) and vice versa. Moreover, this modification will have already occurred; the 'encounter' has already happened. I am arguing, then, that gossip is a constitutive necessity: which is, as I will explain, very different from saying that it plays an important role in society.

THE FUTURES MARKET: INVESTING IN THEORY

What I want to propose here, and what I think is lacking from previous accounts of gossip within cultural studies (and the humanities and social sciences generally) is that gossip, far from being a contaminating force that needs to be kept in check or an aberrant, improper form of knowledge external to knowledge proper, is at the heart of cognition, conditioning any history of knowledge or claim to knowledge put forward within the socio-cultural sphere. Such a configuration will force us to reconsider the opposition between 'illegitimate' and 'legitimate' knowledge. I want to begin to explain my position by turning to an interesting earlier attempt on the part of cultural studies to redraw the relationship between academic discourses and popular, everyday discursive culture (one that I've found to be a useful springboard from which to think about these issues): that provided by Toby Miller and Alec McHoul in *Popular Culture and Everyday Life* (1998).

I want to consider Miller and McHoul's book to further my discussion at this stage for three main reasons. First, it presents one of the few attempts in recent cultural studies to move the 'discipline' beyond what Miller and McHoul call 'speculative readings' (that is not just a proposed return to political economy). A 'speculative' cultural studies, as they see it, produces unsubstantiated speculation via critical theory on the meaning and importance of everyday culture. I too feel that a certain kind of 'speculative' reading is problematic and I want to test the apparent escape route presented in *Popular Culture and Everyday Life*. Second, in using the term 'speculative' when referring to the kind of cultural studies that they want to challenge, Miller and McHoul prompted me to think about the connection between cultural studies, theory and gossip, if we think of all three as (albeit very different) forms of speculation. Third, in fashioning 'critical theorizing' (Miller and McHoul 1998: 181) as the villain of the piece, Miller and McHoul present an opportunity for me to explain exactly why I think 'theorizing', for my money, is a better investment than their own ethnomethodologically inspired cultural studies (EMICS), political economy approaches, or the kind of 'speculative', politically determined accounts they critique. In particular it offers me the opportunity, which I will take in the following chapter, to explain why deconstruction can offer a more responsible, more *political* even, future for cultural studies.

To divulge some academic gossip of a kind, one respondent to an earlier paper version of this chapter suggested that nobody takes Miller and McHoul seriously (implying, of course, that I shouldn't either).[6] I think that a comment like this misses the point. First, it raises all sorts of questions about academic legitimacy, some of which I want to address further below. Second, whether or not they have been taken particularly seriously, I nevertheless found Miller and McHoul's book productive for helping me think through some of these issues and ideas (even if this 'thinking through' has often been in the face of or against their ideas). And third, while I certainly don't think we necessarily need take Miller and McHoul's answer very seriously, I do think that the question they raise in their book is in fact the right one to ask: how to move cultural studies beyond readings of culture that arrive with an *a priori* politics that is then revealed in some cultural product or practice.

This question of the aptness of politically determined speculative readings, of course, enters a well-established debate between cultural studies and political economists best exemplified by Nicholas Garnham and Lawrence Grossberg's exchange in the 1990s (see Gary Hall (2002) for a provocative examination of this debate). Garnham expressed a distaste that many political economists held for cultural studies and what they saw to be its tendency to produce politically 'optimistic' readings of subversive or resistant culture (what Miller and McHoul are calling 'speculative readings'), and not paying sufficient attention to the economic conditions of cultural industries and their ensuing constraints. Grossberg defended cultural studies against these attacks, pointing to the work of those in cultural studies (such as Meaghan Morris and Angela McRobbie) who do pay attention to questions of production. More recently, as I have mentioned in Chapter 1 already, Grossberg has insisted that the way forward for cultural studies is to 'do' politics and economics 'better than' the political scientists and economists: that is to say, since the agent of change no longer resides in popular culture, we need, Grossberg argues, to turn to political and economic culture where it does (2004). A radical rethink of the relationship between culture and the economy, Grossberg hopes, will help us to arrive at an adequate, cogent and even ethical analysis of the contemporary conjuncture.

While it risks being reductive of Grossberg's nuanced argument, it is still worth quoting an anonymous reviewer of the conference at which Grossberg aired these views: 'At Crossroads, accompanying the praises sung to the "economic turn" was another refrain. One good turn deserves another, and in this case it meant a turn away from "theory." It seems that turning the clock back to Stuart Hall, Gramsci, and Policing the Crisis meant turning our backs on deleuzians of grandeur (and other speculative indulgences)' (Interactivist.net 2004). Grossberg's turn to cultural economy, along with the general mood of the 2004 Crossroads in Cultural Studies Conference, is interpreted here as a warning against the excesses of theory and speculation.

Miller and McHoul's intervention into this general debate is interesting, it seems to me, precisely because, in lambasting 'speculation', they express an aversion to theory that seems to be, albeit with different emphases, an increasing commonplace among cultural studies departments today. As I have suggested in Chapter 1, there has been an identifiable shift in cultural studies towards sociology and political economy and what Paul du Gay and others have called 'cultural economy' (see Amin and Thrift 2004; Du Gay and Pryke 2002; Merck 2004; Hesmondhalgh 2002). And as an indicator of this general climate, the revision of Raymond Williams' seminal text, *Keywords*, edited by important figures in cultural studies – Tony Bennett, Lawrence Grossberg and Meaghan Morris – includes an entry for theory that ends thus:

> If theory was, on the whole, victorious in these [theory] wars, it has, like all victors, taken on much of the coloring of the conquered population, and has entered into a compromise which guarantees its formal authority at the expense of substantial, but tacit, concessions to its opponents. It is not certain that this victory was not a defeat, and the mood of its erstwhile proponents is perhaps best summed up in book titles such as *What's Left of Theory?* (Frow 2005: 349)

Presenting theory both as having passed its sell-by date, and as being irredeemably compromised, John Frow's entry airs a familiar sentiment. Miller and McHoul's distaste for theory has a slightly different, if equally familiar, inflection. They find speculations on the meaning and political importance of popular culture abhorrent because for them it suggests an irresponsibility towards the 'member', as they call their subject, who is not allowed to speak in this scenario. Theorizing takes the place of 'real' experience. I will challenge such notions of irresponsibility in the next chapter but for now I want to suggest that at a time when speculation is being lambasted we need to be *more* not *less* speculative, or at least to pay more attention to what is involved in speculation. I will explain further after outlining Miller and McHoul's argument.

One response to speculative readings that take cultural phenomena always to stand for something else on a socio-political level – for example, reading gossip as a form of empowerment for the politically marginalized – is to declare an aversion to external judgement. That is to say, if meaning is produced by and within the social practice under consideration (here, gossip), the risk of imposing meaning is apparently averted. Such an attempt to avoid speculating upon the importance of people's everyday actions from the outside is suggested by Miller and McHoul. They are ill at ease with a cultural studies that equates 'mundane transgressions with general social tendencies' and assumes 'that everyday cultural objects stand on behalf of, or represent, wider social forces' (Miller and McHoul 1998: ix). As well as the 'urgent hunt (characteristic of cultural studies) for resistive readers who can delegate their wildness to researchers' (Miller and McHoul 1998: 25), Miller and McHoul, then, find politically determined pronouncements on human subjects mired in a state of false consciousness problematic.

Miller and McHoul provide an example of what they mean by speculative cultural studies in the form of Cindy Patton's reading of MTV and Madonna. They are concerned that her reading begins with a speculative claim – in this case, that MTV is 'an important site for the struggle over control of popular memory' (Patton 1993: 91) – which steers the rest of the argument. At the troubling heart of Patton's proposition and others like it is a speculative statement that seems to Miller and McHoul more guided by politics than observation. What is at stake in speculative readings is what status the political as analytic or speculative force is allowed to have when confronting everyday phenomena.

Miller and McHoul do not single out and discuss speculative readings of gossip, yet we can guess that such readings would make speculative assertions concerning gossip's political or moral import. Gossip would be made to perform as a symptom of something else, in the way that both the positive and negative readings of gossip have done above. As a psychoanalyst seeks to find the hidden traumas indicated by an eruptive symptom, so Spacks, for example, reads gossip as a symptom of women's experience of patriarchal constraints. In other words, gossip is never (or never *just*) gossip here; it's always a symptom of something else. Gossip is women's challenge to established thought (Spacks 1985); an attempt at mastery when other avenues are blocked to us (Ayim 1994); like jokes, according to Freud, it is displaced aggression (Spacks 1985: 50); or gossip is connected to the unconscious Oedipal wish for patricide (see Rosenbaum and Subrin 1963: 829). The same is true for the sociological accounts that think of gossip in terms of its societal function – of what it does within or for communities, and it is especially evident in the negative accounts of gossip in which it represents a malignant and corrupting force. In this way, gossip has signified a number of societal 'ailments' or 'desires'. Miller and McHoul are concerned with approaches that read these kind of symptoms at a cultural-political level.

As an alternative to the speculative cultural studies they see as currently dominating the discipline, Miller and McHoul want to 'look at the everyday in its *historical particularity* and in its *utterly mundane character*' (1998: x). The speculative drive within symptomatic readings of cultural studies is to be countered by an attention to context, empirical data, and an acceptance of banality, giving *un*spectacular popular culture the attention that has hitherto been limited to spectacular forms. Miller and McHoul call upon a two-pronged approach as a way of combating speculation and its dubious authority. (Who is allowed to make pronouncements upon others? On what authority are these speculations based?) This ethnomethodologically inspired strategy involves both securing context via 'factual' historical detail in the guise of political economy, and observing and talking to people (or 'members') in everyday environments. Ethnomethodology approaches everyday interactions as acts which engender knowledge in participants. A close relationship between context and cognition is therefore emphasized. Understanding does not come from somewhere outside of the action, practice, or analysis itself, but is experienced through the process.

I do, as I've already said, sympathize with Miller and McHoul in their criticisms of speculative readings that assume a political agenda prior to an encounter with culture. I would go even further by repeating something I have already said in earlier chapters: that not only is a politics assumed, but the question of what politics 'is' is left unasked. This can lead, as we have seen with reference to the work of Wendy Brown (2001) in Chapter 1, to a certain kind of moralism. Nevertheless, while I have sympathy for Miller and McHoul's concerns about speculation in the way they set it up, I want to retrieve the trope of 'speculation' from their grasp. In their hands, 'speculation' becomes a lapdog to an already decided politics. Their answer to the question of how to move beyond politically optimistic readings (what, in the Garnham-Grossberg debate would fall on the 'cultural studies' side) is to drive out the 'speculative' elements of cultural studies. Yet this has serious problems, which I hope will become clear through a meditation on speculation.

While Miller and McHoul are using 'speculative' to primarily refer to readings that are dogmatically or reductively guided by politics, the term is far richer and more suggestive. The elements of speculation Miller and McHoul object to can certainly be found in the dictionary definition of speculation. (And while there is a certain irony in invoking this apparently authoritative source in the midst of an essay contesting the purity of such appeals, it should be noted that the *OED* is an assembled record of casual language usage not opposed to gossip as a social indicator of signification.) The *OED* includes references to the way in which 'speculation' is used in a derogatory way – as in *mere* or *pure* speculation; and also to the idea of speculation as opposed to practice, fact, action. To speculate is to engage in thought or reflection especially of a conjectural or theoretical nature and it is this element of speculation that Miller and McHoul object to: in the concluding paragraph of *Popular Culture and Everyday Life*, they insist that their method (that could be said to emphasize 'practice, fact, action') is a better alternative to 'critical theorizing as a way of beginning any cultural study' (1998: 181).

All of which sounds like a form of risk aversion. Indeed, speculation involves risk. The *OED* tells us that to speculate can also mean, 'To engage in the buying or selling of commodities or effects in order to profit by a rise or fall in their market value; to undertake, to take part or invest in, a business enterprise or transaction of a risky nature in the expectation of considerable gain.' When we invest in the 'right' theory, then, speculation can provide a profitable return. But it can also, if we have not done our homework so well, or if we are unlucky, result in a loss – a bad return. It is not just theories about the political importance of cultural products and practices that propel an idea out 'there', into a realm beyond fact and fiction. *All* theory could be said to be speculative in the sense that it is about an unguaranteed future return, a beyond that is unfixed. Such a characterization resonates with Stuart Hall's description of theoretical work as 'interruption' (1992: 282), for an interruption posits something unexpected, something which the existing paradigm cannot easily subsume even while it might have given rise to it. Hall suggests feminism as one such interruption to cultural studies, positing feminism as a thief in the night. But while 'thief' might connote something totally foreign invading the safety of the 'home', Hall acknowledges that thieves are produced, of course, by the society they steal from. In this way, he describes how the male-dominated Centre for Contemporary Cultural Studies in Birmingham sought out 'good feminist scholars' (Hall 1992: 282), and how feminists rightly resisted this polite invitation, preferring rather to break in. The CCCS speculated on feminism but had to radically change when its unruly 'profit' arrived. There's no telling what form the interruptive return from a speculation will take.

What might be more unsettling about speculative or theoretical approaches in *Popular Culture and Everyday Life* than the political commitment such approaches display in their conjectural leaps is the risk of a bad return that is opened by the theoretical speculation. The risk is higher for Miller and McHoul when people are at the heart of this speculative drama: when speculation takes the place of the actual experience or voice of people. (It is too much like hearsay in court, perhaps. Why listen to a witness' second-hand account of someone else's statements, when that someone can be made to testify him/herself? A speculative cultural studies is too much like Heidegger's idle talk, then, unable to get to the thing itself thus mistaking secondary interpretations for real understanding.) I want to think more about where this connection between speculation and theory might lead us to make an interruptive intervention into the debate about the practice and identity of cultural studies. I hope it will provide an alternative to: firstly, the cultural studies versus political economy divide; secondly, the solution provided by Miller and McHoul; and lastly, and most importantly, to the stagnant moralism (Brown 2001: 18–44) that those approaches might unwittingly foster (especially those which cast theory/speculation as politically irresponsible).

This involves a move 'nearer to' rather than 'away from' speculation to come to a new formulation of cultural studies' relationship to gossip, and, I would argue, all cultural phenomena. Rather than defend cultural studies against the accusation of speculation put forth by Miller and McHoul, then, I want to invest further in the idea of speculation, towards a more radical formulation, to see what kind of return we will get. Far from repeating a theoretical inflection of past phases in cultural studies, I concur with Sadie Plant, Gary Hall, Wendy Brown, Neil Badmington, Johan Fornas and others, that cultural studies has yet to fully think through the implications of those aspects of theory that are not easily reducible to the overtly political project of cultural studies. That is to say, while cultural studies of the 1980s and 1990s readily took up notions of social and discursive construction in terms of gender, sexuality, class, race and so on, to take one example, it was less eager to explore the conditions of (im)possibility for making statements about social constructionism, about politics even, in the first place. Gary Hall quotes Sadie Plant making this very point (Plant 1995; cited in Hall 2002: 2). Plant feels that cultural studies has employed elements of psychoanalytic theory, deconstruction and Foucauldian analysis 'in the service of an idealist and humanist tradition, and any ideas that might have disturbed this picture have been left on the shelf' (Plant 1995: 100). Wendy Brown finds that even though we live in a post-sovereign and post-literal theoretical regime, a hypersovereignty and literalism pervades within cultural politics (Brown 2001: 22), suggesting that many of the lessons of post-humanism and post-structuralism have yet to be rigorously taken on board. Thinking about speculation is my way of contributing to this unfinished project. I want to suggest that we need to take on board the way in which speculation is at work whenever principles are put forth, displaying the redundancy of being anti-speculative.

YOU GOTTA SPECULATE TO ACCUMULATE

Despite their safeguards, Miller and McHoul cannot avoid speculation. In a review of *Popular Culture and Everyday Life*, Kirsty Leishman writes, 'the authors' proposed [ethnomethodologically inspired cultural studies] is ... fraught with the same pitfalls of speculation and assumption with which they charge the history of cultural studies' (1999). She provides an example from one of Miller and McHoul's case studies:

> In the case of observing McDonald's, any conclusions drawn are circum-scribed by the EMICS scholar's assumption that this everyday activity is experienced by those who are observed, solely within the discourses the scholar nominates, in this instance those around food. This approach to the study of culture relies on a peculiar negation of the intersection between political, social, economic and cultural spheres in any given situation. (Leishman 1999)

She rightly points out that subjects call upon a range of discourses – at micro *and* macro levels – when going about their everyday business. To cut off the macro, speculative, political level of everyday life (say, the way gender or race or our awareness of political issues inflect our everyday conduct), is to be false to that experience. Leishman (1999) claims that doing so 'denies the way cultural texts are produced in the first instance by people who participate in the culture at *many* levels'. And so the premise of the project is limited by the authors' predetermined speculations as to the political importance of one discourse over another.

While I wholeheartedly agree with Leishman's analysis, I want to push it further, drawing out the full implications of what she merely identifies as an 'irony'. I want to suggest that speculation/theory is not a deviation from either a factual path of enquiry or an investment in 'real' political action left intact, one that is just waiting for the speculator to return when s/he has finished with the realm of chance and guesswork of 'mere' speculation. Rather, I will argue, speculation, as the 'motor' of knowledge, is already present in the path of, say, empirical or ethnomethodological enquiry. 'Non-theoretical' work is already drawing on theories of the non-theoretical, or of agency, or of politics. Speculation, I want to suggest, has always already begun.

I will begin by restating the logic of Leishman's observations in slightly different terms. In their preface, Miller and McHoul stress that theirs is an 'extremely data-driven' approach attempting to show 'what these [popular cultural] objects actually look like in their everyday situated places' (1998: xi). They will attempt their project by 'actually going out and collecting relevant data' (Miller and McHoul 1998: xi). Miller and McHoul tell us that: 'The historical parts are rigorously based in the factual bases of cultural phenomena. The analytic parts are, equally, rigorously based on empirical data' (1998: xii). They promise to 'refrain from speculative conclusions' (Miller and McHoul 1998: xii). That may well be the case, but in avoiding speculative conclusions Miller and McHoul do not automatically free themselves from the speculative altogether. In the very first chapter, they say that their focus is on 'subjectivity' and 'power'. They explain: 'By "subjectivity" we mean the ways in which people experience themselves as human: what it means to be, for example, exercised, fed, and counselled; and how individuals move through society inside these and other categories. By "power" we refer to the exercise of knowledge and agency to construct and police such identities' (Miller and McHoul 1998: 1). They *begin* with these philosophical concepts that have a history in speculative assumptions about subjects' relations with themselves, the nature of experience, of agency, and the relationship between knowledge and force. Just because they choose not to do the speculative work themselves does not free them from speculation.

But in order to extend Leishman's observation, we need to think about the role of speculation in knowledge processes. We can see that the principles of ethnomethodology inform Miller and McHoul's study. These principles involve *observing* and *reporting*, rather than *interpreting* what people do. Miller and McHoul feel that 'everyday popular culture is too important a social phenomena to be dealt with speculatively' (1998: x). In seeking to reject or avoid speculation, they position their whole project against it, but speculation is nevertheless 'there' in the 'data', the knowledge they produce. This is because knowledge is subject to principles. Certainly, the knowledge produced through an ethno-methodological approach is subject to principles regarding the observation of mundane situations in order to view the way people use their culture. But a principle, a law governing the enquiry, is transcendental and in being positioned away from or before the action non-speculative ethnomethodology is presented as a sealed entity. In this way, it only goes into contract with itself, we can call on no higher law to help us, and it apparently doesn't need anything 'below' it in order to organize and operate. Now because of this self-reliance, because it is 'everything', it unleashes otherness within itself – a radical alterity.[7]

This alterity, the non-self-identity or non-belonging of the principle, this 'relation to itself (as other) which binds it to itself' (Bennington 1993: 142) constitutes what we can name ethnomethodology (or political economy, or ethnography and so on). This is all that identity is. No identity, then, without a relation to the other, rendering identity 'impure'. In a very different context, Derrida writes, such an always already interrupted relation, or 'non-belonging[,] unleashes speculation' ([1980] 1987: 283). Speculation is 'unleashed' because knowledge gives rise to, but cannot be ultimately secured by, recourse to a stable concept or organizing principle, and so a proliferation of possibilities opens the field. No mastery is afforded to a principle or, for that matter, to an author. Speculation 'infects' and has always already 'infected' texts, even when the 'principle' is one of doing justice to the experience of people and of anti-speculation.

So Miller and McHoul unwittingly speculate. They are investing in a set of ideas, concepts and principles but without paying the necessary debts. They claim allegiance to an ethnomethodological 'camp' (as well as cultural studies, even while stating their problems with it), and pay their dues to these precursors. But in disclaiming the speculative, they cannot pay their debts to, firstly, the speculative work that has produced the concepts (of politics, or power, say) and also principles (of the anti-speculative) that they use, and, secondly, the play of speculation through the possibility of iterability that causes texts, including their own, to reach beyond the boundaries designated for them.

Derrida claims that speculation is always already in operation where know-ledge or reason is concerned, because 'to borrow is the law. Within every lang-uage, since a figure is always a borrowed language, but also from one discursive domain to another, or from one science to another. Without borrowing, nothing begins' ([1980] 1987: 384). In other words, because organizing principles or authors cannot completely master knowledge or reason, cannot contain meanings moving beyond the limits set up, and because of a radical intertextuality, there is already something 'foreign' that has been 'borrowed' from elsewhere, from the other, within a text (and this includes cultural texts of all kinds, not just written). On a practical level, like Miller and McHoul and their unacknowledged speculative precursors, we cannot help but borrow (figures, ideas, language and so on) and incur interest: 'Everything begins with the transfer of funds, and *there is interest in borrowing*, this is even its initial interest. To borrow yields, *brings* back, produces surplus value, is the prime mover of every investment. Thereby one begins by speculating, by betting on a value to be produced as if from nothing' (Derrida [1980] 1987: 384). But because this debt from borrowing is generalized (is the general state of beginning and thus is everyone's debt), it is neutralized. In borrowing, we are caught up in a speculation – which, if we recall, can mean: 'To engage in the buying or selling of commodities or effects in order to profit by a rise or fall in their market value; to undertake, to take part or invest in, a business enterprise or transaction of a risky nature in the expectation of considerable gain.'

If we accept that knowledge is indefinitely subject to speculation because it cannot ultimately either 'belong' to anyone or be contained by any principle, this means that Miller and McHoul's endeavour to limit speculation (and consequently deny alterity and a 'primary' borrowing) is fraught with problems. From this point of view, a cultural studies free from speculation is impossible. It is hoped that the commitment to observation or material conditions will produce an account uncontaminated by speculation. But Miller and McHoul are caught up in a speculative exercise in both the sense that Leishman uses and that which I am identifying here: they repeat what they seek to escape.

Miller and McHoul, and other critics of a theoretically inflected cultural studies, characterize cultural studies as being lost to speculations upon the political meaning of cultural phenomena: dominated by an approach that owes too much interest after borrowing from a pre-existing (usually political) ideal. But if borrowing and thus speculating is something that inheres in knowledge, is something that makes the positing of knowledge possible (because without the possibility of repeating knowledge, we would not be able to recognize it as knowledge); if knowledge moves beyond the realm of mastery, beyond any speculator who may have placed the speculation in circulation, then any attempt to keep speculation at bay is obviously futile.

Critics of a theoretically inflected or speculative cultural studies borrow ideas and language and are therefore always already caught in a system of debt and speculation. Their own assertions, even when based on political economy, case studies, or ethnographic work, are already borrowed, subject to alterity, and open to further borrowing and signification. They are in as much debt to predecessors as I am. The problem is that such positions are so busy rooting their work in 'real' politics or ethnographies, and positioning this work as some kind of alternative to speculation, that they do not acknowledge the speculative 'nature' of their own work. They are, therefore, caught up in repeating or borrowing from these models of speculative work without acknowledging it. This blind repetition leaves such positions open to the kind of conservative moralism that I discussed in Chapter 1. For without a consideration of what conditions our assertions – what enables us to say anything about politics or the 'real' experience of people, say, in the first place – or an account of the alterity within the identity of politics (or, indeed, identity politics), we risk solidifying the terms of the debate in order to use them against anyone who dares to question them. However, all is not lost. Cultural studies *can* be thought otherwise. By recognizing the way in which speculation is central to cognitive, textual, discursive and even disciplinary operations, it is possible to open up a cultural studies beyond suspicion of the theoretical.

But of course, theory is not the same as speculation. As I have already said, Miller and McHoul are right to think that what they identify as speculative cultural studies is problematic. But in turning away from all speculative work in the process – in allowing 'speculation' to stand for all 'critical theorizing' (Miller and McHoul 1998: 181) – they close down the possibility that some theoretical, speculative work might be needed if we are to come up with an account of popular culture that takes it seriously, as they profess to want to do. I am imagining a cultural studies that can try to trace some of the ways in which that popular culture exceeds itself: a radically speculative cultural studies that can take on board the speculative drive – a necessarily risky investment, to be sure. Rather than thinking of speculation in Miller and McHoul's limited sense (as speculations upon the political meaning of texts), we could try to think of the speculative in a more athetic way. That is to say, a kind of speculation that doesn't involve positing a firm thesis or which operates under a stable principle.

In order to get to the speculative in this more radical form, I want to turn more explicitly to a text that has been informing my discussion so far. It is a text in which speculation is speculated upon most famously, rigorously, interestingly, and *speculatively*: this is Jacques Derrida's 'To Speculate – On "Freud"', a close reading of Freud's attempt to account for the experience of unpleasure in the face of an apparently dominant or master principle – the pleasure principle.[8] In this essay, the issue of philosophical speculation arises because Derrida detects an anxiety on Freud's part about the threat it poses to the scientific claims he wants to make for psychoanalysis. At first it would seem that Derrida in 'To Speculate – On "Freud"' is concerned that Freud, in *An Autobiographical Study* (1925), avoids paying a debt – to Nietzsche and Schopenhauer, and philosophy in general. Freud invokes these philosophers only to deny them a place in the genealogy of his ideas. He rejects them as influences upon his psychoanalytic theories of the mind because he does not want philosophical speculation to infect psychoanalysis. In *Beyond the Pleasure Principle*, Freud flatly states, it is 'of no concern to us ... to enquire how far, with this hypothesis of the pleasure principle, we have approached or adapted any particular ... philosophical system. We have arrived at these speculative assumptions in an attempt to describe and to account for the facts of daily observation in our field of study' (1920: 7). To paraphrase, Freud is saying something to the effect of, 'I might well have inherited this idea of the pleasure principle from philosophical notions, but this is of no interest as I am not in the business of claiming originality; I am interested in getting results.'

Freud cannot acknowledge the debt he owes to Nietzsche and Schopenhauer because Freud, according to Derrida, feels that the inheritance is empty – comparable to 'counterfeit money'; the philosophers' notions may resemble those found in psychoanalysis, that is, but they 'lack the equivalent of a content proper to psychoanalysis, which alone can guarantee value, usage, and exchange' (Derrida [1980] 1987: 266). The philosopher has not gained the insights through the hard work of psychoanalytic observation. Consequently, these philosophical notions remain for Freud, mere simulacra ([1980] 1987: 266), just philosophical speculation, and hence intolerable. Given this dismissal of philosophical speculation, when Freud later admits in *An Autobiographical Study* that he eventually gave 'free reign to the inclination, which [he] kept down for so long, to speculation' (Freud 1925: 57, quoted in Derrida ([1980] 1987: 272), Derrida has to conclude that Freud's speculation is of an order different to 'philosophy or scientific or clinical experimentation in their traditional modes' ([1980] 1987: 272).

Rather, the speculation at work in *Beyond the Pleasure Principle*, is athetic – a term Derrida employs to indicate the way in which Freud's text, in trying to take a step 'beyond' the pleasure principle, cannot quite posit another theory. Derrida uses the phrase *pas au delà*: the idea of 'steps for nothing' ([1980] 1987: 296), referring, translator Alan Bass tells us, to 'Freud's repeated gesture of taking another step forward that goes nowhere, the rhetoric of the athesis' (in Derrida [1980] 1987: 292 fn1).

So, we are not dealing here with 'the speculative of the Hegelian type' (an argument that propels itself forward via the Hegelian dialectic – thesis, antithesis, synthesis – speculation as a synthesis of known parts), nor with inductive science: in fact, 'Freud does not, under the name of speculation, call upon a pure and *a priori* theory that simply precedes the so-called empirical contents' (Derrida [1980] 1987: 277). Freud's step beyond the pleasure principle never quite happens, he never finds a sure footing; he can only speculate without positing a thesis.

Unwittingly – and Derrida is quick to point out that Freud in no way '*elaborates* this inconceivable concept [of speculation] for itself ... or works in order to *present* its properly theoretical originality' (Derrida [1980] 1987: 277) and admits that he is 'corrupting the "properly Freudian" usage of "speculation"' ([1980] 1987: 283) – Freud's text points towards a notion of speculation altogether more unsettling than its traditional meanings within philosophy. Derrida's allegation that 'speculation is not only a mode of research named by Freud, not only the oblique object of his discourse, but also the operation of his writing' ([1980] 1987: 284) shows the speculative operations of Freud's text.

Of course, Freud did not *choose* to produce an athetic text. He *wanted* to get 'beyond' the pleasure principle, to a new thesis, but could not quite manage to because of the speculative excess of his speculations. But I still think we can draw on this model – not to produce frustratingly evasive essays that never quite say anything – but as a way of being more in tune with the speculative. What is unhelpful about 'speculative cultural studies' (in Miller and McHoul's opinion) is the overly thetic nature of its readings – for example, the way in which these readings try to master popular culture with, for example, identity politics. To avoid the problems that I have identified with this anti-speculative stance, deconstruction can be useful (and I use the word 'useful' here as a deliberate rejoinder to those who lambaste it for its 'uselessness'). For in paying attention to the quasi-transcendental movement of its terms (like *différânce*, or dissemination, but also, speculation), any firm thesis is denied in turn. That is not to say that meaning is not posited in deconstruction; it is, but the 'quasi' recognizes the way in which absolute meaning is deferred, in the same way that we have seen a principle to at once seal itself – become posited – *and* unleash alterity, something that is anything but 'itself', which is already inside 'itself'. Not all kinds of speculation are thetic.[9]

GOSSIPING AGAIN

Derrida names the athetic operations of Freud's text 'speculation'; it is the name he gives to the in-between, undecidable, faltering status of the knowledge/non-knowledge in *Beyond the Pleasure Principle*. Because in *Knowledge Goes Pop* I am looking at popular knowledges, I want to think about such knowledge/non-knowledge (or what *exceeds* knowledge) as gossip. Like Derrida's terminology, it is a strategic employment of a word (here, to name the undecidability of knowledge) coming out of the texts I am encountering. As such, I want to argue in this section that the uneasy position Freud unwittingly assigns speculation in his text, is comparable to the strange place or status gossip has hitherto been given in cultural studies and the humanities more generally (the implications of which I will make clear shortly). While gossip has been treated as an alternative mode for desperate times to be selectively employed, or as an external object of study, I want to argue that gossip is actually already 'within' the cognitive practices and knowledges associated with more 'legitimate' endeavours.

Now, commentators on gossip, usually in their preface or other some such aside, often acknowledge the saturation of academia with gossip. In the university, we find an institution that is at once founded upon ideals of knowledge, dedicated to its discovery and exchange, and yet also very much involved in a less 'legitimate' knowledge – that of gossip. Mellencamp, in *High Anxiety*, muses, 'I often wonder if any profession is as gossip-prone as academia, where words are the biggest, if not only, commodity' (1992: 172). In Spacks' book, *Gossip*, she describes the central role and lure of her daily gossip sessions with a female colleague at her university (1985: ix). Ayim is interested in the central place that what is, in effect, gossip assumes in official university business such as selection for tenure in the US, or grant applications:

Hiring committees at universities ... frequently totally disregard formal letters of support for applicants, assuming that such documents, becoming as they do part of the file, are always liable to the possibility of falling into the hands of the candidate. Consequently, the committees often believe that such a format is not conducive to receiving either substantive or even reliable information about the candidate. In such cases, a committee member is likely to telephone the referee and informally report the conversation to the rest of the committee. (1994: 97–8)

The point – academics bitch and gossip – might be an obvious one. And I don't want to suggest that cultural studies is subject to this kind of gossip more than any other 'discipline', but I do think that cultural studies is in a good position to explore this relationship with gossip further. Not least because it shares much with gossip. Both, for example, can be considered a knowledge-producing discourse of uncertain position within the academy (despite cultural studies' increasing institutionalization). That is to say, the legitimacy of cultural studies as a knowledge, like that of gossip (and conspiracy theory, as we have already seen), is often questioned or indeed under attack from inside and outside the university. Its legitimacy comes under attack partly because, like gossip, cultural studies opens itself to being speculative – cultural theorists make inferences about the world from a necessarily limited amount of information. Like gossip, cultural studies is often not about being 'factually' right or wrong but about communicating something that has resonance with the reader about the world around them. Like gossip, cultural studies is often accused of decontextualizing information and repeating it without the 'authority' to do so. The 'knowledge' that cultural studies produces is, then, of an uncertain status – what authority do our speculations about culture have? How should they be read? (To emphasize this point, it is worth noting that academics from disciplines outside of the social sciences rarely quote from cultural studies to back up their points, whereas different strands of cultural studies, including my own, insist on borrowing from philosophy, physics, biology, linguistics, psychoanalysis and so on.)

Pointing out the affinity cultural studies has with certain popular knowledges is in no way meant to discredit cultural studies; rather, it acknowledges the unique vantage point of cultural studies to address the issues of marginality and legitimacy that I have already broached in Chapter 3. I think that there are several lessons that cultural studies can learn from what gossip puts on display, not least that gossip forces us to judge the knowledge we encounter at every step. This is lost when we overlook or underplay the uncertain status of the 'knowledge' each produces. In order to show up the limitations of thinking about gossip as just an object of cultural studies, or as something that cultural theorists do among themselves when no one is watching, I want to highlight how gossip, as a form of 'illegitimate' knowledge, conditions more legitimated knowledge, including the knowledge cultural studies draws on and produces.

To show this, I want to return to one of the cultural studies commentators' asides regarding gossip and the university. In her study of gossip in cultural life, Mellencamp stresses that the anthropologists and sociologists who have had much to say about gossip in various cultures, are often on the outside of those cultures, 'comparable', she writes, 'to being tourists or foreigners' (1990: 167). She points towards the way in which this outsider status potentially devalues the experience and affect of gossip (ironically at a conjuncture which values experience and affect) but she fails to bring gossip completely 'in', as it were. Certainly, she discusses many case studies that were topical to the writing of *High Anxiety* but this does not stop Mellencamp herself from being a 'tourist' or 'foreigner', as she puts it, to gossip. She may well be discussing the gossip in 'her' culture (American, or 'Western'), the one that she inhabits, but by failing to include her academic context in that culture to any significant extent, the analysis remains one that objectifies gossip.

It is within a brief discussion of a study by the Canadian psychologist J. D. Logan (who likened geniuses to gossips) that Mellencamp includes her comment regarding academia already quoted: 'I often wonder if any profession is as gossip-prone as academia, where words are the biggest, if not only, commodity' (1990: 172). And yet, the implications of this parenthetical aside and Logan's comparison are not followed through. The suggestion is that academia's product – words – cannot be contained by its official knowledges, its official economy, and is always liable to spill over into a black market in which value is subject to new exchange rates, the laws of other knowledges. Though mentioned, the connection between the words produced through academia's 'legitimate' knowledge and this popular, other knowledge is not pushed.

At the end of the paragraph that contains her parenthetical observation, Mellencamp goes on to ponder that she 'could cheekily update' Logan's characterization of the logic of gossip (and genius) as 'one of rhizomatic thinking, or describe the style as a postmodern one of pastiche, eclecticism, and bricolage' (1990: 172) and yet, despite raising the spectre of these theoretical models, the work that this 'updating' would require is never actually done. She makes a hypothetical hypothesis; the theoretical remains merely a theoretical possibility. It would be 'cheeky', somewhat 'illegitimate', too speculative, perhaps, and not completely safe in this context, she implies.[10] Could it be that Mellencamp does not wish to risk the market value of her words through a necessarily insecure speculation? Just at the point where they seem to be allowed 'in', gossip and theory are kept at bay. Gossip is acknowledged as being present in academia but is subsequently still treated as an object to be described at arms length. And theory is a possible route left untaken. Indeed, many of the references to theory and theorists in Mellencamp's book are not followed through. She is certainly not *anti*-theoretical – her book is littered with references to Deleuze, Lacan, Bakhtin, and Baudrillard – but in never quite doing the theoretical readings she suggests are possible, theory appears like an unnecessary detour or risk that one could take if one had time or sufficient funds, rather than an essential endeavour. The knowledgeable performance of Mellencamp's literature review and cultural account is kept distinct from its object: gossip.

I want to argue that this separation between the proper knowledge of the university and gossip is untenable because gossip makes that very idea of knowledge thinkable. This is easily explained with reference to the history of knowledge. This history is not one unified or linear account. It is always liable to moments of splitting off or borrowing. Because textually manifested knowledge can always be cited and quoted (a necessary state if it is to become ratified as knowledge and hold some kind of force), it is subject to misquoting or citing out of context: it is open to 'abuse'. Knowledge is always subject to the possibility of 'degrading' into 'just' gossip, 'mere' speculation, or simply illusion, of moving further and further from its definition of justified true belief. Rather than the possibility of 'degradation' coming after knowledge has been secured, it accompanies knowledge at every step; knowledge cannot be carried forward without this possibility in fact, because without citation, repetition, borrowing (all of the things that make knowledge vulnerable to becoming further from the truth – more like gossip, in fact), knowledge would not count as knowledge – no one would be able to recognize it as knowledge. For example, for us to be able to recognize the authority and force of the knowledge to be found within an encyclopaedia, it has to be open to repetition. This means that knowledge is open to decontextualization, distortion, misquotation. It is open to something akin to gossip, if we are to think of gossip as the presentation of information without recourse to a method of verification, leaving its status 'open' and 'uncertain'. The borrowing and repetition that makes knowledge and a history of knowledge possible in the first place also means that it might only ever be speculation or gossip. Thus the presence of gossip, rather than being opposed to knowledge, is an integral part of it. What, then, is knowledge that is conditioned by gossip?

None of the cultural studies discussions of gossip cited have been able to think through this question. They have not been able to resist reinstating the distance between some ideal of knowledge and gossip even when they appear open to a closer relationship. So Mellencamp glosses over the appearance of gossip in academia choosing, rather, to chart gossip's appearances in popular culture knowledgeably.

Ayim acknowledges the university's use of gossip when more formal modes of enquiry aren't up to the job but still positions gossip as aberrant, and thus merely an aid to knowledge (1994: 99). But because 'legitimated' knowledge cannot be recognized as knowledge without the possibility of gossip (being, as I've said above, repetition out of context, repetition in the absence of any 'author', and a statement lacking any authority or grounding in fact) knowledge and gossip cannot operate as distinct unities. Each identity (knowledge as knowledge, gossip as gossip) is dependent upon a relation to the/each other. Gossip is the speculative possibility of knowledge. This non-unity, this alterity within identity, as I have already explained, opens up the possibility of speculation, meaning that a text or any other apparent unity, is structured by the possibility of speculation.

We can start to think through the implications of this by changing the terms of our discussion a little. Rather than thinking about gossip as a modified form of knowledge, what would it mean to generalize gossip – to think of all knowledge (both popular and 'official') as a form of 'gossip'? This generalized gossip is what makes it possible to think about the relation between gossip and knowledge in the first place – enables us to speculate about any relation at all. A generalized gossip is the condition of possibility and (therefore) impossibility of the 'purity' of knowledge.

In light of this, gossip is not a contamination that needs to be kept in check; nor a form of improper knowledge. Rather, we are trying to think speculatively 'beyond' the oppositions between proper and improper, knowledge and gossip so that gossip is redefined: it is generalized. We are not on stable ground here. This 'beyond' cannot be a firm synthesis of the two opposed terms, from which further (Hegelian) dialectical speculations can be launched, but is something else, something altogether more *speculatively* speculative – an athetic step. In this athetic ground, we can suggest that gossip is a textual and discursive necessity and, as such, inheres in knowledge proper. (We are dealing with the athetic here, because none of the terms that we are dealing with – gossip, knowledge – are stable precisely because of that relation.)

If gossip conditions knowledge, the openly uncertain status of gossip's authority and authenticity (it seems to be accepted, that is to say, on the idea that it may or may not be true) affects the authority and authenticity of all knowledge. Gossip makes us address the 'mystical foundations' of authority (as Kant would have it), problematizing our attempts to trace knowledge back to an ultimate source. It is this question of authority exposed by gossip that I want to consider in the next chapter in relation to a case study. To assist this move into thinking about gossip in culture more closely, I want to conclude this chapter by thinking through all that I have said so far about a generalized gossip in relation to the cultural economy.

GLOBAL GRAPEVINES: THE CULTURAL ECONOMY OF POPULAR KNOWLEDGE

There seem to be (at least) two different (but related) ways of reading the cultural climate in relation to what we have said about gossip. The first reading concentrates on the disruptive effect of generalized gossip on other, more 'respectable' ways of knowing and the wider social, ideological, political structures this knowledge/knowing supports. According to this reading, the trace of gossip (and, as we will see in the next chapter, of the undecidability regarding legitimacy) at the heart of knowledge encourages us to question the ground on which all kinds of official configurations of knowledge stand.

If, as current political thought suggests, we are living and working in a global *knowledge* economy (one only needs to scan government Web sites from 'developed' countries to see evidence of this belief) we could ask what status the signifier 'knowledge' has in light of the challenges set forth by the structuring or conditioning role of a generalized gossip. The connected question that needs to be posed here is (and this relates back to my discussion of Table 1 in Chapter 1): what status does that economy have – and therefore the ideal of the free market it propagates – if its dominant commodity (knowledge) is volatile, unstable, undecidable because it is shot-through with the possibility of being 'only' gossip, of being of little or no value? What happens when a dominant commodity, before any mercantile exchange has taken place, already involves a debt to another (in the way that I have discussed above in relation to borrowing)? Can the constitutive relationship between knowledge and gossip upset, halt, arrest, challenge the economy and patterns of ownership and power? This would be politically desirable to those of us who are opposed to the way in which the knowledge economy privileges a particularly utilitarian notion of knowledge – as opposed to one based on community, for example, or creativity – and the free market policies that often accompany this (see Rutherford 2003 for a number of essays on these issues).

In order to sell knowledge, in order for it to have *value*, the knowledge economy has to disguise the aporetic tension between the impossibility and possibility of legitimate knowledge at the foundation of all knowledge: service providers and retailers have to convince consumers and shareholders to invest in knowledge by presenting it as useful, authoritative, unique, legitimate, and as theirs to sell in the first place. What is in fact risky speculation (investing in a knowledge that holds the trace of its own illegitimacy within it) with no appeal to a final authority, no guarantee of a profit, is presented as a safe investment. This is the difference between, say, playing the stock market and taking out a fixed-rate bond. We imagine through purchasing knowledge that we are the ones who will receive interest, but we are not encouraged to think about the debt that knowledge itself already owes for its indefinite, 'originary' borrowings.

While those who work with knowledge develop strategies (such as appeals to metanarratives, or personal endorsements) to present knowledge as secure, gossip forces us to think about its insecurity. This is because, as I have shown, gossip functions according to an uncertainty, an undecidability, as to its status (is it fiction, is it fact; is it false, is it true; is it playful or serious; is it non-knowledge, is it knowledge?). In this way, gossip is perhaps (potentially) less violent than other forms of knowledge in that it admits its self-instituting, infected structure (as long, of course, as it isn't being presented as something else, which is a problem I will consider in the next chapter). When we indulge in gossip, we are speculating – investing (to a lesser or greater degree, depending on the gossip) in one knowledge over another. Crucially, when we gossip we are usually aware that there are other accounts to consider, that it is highly subjective, and that other ways of knowing are available to us for understanding the information we receive. Likewise, we understand that with gossip comes a debt, that it is borrowed information; we understand that it may be a misquotation, a borrowed fragment, a repetition out of context. We could say, then, that gossip is more 'honest' about the way in which knowledge works: how knowledge is conditioned by those elements which it attempts to exclude such as fallibility, fiction, doubt, undecidability, illegitimacy.

However, this reading only gets us so far; only as far as we have gone with conspiracy theory in Chapters 2 and 3. While this is a valuable and important element of what popular knowledges can potentially provide, to rest with this reading would surely be to risk repeating the conclusions (though not the methodologies) of the celebratory readings we are trying to avoid. I would be able to claim a subversive or deconstructive potential for popular knowledges like gossip and conspiracy theory in advance of any singular instance and leave it at that, happy that there is a force in the world able to disrupt the dominant economic mode (reliant, as it is, upon 'knowledge' networks and commodities). I could sleep easier at night knowing that knowledge was being brought down a peg or two and kept in check by underdogs like gossip. Which brings me, before I get carried away with notions of heroism, to the second reading of knowledge and gossip in the cultural climate.

For rather than gossip interrupting the knowledge economy – and that economy's associated neo-liberal open market and erosion of the value of knowledge beyond a notion of 'utility' – gossip could also be thought to facilitate and be facilitated by the rise of information networks and the knowledge economy. What I mean by this is that it is possible to read the unstable nature of knowledge that gossip puts on display as wholly compatible with the often confusing and complicated networks of knowledge and information in contemporary society. The Internet, for example, can be a useful research tool but more often than not leads us on a wild goose chase to random search results unrelated to our original enquiry or to sites that link endlessly to others, deferring the source of knowledge. Often, even when we find what we are looking for, it is unreferenced, unclaimed, without clear copyright; the knowledge we find there is of an uncertain status, much like gossip itself. We seem more and more comfortable, that is to say, with the idea that knowledge cannot be traced back to an ultimate source (as is often the case with gossip). We seem more willing to allow information to accrue validity simply through circulation. If we read or hear something in enough contexts, it will assume the status of knowledge in spite of an absence of authority or method of verification. A great deal of knowledge today seems to have taken on something of the status of gossip. It is neither true nor false, knowledge nor non-knowledge but somewhere in between. This is precisely why I have chosen to focus on popular knowledges in this book. They seem to me to provide a unique way to understand the nature of knowledge today.

Gossip in this second reading is normalized. It ceases to be an exceptional occurrence or practice, and becomes a dominant mode of knowledge exchange itself, wholly in keeping with the demands of a modern knowledge economy. In fact, although in my first reading I suggested that the knowledge economy relies on ascribing value to knowledge through claims to authority, it can also assimilate popular knowledges as commodities. I mean this not only in the sense of a commodified *content* (a conspiracy culture or gossip industry), but also in the sense that some popular knowledges as *mode* or *form* can be imbued with commercial value. Indeed, if a form of popular knowledge is not codifiable in any clear way, if it has no recourse to a written constitution, if it is based on an undecidability as to its verity, if it is based only on arbitrary decisions as to its identity, it might be all the more profitable for a savvy entrepreneur to assume the position of being (popularly) knowledgeable, as having, after Pierre Bourdieu, popular cultural capital. If knowledge has an uncertain status and is uncodified and tacit, one can cash in most spectacularly – because popular knowledges might need expert readers, translators, and interpreters as much as, if not more than, official knowledges. The entrepreneur can suggest that only through engaging their services can the employer have access to this popular, unwritten, ambiguous knowledge. Think, for example, of style gurus. Retailers of all kinds seek to tap into uncodifiable 'street' level knowledge by employing those who can translate emerging trends into commercial profit.

Gossip becomes normalized through our frequent encounters with know-ledge that cannot, as we shall see in the next chapter, be traced to an ultimate authority. In this way, it does not necessarily present a challenge to the knowledge economy. Rather, it could aid it (remember James Earle's suggestion that gossip is the original knowledge economy?) and increase our reliance upon the commodification of knowledge. Gossip might become normalized to the point that it begins to assume a role like its 'official' counterpart. Popular knowledges, like gossip, become the latest fodder for an ever-expanding economy looking for new products, new markets, and new ways of selling. Even gossip becomes commodified and claimed. I mean this in terms of content and form: content-wise I am thinking of the product sold by magazines like the *National Enquirer* in the US and *Heat* in the UK; with regards to form, what I am arguing is that less formal, stable ways of receiving knowledge are taking centre stage, like the Internet. Thus, gossip becomes familiar as we are increasingly confronted with, consume and learn to think through forms of knowledge of uncertain status and origin.

If we leave aside the commodification of gossip (as content or process) for a moment and concentrate on the normalization of gossip, it becomes clear that this has far-reaching implications, not all of which are necessarily desir-able, progressive or subversive. The more familiar we are with unfounded knowledge, the less surprised we will be to see it included in the news, or as a part of official government procedures (such as the inclusion in the UK governmental dossier entitled *Iraq – Its Infrastructure of Concealment, Deception and Intimidation*[11] that presented plagiarized work from a PhD student as verified intelligence). The breakdown of the opposition between knowledge and gossip in the cultural sphere means that knowledge takes on more and more characteristics of gossip (neither true nor false; neither knowledge nor non-knowledge) so that we get 'faction' on television, narrative science, and uncorroborated intelligence.

It might seem that this state of affairs testifies to the popularity of popular knowledges, justifying the name. People perhaps look to popular knowledges because these knowledges do not pretend that there is an ultimate foundation to knowledge; they don't present themselves as unshakably true. In their playful, provisional, speculative form, popular knowledges hold less connotations of power, force, or violence.

Because of this popularity, the argument follows, the ambiguity of popular knowledges has infiltrated spheres more traditionally associated with official knowledge, perhaps in a way that complicates that distinction. And yet, of course, there *is* 'violence' at work. When a student thesis is unreferenced and presented as sound intelligence, when the speculative is presented as observational – as fact – and when this is given, as I shall be considering in Chapter 5, as a reason to go to war (as it was in the UK's case for war in Iraq, which depended on a single source) there is 'violence'.[12] So we may not be surprised to learn about the infiltration of undecidable gossip into official realms when we find out about it but I think we must be vigilant as to when it is presented as either wholly true or false. Gossip's potential to put the provisionality of authority and undecidability between truth and lies on display, is only that: a potential. It is up to us to realize when gossip is being used not to suspend or interrupt power and authority, but is disguised in order to reinforce it. These will be my concerns in the following chapter.

CHAPTER 5

Sexed Up: Gossip by Stealth

Despite my focus on the relationship between gossip and cultural studies in the previous chapter, I first became interested in gossip because of its ubiquity in cultural and political life. As I became more aware of this gossip I realized that it was rarely named as such. This chapter is my attempt to understand that omission. It is also an attempt to produce a responsible reading of this important cultural phenomenon.

MY GOSSIP

If I told you (one-to-one, in private, in secret, stressing that you not pass the information on, while knowing that you probably will) that the case for war in Iraq hinged on gossip, would you believe me? Would you tell anyone else?

Before deciding, you might ask me to prove it. Now, I could just say, 'trust me' with a knowing look, and a tap on the nose to suggest it's all in hand. Or I could allude to someone else, someone of higher authority, from whom I gleaned the information, thus passing on the burden of authority and proof to a figure you may not be able to question. Or, I could rise to the challenge; after all, gossipers often try to persuade us of the verity of what they reveal ('a friend of mine saw them!' or 'I read it in the paper!'). But it is not a condition of gossip's identity to be proved (or, in fact, disproved) and it may well be more 'gossipy' if the question of its verity is left open.

So I'll tell you my gossip, and as with all gossipees, you can decide whether or not to invest it with import. You might try to elevate my gossip to knowledge and even succeed in doing so but, I will be arguing, this new credibility and identity would still contain the trace of undecidability that structures it. This trace is not just something to sweep under the carpet (if indeed this were possible – a trace, after all, is indelible); it would still organize that from which it was excluded, even from its position 'under the carpet'.

I want to speculate on the way in which popular knowledges are at the heart of some important contemporary events. Specifically, I want to list the numerous ways in which I think gossip was central to the case for war on Iraq, the ensuing battle of wills between Westminster and the BBC in Britain, and the subsequent

questioning of how intelligence was handled in the lead up to the second Gulf
War in both Britain and the United States.

*Before charting this territory, I want to come clean. In an attempt to approx-
imate the experience of gossip, I have suspended references and footnotes for
the duration of this gossip transmission.*

*Maybe I shouldn't have told you. Maybe you would have found yourself
feeling uneasy or sceptical half way through without quite knowing why.
Maybe you would have realized soon enough that there are fewer avenues of
authentication to follow.*

*Of course, this is not to say that the work in the rest of this chapter that
does have guiding parenthetical references and footnotes is exempt from your
scrutiny and scepticism, nor from the problems with legitimacy encountered
here – that would be a mere trick or illusion as my ensuing discussion of
legitimacy and authority will make clear. And I am not trying to demonize
reference systems. I become very frustrated when my students don't use them
– they do, after all, form the backbone of academic research, not least because
they can lead other researchers to the source of material so that they, in turn,
can offer a different interpretation in an ongoing dialogue. Our problems
concerning legitimacy are not circumvented once we stop telling the reader
where our information is from. Nevertheless, this more 'gossipy' discussion
of gossip might help us to keep the question of legitimacy and the status of
knowledge open, at least for a little while. This is but one experiment in the
process of producing an analysis sympathetic or responsible to its subject,
rather than following a recommended or programmatic course of action.*

*A speculative or 'gossipy' reading of gossip (in which facts have a dubious
status, and any claim to authority is unclear) is necessary for the subject of
the case study below – for we will encounter material that has been, or still
is, classified, unverified, or secret. Every way we turn, it seems as if another
piece of gossip arises. That such gossip is made to look like anything but
gossip does little to reassure and reorient us. Because of the nature of this
material, I am dealing with secondary texts and accounts that are themselves
all looking for ways to distinguish gossip from knowledge. I began looking
at gossip in the lead up to the war on Iraq and subsequent events precisely
because of this instability. Perhaps all situations of such international
import are equally opaque, but it seemed more noticeable, more striking,
and particularly ominous, in the post-September 11, trans-Atlantic, politico-
cultural scene. If, as I will go on to argue, undecidability affects any encounter
with, and experience of, knowledge – then it cannot but be the case that the
knowledge being produced by a post-September 11 discourse around security
and terrorism is questionable.*

*I am aware of the problems of trying to produce a more gossipy account
of gossip. For a start, I am still indebted to academic discourses. Which means*

that I am caught in a residual adherence to knowledge hierarchies – I look to fairly reputable sources for my information, for example. I haven't asked my grandmother, or my next-door neighbour what they think. It would, then, be disingenuous and unhelpful to claim what follows to be the same as gossip (although the accounts I draw from are all secondary texts – so, in a sense, I am merely passing on what I have heard or read; and even where I have included the name of the author and publication, we should remember that gossips aren't immune to such tactics of persuasion). I can but flirt with gossip as form rather than content. But, I still want at least to try to create unease about the status of what I write – for such unease or scepticism reproduces our experience with gossip in the way that it forces the question of knowledge and legitimacy upon us. I would like to find ways of going further with this in an attempt to realize one kind of responsible reading: one that lays before us the arbitrariness and, therefore, undecidability of knowledge; and to think through the decisions that we make in spite, or rather because of, these conditions concerning what is and what is not knowledge. It also means, of course, being aware of our own investments in knowledge as we think through those decisions (hence this qualifying, transitional section; in italics, no less, in an attempt to signal reflexivity). This chapter will at worst be read as bad scholarship, at best, good gossip.

Now for that gossip:

- The intelligence that suggested that Iraq could deploy weapons of mass destruction (WMDs) in forty-five minutes was unreliable, uncorroborated and single-sourced. In fact, during the Hutton Inquiry in the UK, established to investigate the events leading up to the death of weapons inspector Dr David Kelly after he was 'outed' as the source of reported doubts about the government's dossier (*Iraq's Weapons of Mass Destruction – The Assessment of the British Government*), it emerged that the 'forty-five minutes' claim was from a single source reporting a single source. In other words, you could say it was gossip. Dr Brian Jones, who managed scientists working at the Defence Intelligence Staff (DIS), admitted at the Inquiry, 'We even wondered when discussing the issue whether [the informant who passed on the "forty-five minutes" claim] may have been trying to influence rather than inform.' Jones thought the informant was bragging: resorting to gossip to gain status. And yet, this gossip was included in the governmental dossier not as gossip, but as reliable intelligence. In Tony Blair's foreword to this document, he states '[Saddam Hussein's] military planning allows for some of the WMD to be ready within forty-five minutes of an order to use them.' Like much gossip, the claim is vague. (Which WMDs? Are we talking nuclear, chemical or biological? Are they short-range or long-range? Who are they intended for?) And it is inflammatory. Like all juicy gossip, this morsel is picked up and passed on by others. In this instance, George W. Bush passed it on in a radio address to the nation: 'The Iraqi regime possesses biological and chemical weapons, is rebuilding the facilities to make more and, according to the British government, could launch a biological or chemical attack in as little as forty-five minutes after the order is given.' The gossip is passed on not as gossip, but as reputable fact from that respectable establishment, the British government.

■ When BBC reporter Andrew Gilligan accused the government of 'sexing up' the dossier that made the case for war (by using single-sourced intelligence such as the 'forty-five minutes' claim) the government counter-accused Gilligan of poor journalism: of reporting an anonymously sourced, uncorroborated piece of gossip. The BBC defended itself by claiming that the fact that someone working closely with those writing the dossier had doubts about its validity and concerns regarding the role of Alastair Campbell, Blair's director of communications and strategy until his resignation in 2003, was a story in itself. The office gossip, when the office is the DIS, is considered worth reporting. Campbell responded thus: 'If the BBC are now saying that their journalism is now based on the principle that they can report what any source said, then BBC standards are now debased beyond belief.' Campbell's repetition of the word 'now' three times might just indicate nerves in a stressful situation, but it also implies a slippery BBC eager to shift their position as it suits, and also a 'then' in which standards, apparently, were more rigorous. In an unprecedented letter to the then director general of the BBC, Greg Dyke, Blair himself wrote, 'It seems to me there has been a real breakdown of the separation of news and comment.' Campbell and Blair's questioning of the BBC's journalistic practices was a taste of things to come as the effects of the Hutton Inquiry were felt throughout the profession in the UK. A report in *The Economist* reads:

> Mr Gilligan's approach contrasts with that of another BBC reporter, Susan Watts... Her account partly backs up Mr Gilligan's version of what he was told by Mr Kelly; but she felt Mr Gilligan's most explosive allegation – that Alastair Campbell, Tony Blair's communications chief, had personally ordered that the dossier be "sexed-up" – was "gossip" and not reportable.

Susan Watts is set up here as a journalist who has no difficulty distinguishing gossip from grounded knowledge and employing standard professional safeguards to judge the quality and viability of the information she encounters. It would be disingenuous not to acknowledge that, at a certain level, all of the ensuing fuss over Gilligan's report could have been avoided if he *had* been more cautious. But that's not the same as saying that his report was wrong, or, more importantly for us, that it didn't highlight some interesting double standards about the status of gossip in the public sphere (and the *secret* services). For Gilligan *could* have been more sceptical about Kelly's views on the government's dossier, or could have at least made more stringent efforts to record those views accurately, or find others to corroborate Kelly's doubts about the dossier, but the interesting point for us is that the government and intelligence agencies paid just as much credence to gossip (of a sort) as Gilligan, the 'rogue' reporter.

BBC *Newsnight* reporter Watts had also been an informal press contact of Dr Kelly's. In a transcript of Watts talking to Kelly after Gilligan had broken the story about Campbell sexing up the dossier, she admits that she 'missed that one', after which they both laugh. This suggests that, whereas in hindsight it is easy to characterize Susan Watts as the better, more ethical, more professional journalist, she may well have just overlooked the story that Gilligan saw. It wasn't that she tried to find a second source for the story about Campbell, it was that she failed to pick up that there was a story there at all, she dismissed Kelly's mention of Campbell as 'a gossipy aside', as she told the Hutton Inquiry. It's possible that her code of conduct wasn't put to the test in the way that she and *The Economist* report suggests. Gilligan might have listened too closely to gossip but Watts perhaps wasn't listening closely enough.

- During the Hutton Inquiry, Dr Brian Jones said that Kelly would have been aware 'that there was a problem with the sourcing ... just from chatting to us.' In other words, as Kelly hung about at the Ministry of Defence, one or two gossiping acquaintances at the DIS expressed their unease about the 'forty-five minutes' claim. In this way, by talking to Gilligan, Kelly was doing precisely what a good gossip does: passing gossip on. That he later professed ignorance as to the protocols surrounding the relationship between government employees with access to sensitive information and journalists testifies to a lax, *laissez faire* attitude towards secrecy: what is the point of a secret if you can't divulge it to someone who'll appreciate it? It is highly likely that Kelly underestimated the significance of his gossipy revelations over afternoon tea in the Charing Cross Hotel on the 22 May 2003.

- The findings of the Hutton Inquiry and the manner in which Gilligan was treated (the BBC stood by him during the row with No. 10 but he was subsequently dismissed) have had far-reaching consequences for journalism in the UK. As an indicator of the anxious climate, an internal memo at the British broadsheet, the *Guardian*, from editor Alan Rusbridger to his staff is exemplary. He stresses the need to re-evaluate working practices: 'Spooks, politicians, civil servants (and potential moles) will all be re-evaluating their ways of working (or leaking) in the light of the evidence that has been disclosed. So should journalists.' Leaking, a form of gossiping, will be kept in check by those that have something to leak, and journalists will have to cover their backs in a similar way: a higher level of vigilance is required when it comes to encountering gossip (receiving and passing it on). It is not enough, he goes on to say, to be careful with the wording of a *Guardian* article if a journalist is less guarded elsewhere, say on talk radio (Rusbridger cites BBC

Radio Five as an example but he is thinking of Gilligan's article in the *Mail on Sunday* which was even less careful about wording than his original, controversial BBC Radio 4 report). Rusbridger warns: 'On sensitive stories be very careful to stick exactly to what has been agreed in print. That goes for tone as much as facts. And I'm afraid it also goes for entering into email exchanges with people who present themselves as innocent readers. More than one *Guardian* journalist has been lulled into a false sense of security via this route – only to find their words splattered all over some hostile website or weblog.' In other words, be careful who you write to, talk to, gossip with, because you never know who might pass it on, possibly misrepresenting or decontextualizing the information.

- In the wake of the Gilligan/Kelly affair, Rusbridger predicted that the practice of civil servants leaking stories to the press would be kept in check, but a different story has actually emerged from Whitehall. Even the Hutton Report itself, much to the chagrin of Lord Hutton, was leaked to the UK tabloid the *Sun* and its contents were reported before the official publication. A six-month investigation by the Department of Constitutional Affairs failed to identify the leak. This is not unusual. Reporter Julian Glover writing in the *Guardian* says that it is a Whitehall tradition; apparently 'About twenty-five civil service leak inquiries are set up a year and almost none of them finger a culprit.' Gossip here – unauthorized leaking – is used as a check upon governmental control over the flow of information.

- Following Gilligan's broadcast and the ensuing indignant stance from No.10, there was much speculation by the press and Westminster as to who Gilligan's source was. The guessing game was made more difficult because Gilligan had claimed his source to be a member of the intelligence community, whereas in actuality he was a weapons inspector. For a few weeks, the chattering classes exchanged heated gossip as to the identity of the mole. Kelly, having recognized some of what he had said in Gilligan's report, eventually decided to put himself forward to his employers as the possible source of the story. Kelly recognized his own gossip in the content of the gossip of others.

- David Kelly committed suicide after the government leaked his name in an informal manner to the press, adopting a policy of question and answer for journalists to ascertain the identity of Gilligan's source. (One can imagine similar 'games' of partial revelation taking place over the garden fence.) An informal process was favoured over a formal statement because of the sensitivity of the matter. While not exactly gossip, this informal mode of communication sought to 'hedge its bets' in the way gossip at first sight does. That is to say, gossip is commonly thought of as a mode of communication that lacks responsibility: gossipers can always say that they are just passing on something they have heard. (I want to point out, however, that this is a very different configuration of the relationship between gossip and responsibility than the one I will go on to outline at the end of this chapter.) In using this policy of not naming Kelly as such but allowing journalists to run through a list of possible candidates (naming through not-naming), the government's press office can place the responsibility elsewhere – onto the journalist for guessing correctly. Sensitive? Or just plain cowardly?

■ Britain's Butler Committee, set up to investigate the quality of the intelligence on Iraq's WMDs, criticized Blair's 'informal' mode of government, which relies heavily on the advice of unelected special advisers (such as Alastair Campbell) rather than Cabinet ministers, thus 'reducing the scope for informed collective political judgment.' The report goes on to read: 'Such risks are particularly significant in a field like [intelligence], where hard facts are inherently difficult to come by and the quality of judgment is accordingly all the more important.' The report seems to suggest that when dealing with material of an undecidable nature like intelligence (which could always be 'just' unfounded gossip), it is important that the context of reception or analysis be as formal (and as accountable) as possible. Gossip is better handled, the report indicates, if its informality is not seen to infect those around it. The image here is of a stable, unmoveable, reliable, credible ground that can receive material of an opposite nature, but what Blair's preferred style of government shows is that formality can be considered too time-consuming and rigid.

■ In the US, according to a report in the *New Yorker*, Bush and his cohort established the habit of circumventing CIA analysis, to obtain raw, unassessed intelligence. Reporter Seymour M. Hersh records his conversation with Greg Thielmann, a former director of the Strategic, Proliferation and Military Affairs Office at the State Department's Intelligence Bureau. Hersh tells us what he heard Theilmann reveal regarding what the CIA thought of this intelligence once it did reach them: 'They'd pick apart a report and find out that the source had been wrong before, or had no access to the information provided.' The trustworthiness of Ahmed Chalabi, who led the foremost Iraqi opposition movement, the US-backed Iraqi National Congress, before the fall of Saddam Hussein, was a particularly sensitive matter: the White House liked what it heard through Chalabi's defector reports even though they were discounted by the intelligence community. Theilmann tells Hersh: 'There was considerable skepticism throughout the intelligence community about the reliability of Chalabi's sources, but the defector reports were coming all the time. Knock one down and another comes along. Meanwhile, the garbage was being shoved straight to the President. A routine settled in: the Pentagon's defector reports, classified "secret," would be funnelled to newspapers, but subsequent CIA and INR [Bureau of Intelligence and Research] analyses of the reports – invariably scathing but also classified – would remain secret.'

On the basis of these defector reports and uncorroborated Italian intelligence that suggested that the Iraqi Ambassador to the Vatican, Wissam al-Zahawie, might have purchased uranium in Niger in 1999, Hersh reports:

On August 7th, Vice-President Cheney, speaking in California, said of Saddam Hussein, 'What we know now, from various sources, is that he ... continues to pursue a nuclear weapon.' On August 26th, Dick Cheney suggested that Hussein had a nuclear capability that could directly threaten 'anyone he chooses, in his own region or beyond.' He added that the Iraqis were continuing 'to pursue the nuclear program they began so many years ago.'

US foreign policy concerning the Gulf was built upon shaky intelligence; or if you like, war against Iraq was justified using the gossip President Bush et al liked the sound of even if the CIA discredited it.

■ I want to pause for a moment on the final piece of evidence taken up by the White House to make a case for war: the documents indicating the sale of uranium to Iraq. For gossip within the CIA has been floating the idea that an ex-officer, disgruntled at the way CIA analyses of intelligence were being disregarded by Iraq hawks in the White House, faked the documents in order to expose the folly of the hawks. Hersh writes: 'Like all large institutions, CIA headquarters, in Langley, Virginia, is full of water-cooler gossip.' A retired clandestine officer talks to Hersh: 'What's telling ... is that the story, whether it's true or not, is believed.' Hersh interprets this as 'an extraordinary commentary on the level of mistrust, bitterness, and demoralization within the CIA under the Bush Administration.'

End of gossip transmission. End of gossip detection. (As if it were that easy to demarcate gossip's beginnings and ends...)

I could go on but I don't want to get lost in a list of instances in which gossip has arisen. As our encounter with conspiracy can tell us, the more we look for something, the more likely it is we'll find it. Collecting these examples under the name of gossip involves a certain amount of elision but I think it is important to name them as such for its presence makes us acutely aware of the fragility of information and (mis)uses of authority. But I should say more about this category of 'gossip' used with such liberty above. In using the name of gossip to gather these examples, I don't wish to convey an overriding homogeneity. Repetition of the same snippet of gossip doesn't even have internal homogeneity; that is to say, even when gossip passes information on, iterability ensures that it is haunted by the trace of the possible 'death' of the source of the gossip, making it always 'other' from the 'original' in that repetition (and this is before we take the 'Chinese Whispers' effect into account). And so the possibility of homogenous relations *between* instances of gossip is also problematic. Rather, I think that this category of gossip can be usefully thought of as a play of heterogeneity. Different in each instance, the examples cited above cannot be reduced to one account or explanation, to one grand theory. Just as my discussion of the economy in relation to gossip in the previous chapter gave rise to very different readings, so here it is difficult to pinpoint the politics of gossip. In some of the scenarios gossip serves as a check on official stories, performing a 'fourth estate' role, exposing secrets and calling authorities to account. In others, however, gossip is taken up by those authorities and forced into a more reliable and airtight identity. But rarely, on either side, is gossip admitted, claimed, stood by. Gilligan made journalistic inferences and took chances; Kelly aired concern over the quality of the dossier perhaps out of an ethical duty – what we call 'whistle blowing'; Blair's government employed informal modes of government; Bush endorsed and used uncorroborated and discredited intelligence. Gossip, named such, rarely arises, and so the way in which gossip forces the question of knowledge upon us is downplayed.

From these examples of gossip, as well as from our reading of the economy in Chapter 4, it is clear that gossip, like conspiracy theory, can have both conservative and radical manifestations. Irrespective of political allegiance, many of the forms of gossip that I've been gossiping about show the key players paying attention to gossip because of the story it can support: because it corroborates something they already suspect for whatever reason (personal, political, religious, social and so forth). I am, of course, just as susceptible to this and my own opinion is clearly evident in the way I have conveyed the gossip (well, gossip is never neutral). This involves playing down the undecidability of knowledge and gossip and presenting information as either firm thesis or fact. And yet, despite the conscious efforts to limit the undecidability that accompanies gossip (by not admitting that it is gossip in the first place, or by attributing more authority to the gossip than it deserves, for example), it seems to me that collectively these instances still have the potential to put on display the unstable nature of authority. To illustrate, I want to examine the 'scandalous' nature of the Gilligan/ Kelly affair.

What, we could begin by asking, was the most scandalous aspect of the Gilligan/Kelly affair? Was it that a weapons inspector had doubts about the British government's claims concerning Saddam Hussein's WMD? Was it the revelation that workers with relatively high security clearance regularly, and sometimes unguardedly, talk to members of the press? Was it that Gilligan failed to clear his radio report script with his editors? Or that the BBC failed to enforce a system of double-checking stories? All of these are certainly scandalous on a local scale. But I want to suggest that it was the central role of gossip in the affair (even if it remained unnamed) that determined the heightened level of anxiety. That is to say, because gossip suggested that Iraq possessed WMD, it was impossible to trace the information back to an ultimate source. The Hutton Inquiry ascertained that the information had come via a single source reporting a single source, so that would be a difficult lead to follow even if the first informer weren't secret; finding Saddam hasn't resolved the issue of WMD and the actual weapons, if indeed there are any, haven't been found either. The presence of WMD has not been proved (nothing has been found) or disproved (there is always the slim possibility that stockpiles were destroyed or sold). The WMD scandal cannot find closure. Certainly, it will blow over, become a footnote in history, become less important, but closure will continue to elude because so many of the elements in the puzzle are based on gossip. Gossip keeps the scandal scandalous (I will explain what I mean by this below).

Of course, many of the key players found it necessary to suggest certain points of closure. So Alastair Campbell et al., for example, concentrated on identifying the mole who raised the concerns in the first place (eventually identified as Kelly) and on the legal status of Gilligan's report. By focusing the story on exposing and discrediting the mole and the journalist, Campbell could present a provisional point of closure for the story in the not wholly successful attempt to prevent it from becoming one about the questionable authority on which war was waged. (I say not wholly successful for the anti-war coalition in Britain certainly 'challenged the government's authority to wage a war with Iraq,' as Tony Benn phrased it at the People's Assembly for Peace held at Central Hall, London, in March 2003, although I will go on to address the limits of this challenge.) Campbell's game was always a dangerous one: as he questioned the authority of one British institution (the BBC), the same questions could be asked of his own (the government).

Which brings me back to the issue of the scandalous scandal. I want to suggest that the most scandalous element of the Gilligan/Kelly affair might be the infinite regress of authority that conditions all decision making and claims to legitimacy (which is another way of saying, as I did above, that gossip keeps the scandal scandalous). With reference to his conversation with Kelly, Gilligan accused Campbell of altering the essence of the dossier to make it a more powerful document in a bid to gain support for war. Much of the ensuing debate and focus of the Hutton Inquiry concentrated on, firstly, Gilligan's accuracy and journalistic conduct and, secondly, the government's role in the presentation of intelligence in the dossier to the public. But in concentrating on these questions, a more fundamental one concerning the nature of authority was left unasked even though the presence of gossip raised it, and the anti-war coalition was certainly concerned about legality. Such obfuscation, of course, is far from surprising: it is necessary for governing to take place.

'TRUST ME, I'M THE PRIME MINISTER'

In order to get a clearer sense of how gossip alerts us to this problem with authority, I will need to examine the classical formulation of knowledge. As I have already suggested in Chapter 1, 'knowledge' is commonsensically understood as justified true belief. If we recall the necessary conditions for knowledge are as follows: *the proposition* has to be true; I have to believe that the proposition is true; and I have to be justified in believing the proposition. Epistemologists have debated the assumptions at the heart of these conditions for centuries, particularly concerned with definitions of truth, the nature of belief, and what constitutes adequate justification for knowledge.

What is striking about the classical formulation is that it leaves open the question of authority -- of who authorizes the justification for knowing something and whether that justification can be scientific *only* or could also be ideological. 'Justification', after all, suggests both rational (disinterested) and non-rational (interested) motives. And there is a more fundamental issue with the authorizing of knowledge, which rests on the question of who authorizes the authorization, and so on, *ad infinitum*. That infinity is the space of the mystical: there is no point at which the question of justification comes to a standstill, no final ground of justification, thus keeping the question of authority open as fundamentally unknowable, or mystical. This means that knowledge cannot be justified in any rational, or should I say, knowledgeable way; it can never be legitimately legitimized in the first place.

Knowledge leaves itself open to a self-authorizing legitimacy or justification. Jean-François Lyotard elaborates on this issue:

> Authority is not deduced. Attempts at legitimating authority lead to vicious circles (I have authority over you because you authorize me to have it), to question begging (the authorization authorizes authority), to infinite regression (x is authorized by y, who is authorized by z), and to the paradox of idiolects (God, Life, etc., designate me to exert authority, and I am the only witness of this revelation). ([1983] 1988: 142)

Knowledge, despite its attempts to the contrary, cannot do anything to stop this regression because it just inheres in the logic of authorization. It can seek to limit or mitigate the 'madness' that such a state of affairs implies by making sure that its objects are at least as scientifically robust as possible, but it will never stop the 'madness' per se. An appeal to one's position within an institution ('Trust me, I'm a doctor' or 'Trust me, I'm the Prime Minister') doesn't avoid this problem, as the founding moment of an institution too is shot-through with this problem of authority (who bestowed authority to the institution and who bestowed authority on the person bestowing authority etc.). To become knowledge, therefore, knowledge has no choice but to cut 'arbitrarily' into that regressive chain, and to posit something – to posit knowledge that will contain an irreducible and ineliminable trace of the arbitrariness that affects it. Clearly, this is a regrettable set up for knowledge, not least because it means that knowledge can never finally distinguish itself from gossip, a supposed sub-species of knowledge that spawns itself precisely on arbitrary positings of 'knowledge'. On the other hand, without this arbitrary moment of a violent decision, knowledge would not exist at all. In taking its decision to cut into the infinite chain of regress, knowledge becomes itself, and ultimately part of its authority derives just from this act of decision. But the cost is that knowledge is shadowed by the gossiping twin that has the same parent. Because of the arbitrary decision at the heart of knowledge and gossip, legitimacy (the question of whether what we encounter is gossip or knowledge) is irreducibly undecidable. Of course, in one sense, we are *only* dealing with decidability (only a decision can make gossip gossip, or make knowledge knowledge), but the trace of the undecidable remains. This undecidability does not disappear once the decision has been made as to the verity/credibility/import or otherwise of particular content. Derrida tells us: 'The undecidable is not merely the oscillation or the tension between two decisions' (2002: 252). Rather, it is a structuring impossibility at the heart of the question of authority. This means that while we *can* make local decisions as to whether a singular instance is knowledge or gossip, such a decision is shot-through with a more radical undecidability as to this opposition. We make provisional decisions according to laws, rules, and criteria, but the violent establishment of any authority that assures those laws, rules and criteria renders them unstable.

The undecidability of knowledge's legitimacy remains as a trace even when knowledge functions perfectly well. Gossip can serve as a reminder of this. It is important to recognize that knowledge effects are produced – we live by these effects in everyday life, indeed, they are necessary to function – but the risk of gossip (of these knowledge effects being unfounded or of uncertain status) is never far away. Certainly such a trace became important in the cases I've been looking at, for the forging of intelligence into stable knowledge became unsustainable – it could be argued that intelligence, as *secret*, was never intended to be used in the public form it took around the issue of Iraq. The ghost of undecidability between founded or unfounded knowledge, and of the arbitrariness of knowledge's positing, haunts anything that can be thought of as knowledge. When the details of the Gilligan/Kelly affair and the making of the dossier came to light, this simply brought the spectre of gossip into our line of vision. Gossip, then, is not a marginal mistake, self-contained, and unconnected to the 'real' business of knowledge and truth; it both shares the condition of the arbitrary with knowledge, and, as a name we can strategically give to un-decidability, has a conditioning role to play itself in knowledge.

On one hand, this state of affairs makes it easy for Blair to take us to war more or less on the basis of gossip – uncorroborated and unreliable intelligence (concerning the 'forty-five minutes' claim, the procurement of uranium in Niger, and the presence of WMD in general), and a plagiarized student thesis (in the first dossier titled *Iraq – Its Infrastructure of Concealment, Deception and Intimidation*). On the other, it meant that Blair had to do something to secure the regress: he chose to assert his authority. In an attempt to counter the infinite regress of authority and the instability of his intelligence, Blair told BBC's *Newsnight* audience in the February of 2003 that military conflict is 'what I believe to be the right thing to do'. He did not say that it 'is' right, but that he *believes* it to be right. But what founds this moral belief? Well, his self-conviction and sense of moral duty and certainty is seen by many to be a result of his strong religious beliefs. Matthew D'Ancona, deputy editor of the British broadsheet, the *Sunday Telegraph*, is quoted in a US made PBS documentary as saying, 'I think Blair's entire political behavior has to be linked to his private religious beliefs. He doesn't talk about his religious beliefs very much but they are fundamental to anything and everything that he does.' Likewise, Charles Powell, former adviser to Margaret Thatcher, and Conservative member of the House of Lords, says, 'I think it is true to say that President Bush and Prime Minister Blair do share a certain moral certainty about the way the world is going... Now, one has to be careful here. Morality and diplomacy are not easy bedfellows... You can't just run a foreign policy on a moral basis. But there's no doubt that the impulse with both of them is strong. And it is what has led to the vigorous prosecution of the war against terrorism, and now the impending war against Iraq.'[1] Indeed, when asked who he would answer to for the deaths of British soldiers, Blair replied: 'My Maker' (see Ahmed 2003). Blair's political authority is elided with a moral 'duty'. He relies on his legally elected status to authorize his personal moral beliefs and, conversely, draws on his Christian morality to persuade his political constituents. I am not suggesting that any political decision is divorced from an ethical perspective (nor am I saying that it should be, necessarily, although we could separate moralism from morality here, and question the status of the 'ethical' in this context) but in appealing to this register, Blair looks to be scrabbling for authority in all directions (political authority, moral authority, any authority that can arrest the regress that gossip signals).

Blair follows through with his decision to go to war even though some of the people he represents are against it (a perfectly democratic thing to do, of course). We have authorized him to make decisions like going to war but pro-test against this particular exercise of that authority (the protest also being a perfectly democratic thing to do). Blair sticks to his decision and appeals to a moral register in the hope, perhaps, that we will not think too much about this issue of political representation, the message being something like, 'Look, I am listening to you, the public, but I also have to listen to my religious moral code that I represent here on earth.' The result is an embarrassing logic ('Britain has to go to war because, as your elected leader, I have to protect you from Saddam's WMD that can kill us in forty-five minutes, and even if that isn't true, we have to go to war because Saddam is the kind of dictator who *would* kill us in forty-five minutes if he *could*'). By looking to legitimize his actions through both a pol-itical and moral authority, Blair increasingly appears as though he is acting with neither. Rather, he seems to be behaving, as old style Labour politician Tony Benn described it, like a 'medieval king' (quoted in Davies 2003). And medieval kings were, of course, earthly representatives of God's will, rather than the people's.

Now, we are faced with a precarious social-democratic contract here. Benn goes on to say that through Blair's lack of adherence to international law, 'he has released us from our moral obligation to accept decisions and we are now free to follow our consciences' (quoted in Davies 2003). Benn recognizes that the contract, in legal terms, has been fractured: if Blair doesn't act democratically (adhering to international law) then those in a minority don't have to act democratically (by being obliged to support his decisions as the elected leader). Sidestepping the issue of whether what we are really talking about here is a democratic rather than moral obligation, Benn's call to 'follow our consciences' is interesting because of the way it challenges Blair's authority by re-emphasizing the authority of citizens. He doesn't, that is, question why any claims to authority are fragile but relocates authority firmly with the people. Authority isn't questioned, just transferred. On one level, no-one would expect an anti-war protester like Benn to begin raising the question of authority in this way – it wouldn't serve his immediate purposes. But I do think that this question can embolden arguments against the arrogation of power. I want to, then, retrace my steps more slowly with regards to this question of authority and representation.

It is, of course, true to say that at the time of going to war in Iraq the British public voted for Blair and the Labour party to represent them in 1997 and again in 2001 (the case is more problematic in the American context with disputable 'chads' on Florida's ballot papers during the Presidential election in 2000) but that authority is local and provisional: our votes, that is to say, bequeath authority on the Prime Minister or President in a democracy but the right to vote is secured by a number of historical contingencies rather than universal certainties. The right to vote is dependent on citizenship; citizenship is subject to birthplace or a successful application for citizenship. Article 21 of the Universal Declaration of Human Rights states: '(1) Everyone has the right to take part in the government of his country, directly or through freely chosen representatives' and later, '(3) The will of the people shall be the basis of the authority of government; this will shall be expressed in periodic and genuine elections which shall be by universal and equal suffrage and shall be held by secret vote or by equivalent free voting procedures.' But the debate as to whether this right (or any right, for that matter) is inalienable has a long history. What is clear is that the legislative moment that authorizes the right to vote, that in turn bestows power upon the elected person to govern as s/he sees fit (including going to war on the basis of gossip), is a moment of violence, for the legislator who declares voting to be a 'right' could not have been elected democratically. This is the scandal that the gossip we have been looking at can point us towards: it has the potential to show up such 'violence'. Unlike localized scandals which are easily assimilated into public discourse, this kind of scandal does not have a place in the public sphere, which is invested in what Jodi Dean calls 'the rhetoric of publicity', which propagates the idea that 'democracy is a system through which free and equal citizens rationally discuss and decide matters of public concern' (2002: 53). And so, the 'violence' of Blair taking Britain to war on the basis of gossip is only publicly evident in the 'violence' exercised against Kelly, the BBC, and Gilligan. The Kelly/

Gilligan affair served as a convenient scandal to obscure the more scandalous scandal that 'just' is the infinite regress of authority.

What we should take from this particular case is that the lack of authority revealed in Bush and Blair's reliance on gossip is not an exception. Rather, this case simply makes the situation clearer, putting on display the way in which decision-making in government is always based on a 'violent' founding authority. Of course, the necessarily or inherently 'violent' stature of that authority can be experienced without the presence of gossip (we might, for example, experience a general sense of disenfranchisement when decisions we don't agree with – like going to war, perhaps – are made) but the gossip in this case puts the 'violence' to the foreground regardless of political allegiance (and, yes, we would also have to think about the implications of this argument for the way in which Gilligan forged Kelly's gossip into reportable fact). In other words, in everyday governmental decision making, we might only experience the 'violence' of authority when the politics of those decisions sits uneasily with us; but the undecidability that permeated the gossip (disguised as knowledge) Bush and Blair relied upon potentially moves an experience of the 'violent' nature of their decision beyond political affiliation. Irrespective of whether we supported the war or not, the way in which Blair and Bush invested that gossip with legitimacy and force (since gossip does not inherently have those qualities and can only be endowed with them by an adjudicator or advocator), shows up the violence of their decision.

That is not to say that the violence that gossip can potentially expose was recognized or discussed explicitly. In line with traditional theories of ideology, we could say that what has become known as neo-liberal capitalism likes to keep such 'violence' under wraps. Democracy depends on voters believing that they, as self-present, rational, sovereign subjects, legitimately bequeath authority to their elected representatives, not questioning where in fact that authority comes from in the first place. For example, when I marched with over a million people against the war in Iraq in London on 15 February 2003 we perhaps experienced the violence of decision-making authority. But this was translated into a frustration at not being listened to by our government. The war on Iraq was being waged without our specific consent and so, for us, Blair had acted without authority. The banners read, 'Not In My Name'. Blair's action was not, unsurprisingly, discussed as an infinite regress of authority (Blair can't authorize war because we haven't authorized war and besides nobody has authorized us to authorize war in the first place). Rather, it was positioned as an action that just happened not to have been endorsed by us this time (but, given different politics, or different politicians, *could have*). This keeps the secret of authority's regress safe (and the secret of legitimacy I wrote about in Chapter 3), as well as the undecidable nature of knowledge. The democratic process is dented but survives because the idea of the self-present democratic subject is left unquestioned. Through the presence of marches and demonstrations this form of democracy is, even, renewed. Wendy Brown is helpful in this context. She writes, 'expressions of moralistic outrage implicitly cast the state as if it were or could be a deeply democratic and non-violent institution' (2001: 36). Moreover, expressions of moralistic outrage render resistant movements (including, presumably, anti-war movements) as if they were not 'potentially subversive, representing a significant political challenge to the norms of the regime, but rather were benign entities ... entirely appropriate for the state to equally protect' (Brown 2001: 36). Brown is concerned that such moralistic outrage misunderstands and misrepresents the nature of state power.

The war on Iraq was conducted without authority. I mean this in localized ways: much of the public didn't support it; the evidence was flimsy to say the least; no second resolution was granted by the United Nations; and its legal status was hotly debated in the lead-up to the British general election in 2005 after the Attorney General's previously unseen, and highly ambiguous, advice prior to action was leaked to the press.[2] But also in the radical sense that I've been discussing. Yet, such a state of affairs is not an aberration in the democratic process; it is simply an overt example of the way in which power operates. All of which should not sound like an attack on democracy in favour of something else: totalitarianism, say, the authority of which is, ethically speaking, even more violent. Yet the ironies of exercising and privileging one's democratic rights to protest a war waged in the name of spreading democracy and protecting freedom are worth raising. It seems to me that if we do not think about these uncomfortable aspects of the democratic process we cannot begin to open up the ground for what Derrida calls 'democracy to come': democracy, that is, as an 'endless promise' to rethink 'itself', politics, responsibility, justice and the nation state; to honour the spirit of critique that the Enlightenment enshrined, but unsettle its metaphysically conceived assumption of the rational, self-present subject and the model of democracy it fosters (see Derrida 1992d: 38).

On the one hand, the 'secret' of the violent positing of authority and know-ledge is always almost exposed. George W. Bush, we could say, is so obvious about the violence of his ideological decisions that the secret can't stay secret for long. But on the other hand, the way in which abused parties experience this violence (as an infringement of their rights) doesn't quite get to the point. In the feature-length documentary, *Fahrenheit 9/11* (2004), Michael Moore expresses his outrage at Bush's heavy-handed presidency; and it was a cleverly timed attempt to prevent Bush from being re-elected. Such efforts are admirable and much needed by the left but they never quite lift the veil I am referring to (such a metaphor, of course, is misleading, because under the veil is 'nothing': only an impasse). And so gossip – often when it goes undetected and not admitted to – serves as the basis of some 'violent' decisions, but gossip also has the potential to reveal the workings of power. The oscillation between moments of 'violence' and moments of exposure are centred, here, around gossip.

ON BEING RESPONSIBLE

Why was the decision to go to war irresponsible and how can gossip, contrary to its usual associations with irresponsibility, point us towards a more 'responsible' response? First, it is important to recognize that it is impossible to establish a rule for a responsible response. This is because a truly responsible response would be singular, particular to the circumstances that demanded it. Derrida claims that the question of what responsibility is 'must remain urgent and unanswered, at any rate, without a general and rule-governed response, without a response other than that which is linked specifically each time, to the occurrence of a decision without rules and without will in the course of a new test of the undecidable' (1992b: 14–15).

In a number of Derrida's texts, but perhaps most forcefully in *Gift of Death*, he puts forward a 'radical form of responsibility' in place of the orthodox 'transcendent experience that relates Platonic responsibility' to the common good ([1992c] 1995: 27). One of the familiar prerequisites for making decisions is having enough knowledge to make that decision, but:

> Saying that a responsible decision must be taken on the basis of knowledge seems to define the condition of possibility of responsibility (one can't make a responsible decision without science or conscience, without knowing what one is doing, for what reasons, in view of what and under what conditions), at the same time as it defines the condition of impossibility of this same responsibility (if decision-making is relegated to a knowledge that it is content to flow or to develop, then it is no more a responsible decision, it is the technical deployment of a cognitive apparatus, the simple mechanistic deployment of a theorem). (Derrida, [1992c] 1995: 24)

A programmatic decision, made as an affirmation of one's own subjectivity and knowledge, in a sense revokes and devolves responsibility to an already decided, calculable way of deciding. I am not making a 'free' decision if I make it according to terms already set. There is no role for us in the decision-making process other than perhaps as passive transmitter. Elsewhere, Derrida explains, 'When the path is clear and given, when a certain knowledge opens up the way in advance, the decision is already made, it might as well be said that there is none to make: irresponsibly, and in good conscience, one simply applies or implements a program' ([1991] 1992: 41). In light of this, we could think about the way in which Bush and Blair's response to the post-September 11 political conjuncture, particularly their decision to go to war in Iraq, was made according to an already established programme and logic.

Why do I feel able to say this? Well, I think it is reasonable to say that Blair's decision to go to war came before the presentation of the 'case' for war to the public. Indeed, minutes of a meeting between Mr Blair and other key figures, including Lord Boyce, Sir Richard Dearlove (then chief of MI6), Jack Straw, the Foreign Secretary, Lord Goldsmith QC, the Attorney-General, and Geoff Hoon, the Defence Secretary held in July 2002, a few weeks after Blair went to Bush's ranch in Texas, were leaked. The contents suggest that the UK was committed to the course of war long before much of the subsequent intelligence came to light. A *Times Online* report claims: 'The leak revealed what appeared to be minuted war preparations at the highest level of government in July 2002, months before Mr Blair received parliamentary approval for military action' (Evans 2005). Similarly, Bush is commonly believed to have decided on military intervention in Iraq long before the public was told war was inevitable. Assistant managing editor of *Newsweek*, Evan Thomas, relates a telling story in the already cited PBS documentary: 'Richard Haass went to Condi Rice, the president's national security adviser, and said, "Well, should I start having meetings or studies about whether we're going to confront Iraq?" And Condi Rice's answer was, "Don't bother. The president has already made up his mind."' Thomas adds his own opinion: 'I believe the president, in a fundamental way, made up his mind on about September 12, 2001, that Iraq was something he was going to eventually deal with.' And so gossip dressed up as knowledge was invoked to justify an already decided path of aggression. (What I said above, then, about Blair taking us to war on the basis of gossip, is slightly misleading: he tried to justify his already decided decision (made according to strategic alliances, political motivations, or a moral conscience) with reference to gossip disguised as something more solid.)

Blair's decision to go to war was (however serious and difficult) not a decision in Derrida's terms. For the Derridean decision involves risk (as does speculation). War, to be sure, involves political risk (Blair's position within the Labour Party and among some of the electorate was shaken by his support of Bush; the UK's standing in Europe might be compromised; the balance in the Middle East might have been irrevocably destabilized and anti-Western feelings fuelled), and, of course, mortal risk (to Iraqi civilians and soldiers and to those sent to fight and 'keep peace') but there is no rupture with an already established logic, say, of American economic, military and political dominance. The 'idea' of war on Iraq was partly inherited from the first Gulf War or from George Bush Snr (who himself inherited it from precursors in socio-politico-military history). And continuity was insisted upon in Britain, too: Blair went as far to suggest that ousting Saddam was wholly in keeping with a morally-conscious Labour tradition of 'liberating people from dictators'.[3] Of course, the decision *not* to go to war wouldn't necessarily have been a radical decision either, because that too remains within the logic of war: a codified option within the discourse of conflict. A rupture might involve bringing a wholly different order of understanding to bear on the Middle East, on terrorism, on post-September 11 global relations. It would not then be a decision between waging or not waging war, because there would be an ordering point of reference outside of war altogether.[4]

Following a programme like this 'makes of ethics and politics a technology. No longer of the order of practical reason or decision' (Derrida [1991] 1992: 45). Bush and Blair's decision to go to war on the basis of gossip was necessarily 'irresponsible' because it was not theirs alone, they borrowed the criteria by which the available knowledge was judged and a decision made. Of course we have to call upon knowledge to get us to the point at which we can make a decision (say, all of the context that Blair and Bush brought to bear on the Iraq issue), but there will always come a moment when a pragmatic, active decision must be made, breaking with (though carrying the trace of) that knowledge. The necessary leap into the incalculable when making a decision posits unreason in the very place where reason is expected: at the heart of an apparently responsible decision. So the kind of radical responsibility Derrida envisages is one that recognizes and takes on board this incalculability (rather than underplaying it, as the lack of caveats in Blair's dossier did, for example, for fear of accusations of irrationality and the threat this poses to classical notions of subjectivity). The decision, in a way, makes us (rather than us making it); we make it *through* the other. Bennington explains:

> responsibility cannot responsibly be thought of as following a programme of ethical (or political) correctness: responsibility can be taken only when such programmes are exceeded or surprised by the event of the advent of the other. Responsibility occurs on the occasion of a singular event which escapes prior normative preparations. Responsibility is responsibility to the other, but is also *of* the other: the responsive decision I must take is not mine, but a measure of 'my' originary depropriation in the advent of the other and other other. The other, we might say, signs my responsibility for me and only thus might I take a responsibility upon myself *as* other. (2000: 159)

Which makes it difficult to tell the difference between this kind of responsibility and the programmatic decision that also seems to be made by another (religious doctrine, say, or etiquette guidance, in our examples of gossip in Chapter 4). And it is in this aporia between two kinds of decisions (both of which are rooted in incalculability and which seem to be made by another) that Derrida locates the force of the responsible response or decision.

Where does this leave us with regards to knowledge and gossip? I can know in advance that knowledge is constitutively 'corruptible' but I can't know before my reading of it or encounter with it whether or not it has actually been 'corrupted'. Equally, once I make the decision as to its 'corruption', I have to know that this is only a provisional decision, haunted, as it is, by the other possible decisions. The decision is only provisional (even if it forces us to make it *as if* it were our final decision). None of this was brought to bear on the case we are scrutinizing. Blair's government assigned the gossip about Saddam Hussein being able to launch WMD in forty-five minutes the status of credible knowledge.

Such a status was assigned according to a particular logic or ideology around Iraq and could not afford to appear to carry the trace of gossip within it.

In terms of our reading of the Iraq issue, I want to argue that what we are strategically calling here 'gossip' – this undecidability between knowledge and non-knowledge – almost presses the question of responsibility upon us. The partial breakdown between 'official' and popular modes of knowing in the cultural sphere, and the way in which gossip foregrounds knowledge's infinite regress of authority, can compel us to assume responsibility (some cases more than others, to be sure). We can no longer, gossip makes clear, rely on someone of authority, like Bush or Blair, to make a decision for us. Do we accept or refute, for example, the validity of a dossier making the case for war that uses unreliable intelligence?

I think that gossip is interesting and important precisely because it exceeds traditional or established disciplinary forms of, and ways of understanding knowledge. As we've seen in the previous chapter, the way in which the philosophical tradition 'writes off' gossip doesn't do it justice, but nor does anthropology's approach which emphasizes gossip's community function. And because it exceeds the categories of undetermined and meaningless, and determined and meaningful, we are forced into making a decision if we are going to understand it more fully. Our encounter with gossip, that is to say, requires us to decide in an incalculable realm whether we think it is true or not, valid or not. The pre-decided, moral codes for judging gossip, and the figures of authority we might wish to turn to for advice, do not help us to face gossip as more than mere object – they do not help us to face gossip *responsibly*.

We could say, then, that the presence of gossip in the government's dossier for war in Iraq was not *a priori* lamentable on moral grounds. Rather, it is concerning because the undecidability that gossip signals is not addressed. Indeed, not naming gossip 'gossip' is one way of leaving undecidability unaddressed. That is why I have pointed out that none of the people employing gossip in the scenarios above would want to give it that name – not Gilligan, nor the government – not even when they accuse each other of what is, in effect, gossip. In recognizing undecidability, in holding knowledge and non-knowledge in tension, we are forced not to follow but go beyond the execution of a rule. Reducing the question of gossip to morality is an attempt to subsume the radical implications of undecidability within more stable discourses and ways of knowing (as happened in the Gilligan/Kelly case). And because these potentially radical implications can always remain unrealized, the presence of gossip can never be an assurance that questions about what knowledge is, and what or who authorizes it, will be left open. The discourses at hand to foreclose or contain these questions are multiple, coming from both the right and left.

I want to make it clear that recognizing the potentially disruptive effects of gossip on traditional ways of thinking (about subjectivity, about responsibility, about knowledge) is not the same as championing actual acts of gossip. Not least because gossip, of course, has been responsible for some heinous crimes in history. A reminder of this arrived on the front page of the *Independent* as I was editing the final manuscript of this book. The headline 'Vigilante Violence: Death by Gossip' lead into an article about the vigilante killing of Paul Cooper, wrongly believed to have been a paedophile. It was gossip and rumour that led his killers to believe he was guilty of sex offences (Herbert 2005: 1).

Indeed, I am not saying that we should be unconditionally open or hospitable to gossip. That would be impractical and undesirable. If we take another emotive example (without implying that the comparison is unproblematic), infinite openness or hospitality to asylum seekers, while radically responsible (in that no *other* others are being excluded in favour of *one* other), is in practice impossible (there would be too many) and undesirable. An infinite openness to all kinds of knowledges is not always practical and yet the implications of this must be addressed. While problematizing humanist notions of responsibility (and associated concepts like forgiveness or hospitality), Derrida is not saying that responsible decisions are impossible. In fact, he suggests that responsibility exists in a constant tension between contradictory demands, as an oscillation between the demands of the wholly other (say, a notion of infinite responsibility or hospitality) and the more general demands of a community (the restrictions imposed on that responsibility or hospitality for the welfare of the hospitable community). If we can tolerate this aporia, we will have acted as responsibly as we can.

What does all that we have said about gossip mean for a discipline like cultural studies, which should make understanding everyday acts like gossip part of its project (especially if it wants to understand how politics works today)? It means, I think, recognizing our own work as knowledge-production, and putting in motion an adequate theorizing of the relationship of this work to other forms of knowledge-production, including popular knowledges like gossip. We might do well to think of our own work as a form of generalized gossip. Far from producing speculations that fail to take seriously the subjects participating in that culture (in the manner Miller and McHoul and other critics of theoretical approaches to cultural studies are concerned about), we might, in recognizing the undecidable 'nature' of gossip, just be better positioned to trace the links between knowledge, politics and power. And rather than thinking of theory as a pre-existing system through which various cultural acts and artefacts can be read (which would be more like a form of moralism, the perils of which I have made clear), we should look to athetic speculation: which is about taking risks, and as such, somewhat counterintuitively, puts us in a better position to make responsible and singular decisions.

A politically committed cultural studies should be interested in a popular knowledge like gossip because it can force judgement upon us and make us wary of the knowledge we want to utilize to help us make that judgement – that is, if we recognize gossip as undecidability, it forces us to decide what is and what is not knowledge at every step of the way. And this decision making about the knowledge we encounter is one possible description of politics. It is part of the work of an ethical and responsible analysis of culture.

Conclusion: Old Enough to Know Better? The Work of Cultural Studies

SCENE ONE

It is exactly one week after the bombings by Islamic extremists on the London Underground. The usually sober BBC Radio Four *PM* news show moves from a serious report about Muslim scepticism towards the findings of the police investigation to a lighthearted item about conspiracy theories with author Jon Ronson. No one explicitly suggests that the Muslim communities interviewed are peddling conspiracy theories but it is implied through the juxtaposition.

SCENE TWO

It is June 2005 and Tom Cruise and Katie Holmes are having their very own summer of love. Cruise, a Hollywood A-lister, announces his engagement to teen soap television actress Katie Holmes who is trying to make a career for herself in the movies now that she is too old to play young Joey Potter in *Dawson's Creek* (1998-2003). The grapevine gossip sounds something like this: Cruise, long rumoured to be gay, has allegedly paid Holmes millions of dollars to act as his wife to secure his heterosexuality and astronomical salary. Worse, the rumours say Holmes wasn't first choice, but eighth. The gossip is everywhere, except in print.

SCENE THREE

It is 1994, Harvard Professor John E. Mack has just published his controversial study on alien abductions, *Abduction: Human Encounters with Aliens*. Mack is sent a letter informing him that there will be a formal inquiry into the validity of his research. It is the first time in Harvard's history that a tenured professor will be subject to this form of scrutiny. Mack does not yet know that the investigation will take fourteen stressful months, propel him to stardom in UFOlogy and abductee circles, and that the Medical School committee will be forced to retract any disparaging remarks.

SCENE FOUR

It is July 2005 and the European Union decides to ban various mineral supplements and restrict the dosage of certain vitamins. The British Health Food Manufacturers' Association, alternative health practitioners, and self-dosing consumers who swear by the benefits are up in arms. The challenge is also supported by a number of high-profile celebrities, including the actress Dame Judi Dench and the American filmmaker Kevin Miller, who claims that reducing vitamin dosages limits their therapeutic effect (see Saini 2005). The ban stems from medical evidence that reports the dangers of overdosing on vitamins and minerals.

It is the uncertainty around the status of legitimacy played out in these scenes that I find interesting. Within them, the relationships between knowledge and 'non-knowledge', between legitimacy and illegitimacy, between different appeals to authority, are being negotiated. A reading of each in the way I've tried to do with my case studies in this book could tease out the exact manifestation and effects of these tensions. Of course, what I have also been arguing for in this book is that such issues around legitimacy are not just played out in the cultural arena, but also 'inside' the academy where its practitioners are often wedded, consciously and unconsciously, to rationalist discourses.

I have suggested that the questions concerning legitimacy that popular knowledges raise are particularly interesting in relation to cultural studies given its historically uncertain place within the academy. This might account for some of its reticence to (a) trouble its own conditions of possibility; and (b) get too 'close' to popular knowledges. Indeed, the question of legitimacy generates much anxiety inside and outside cultural studies (although, of course, such an inside and outside cannot easily be designated – a matter that also contributes to this anxiety). As I have shown, many attacks from critics of cultural studies and cultural theory strike at the heart of this concern. In generating statements without the necessary authority, cultural studies opens itself to accusations of being like a popular knowledge itself. Not only does the lack of authority render the credibility of statements unstable, but the very mode of discourse, the kinds of questions cultural studies wants to address, inevitably veers further away from a concern with scientific factuality, leaving the field exposed, again, to a connection with more interpretative forms of knowledge that in some eyes do not count as knowledge proper at all.

We could borrow from a different register to think about what kind of position cultural studies finds itself in. We could say that cultural studies, the bastard child of the humanities and social sciences, lacks a responsible father. There is no proper name behind cultural studies (in the way there is, for example, behind psychoanalysis, even when one considers the many precursors to Freud and his debts). Cultural studies might have many contenders for the role of the founding father (Mathew Arnold, F. R. Leavis, Raymond Williams, Richard Hoggart, and latterly, Stuart Hall), but the definitive paternal figure that proffers a degree of 'legitimacy' remains in question. This is not, of course, to suggest that disciplines that do have a definitive 'father' unproblematically attain legitimacy, but that the father (as one of the means by which the field or discipline seeks to institute and reproduce itself and its original guiding idea, along with its canon and pedagogical techniques, its various forms and styles of writing, publication, research, assessment and so on) makes legitimacy more culturally accepted and is called upon to arbitrate in disputes concerning identity and belonging. There is no definitive father to appeal to that can assure us that cultural studies is not mere speculation, mere conspiracy theory, mere gossip. Indeed, the one living paternal candidate – Stuart Hall – continually refuses to accept this role and the responsibility that comes with it. In 'Cultural Studies and its Theoretical Legacies', he writes, 'I don't want to talk about British cultural studies ... in a patriarchal way, as the keeper of the conscience of cultural studies, hoping to police you back into line with what it really was if only you knew' (Hall 1992: 277). There is no father. In fact what I have tried to reiterate throughout this book is that what is true for cultural studies is also true (albeit in different and singular ways) for other disciplines; the precarious position of cultural studies merely exposes a general rule (in a similar way to how we have seen popular knowledges function).

All this might seem to leave cultural studies in a perilous position – its proximity to gossip, conspiracy theory and the rest – is all the more apparent in the absence of a father who would not tolerate such behaviour. But this vacant paternal role, this lack of a master, could be considered as that which allows cultural studies to innovate and explore. All of which might just be another way of explaining that cultural studies is in a good position to address the question of legitimacy, to embrace radical rather than restrictive forms of speculation and to brush shoulders with, understand, and learn lessons from apparently 'illegitimate' popular knowledges. Without the punitive presence of the father, cultural studies has less to risk and lose.

Cultural studies' willingness or otherwise to deal with these issues has to be seen in the context of the university. The questions raised by popular knowledges in this book, of course, have serious implications for the university as an institution devoted to the pursuit of knowledge.[1] Institutions like the university are interesting because they have to posit knowledge despite its arbitrariness: they have to make decisions all the time about knowledge without this decision-making process necessarily being transparent. How does this work in practice?

Institutions function, as Samuel Weber has explored, on the invisible exclusion of certain elements. He is thinking particularly of the way in which
founding or instituting principles are placed in a position of otherness once
they have served their purpose. Institutions and disciplines then owe a debt to
this other, which often goes unacknowledged. Weber considers the way in
which professionalism was instituted as an example of how such 'demarcation'
works:

> limits and limitation were indispensable for the demarcation of the profes-
> sional field, but once the latter had been established, the attention to borders
> (founding principles) became increasingly the exception rather than the rule.
> Attention was focused on the problems and questions emerging *within* the
> field, the coherence and even history of which was taken increasingly for
> granted. (1987: 30)

This is not far from what we have already demonstrated through a 'deconstructive'
reading of popular knowledges (for example, that gossip, as an excluded element
of knowledge proper, is the condition of knowledge's possibility, already part of
its foundation). When we introduce the university (as the institutionalization of
knowledges) into this equation, the ambivalent relation that it has with popular
knowledges like gossip becomes definitive. On one hand, the university draws on
popular knowledge to function when more transparent methods are too lengthy,
formal, and one dimensional. So that, to draw on an example already cited in
Chapter 4, committees granting tenure (in the US) or making appointments call
on less formal modes of communication like gossip to find out the calibre of
candidates. On the other, popular knowledges are formally frowned upon (to
follow through the example of gossip, it is not in keeping with an ethos of equal
opportunities for a start); and in terms of research, accusations of someone's
scholarship being 'gossip' or 'conspiracy theory' would be highly derogatory,
indicating a lack of substantiated evidence, inadequate referencing, or other
methodological mishaps. Popular knowledge becomes less and less desirable
the closer it gets to the realms of teaching and research. If popular knowledge is
kept in its place as a method of enquiry reserved for decisions made outside of
research contexts, or as an object of study for particular disciplines, no problem
is encountered.

The employment of popular knowledge is seen as a special circumstance,
fashioned by an understanding about that 'special' status before, during and after
the encounter. But in light of what I am suggesting – about the conditioning role
of popular knowledge – this aberrant status does not tell us the whole story.

Weber is careful to point out that two readings of institutionalization should
be held in tension: it is not just to be seen in terms of a structure that maintains
the status quo, as in '*instituted* organization', but also as a creative development
that breaks with the old, as in '*instituting* process' (Weber 1987: xv). These two

takes on institutionalization are 'joined in the relation of every determinate structure to that which it excludes, and yet which, qua excluded, allows that structure to *set itself apart*' (Weber 1987: xv). In other words, the instituting moment leaves an excess: as something is created or instituted the future is left open for other events to take place. The risk, of course, is that these future events might disrupt or threaten the institution, and so they are excluded; this exclusion, this setting apart, conferring identity upon the institution. The exclusion helps the institution to maintain the status quo as if institutionalized functioning could exist free from an instituting act. Wlad Godzich describes the situation thus: 'the instituting moment, which endows the entire institution with signification and meaning, is held within the institution as both proper to it and yet alien: it is its other, valued to be sure yet curiously irrelevant to immediate concerns' (1987: 156). After Weber's careful framing, I don't wish to posit the university as a tyrannical agent, keeping unruly popular knowledge at bay; rather we should see the exclusion or management of popular knowledge as structural, an effect of its instituting ambivalence. Popular knowledge is othered, placed on the outside of the university and its prime resource – knowledge – even while making it possible. Weber calls this 'ambivalent demarcation':

> The demarcation is ambivalent because it does not merely demarcate one thing by setting it off from another; it also de-marks, that is, defaces the mark it simultaneously inscribes, by placing it in relation to an indeterminable series of other marks, of which we can never be fully conscious or cognizant. (1987: 145)

Popular knowledge is not placed just in opposition to knowledge; the dividing line joins as well as separates and is, in any case, unstable because the terms it demarcates are in flux, dependant upon a whole series of relations to other terms within and beyond our conscious horizon.

Irrationality is not being set up as a better rule by which to live (Embrace gossip! Be conspiracy theorists!); rather, I think it is important to interrogate knowledge in order to explore the limits of reason. The answer is not to institutionalize popular knowledges, to act as if the demarcation were a simple binarism that can be rectified by crossing popular knowledge over to the 'other side' to make it respectable and ascribing it some kind of 'rightful' position (creating disciplines called, perhaps, Scuttlebutt Science or Conspiracy Studies). This has meant recognizing that the ambivalent relationship between the university and popular knowledge has implications for how we are to: first, ask the question of legitimacy within the academy; and second, approach our objects of study. Which is why cultural studies is so important in this context. Weber writes, 'a discipline legitimates itself through the operations it performs upon objects (whether objects of study, or other disciplines) held to be *different* from it' (1987: 146–7). Weber claims that 'the regulative idea of the [professionalist paradigm of knowledge] is that of the *absolute autonomy of the individual discipline*, construed as a self-contained body of investigative procedures and of knowledge held to be universally valid within the confines of an unproblematized field' (1987: 147). Yet, cultural studies is supposed to be very much open to objects that are different from it, whether this is in terms of other disciplines (cultural studies is based on an ideal of interdisciplinarity or post-disciplinarity, even if in practice, this proves difficult for the reasons Weber cites), or non-traditional objects of study (like gossip and conspiracy theory, to be sure, but also pop music, subcultures, street fashion and so forth). Cultural studies, however, has not necessarily exercised this openness in a way that sufficiently challenges the positioning of those 'different' objects as being still 'other' in some way.

Nevertheless, because of its potential openness to doing so, I want to argue that cultural studies is still in a better position to take on this challenge than many disciplines (precisely because of its long history of considering the subjects of disciplinarity and canonization).

If cultural studies is to be a discipline capable of doing more than merely analysing any popular knowledge as an external object, it will need to address the questions raised by this ambivalent relationship between the university and popular knowledge. For cultural studies' relatively marginal position, its status as the university's whipping boy (as evidenced by all the references to cultural studies as a 'Mickey Mouse' subject, for example, or lambasted as having no legitimate methodology) means that it shares at least some of the cultural value ascribed to popular knowledge. As I keep reiterating, rather than being concerned by this and trying desperately to assert its legitimacy in different ways, cultural studies could use this position to its advantage.

At the end of his book challenging previous cultural studies positions on fan cultures, Matt Hills writes, 'Cultural studies may be keen to critique and re-make the world, but it has become amazingly adept at ignoring its own power relationships, its own exclusions ... and its own moral dualisms' (2002: 184). I think that popular knowledges make such blind spots more noticeable for cultural studies. For an encounter with popular knowledge highlights perfectly the need for cultural studies at its best: as a 'discipline' able to analyse the institutional anxiety that attends popular phenomena and its own position in the crossfire. Cultural studies in this vision opens us up to the possibility of a radical responsibility when it comes to making decisions about knowledge in particular, and cultural phenomena in general. Some of these decisions will matter and some won't. What will have been important, even in the most trivial example, however, is exercising a responsible response to knowledge and culture. It won't make it any *easier* next time – for all decisions, as we have seen in Chapter 5, are forays into unknowability; if they are not, they cease to be decisions – but we will have acted as responsibly as we can.

Some will dismiss my enquiry as relativism. I would argue that we have become very accustomed to playing down this question of relative knowledge as if it were simply a case of personal psychology. Saying, as I have, that there is an infinite regress at the heart of authority (this issue of who authorizes the person that authorizes knowledge) certainly means that knowledge is dependent on cultural circumstance and 'individual' decision. But, crucially, the non-sovereignty of this individual who makes the decision means that the decision that is made is not based wholly in knowledge – it is, rather, without any safeguards at all, without any final recourse; it is made in a realm of the other, in a realm of generalized gossip or conspiracy theory and the like (at least in the way I have rethought and strategically positioned them in this book).

Knowledge cannot be posited without this non-knowledgeable decision. The identity of knowledge is rendered non self-identical, is shot through with alterity and decentred because it always already contains non-knowledge (gossip, conspiracy theory and so on) at its heart. It is a mutually contaminating relationship: they are both inside and outside each other at the same time. This means that the relativity of knowledge is only one element of a much larger story.

So rather that get stuck on this point of relativity, I have tried to think about the way in which some knowledges put on display epistemological undecidability. That knowledge rests on non-knowledge, on a regress, rather than clear criteria for certainty does not signal a collapse into meaninglessness (or madness as Derrida would have it, following Kierkegaard) but it does force us into making a decision about the information we encounter. As I have explored in this book, the 'legitimacy' of knowledge (the question of whether what we encounter is in fact knowledge at all or 'just' gossip; whether it is sound interpretation or 'merely' conspiracy theory) is, while in one sense wholly subject to decidability (after all, only a decision can posit knowledge) also irreducibly undecidable because of its 'impure' beginnings. It is in this realm of the undecidable that we have to make responsible decisions. In response, therefore, to accusations of relativism, it is not the case that there is no knowledge, or alternatively, that all knowledge is valid. (Knowledge *will* be posited just as meaning *is* communicated, and events *do* take place.) But it is the case that a certain *restance* – unique each time – will ensure that the future, even when it apparently 'arrives', will always be yet 'to come'. This means that the question of what knowledge is will need to be asked, again and again, for we will not, and should not, always be able to recognize it.

Endnotes

CHAPTER 1: KNOW IT ALL

1. Stuart Hall usefully uses the terms 'dominant' and 'popular' to distinguish forms of culture. It is on the boundaries between these forms, for Hall, that the ideological struggle takes place (Hall 1981: 227–40).
2. For a cogent discussion of political populism, see Ernesto Laclau, *The Populist Reason* (2005).
3. Key Foucauldian texts in this vein include *The Archaeology of Knowledge* (1969) and *The Order of Things* (1966).
4. See Tyrone Yarborough's manifesto (no date given), which tries to shake up the discipline of folklore to include contemporary examples. A book worth looking at in this context is Linda Dégh, *American Folklore and the Mass Media* (1994). In an attempt to bring folklore and media closer together, or at least to open a dialogue about the tensions of a mass mediated folklore, Dégh observes that: 'with the advent of mass production ... the earlier harmonious give and take between oral and nonoral folklore ceased to exist, and technical reproductivity ... dictated a different pace for folklore communication through new media' (1994: 1).
5. See Younge (2004) and BBC (2003b).
6. See Part Three of Gelder and Thornton's *The Subcultures Reader* (1997), David Muggleton and Rupert Weinzierl's *The Post-subcultures Reader* (2003), and Andy Bennett and Keith Kahn-Harris's *After Subculture: Critical Studies in Contemporary Youth Culture* (2004) for subsequent problematizing of subcultural theory as set out by the CCCS at Birmingham during the 1970s.
7. Ien Ang's seminal text in audience studies, *Watching Dallas* (1985), provides an example of such work.
8. I do, however, argue later that a theoretically inflected cultural studies is a better investment than other forms of cultural studies. But the kinds of thinkers I believe are most helpful, like Derrida and Lyotard, are not, it has to be acknowledged, 'simply' theorists. For in their work they pay attention to what escapes theory (the singularity of literariness or poeticity, the event, the madness of the decision and so forth). So theory itself is subject to the non-self identity that 'beleaguers' knowledge, which means that while the

term 'theory' is something of an institutional or disciplinary one, designed to professionalize a certain set of discourses or modes of thinking, what exceeds theory is always undermining and problematizing that institution, discipline or professionalization.

9. Of course, it would be naïve of me to think I can work outside of the obvious (but often unspoken) hierarchies of legitimacy that operate within the academy (as someone who spanned a rather 'serious' critical theory programme and a cultural studies department that was perceived as being less philosophically 'serious' – at least from the point of view of my fellow critical theorists – during my time as a doctoral student, I am only too aware of those hierarchies).

10. In a similar way, accusations that deconstruction is too 'textual' have missed the way in which 'text' is reinscribed through deconstruction.

11. This analysis leaves many interesting avenues yet to be explored. For example, a consideration of indigenous knowledge (local knowledge, particularly of the land) – its role in communities, and relationship to other, more 'official' kinds of knowledge – would provide a counterexample to the kinds of mass-scale popular knowledges I've concentrated on in this book. Equally, it would no doubt prove fruitful to consider the proliferation of post-colonial knowledges that challenge and subvert colonial narratives such as Orientalism or, for that matter, queer knowledges that challenge heteronormativity. Such investigations would make for a very different book, although some of the points I have made about the structure and conditions of possibility (and impossibility) of knowledge would still be relevant.

CHAPTER 2: JUST BECAUSE YOU'RE PARANOID, DOESN'T MEAN THEY'RE NOT OUT TO GET YOU

1. Of course, it seems as if this is another example of academia arriving 'late'. In some ways, this is a necessary state of affairs: we have to recognize an 'object' of study before we can study it. This is not to deny the fact that academic structures of thought can accompany or inform a cultural movement, moment, or phenomenon, nor to simplify categories of primary and secondary texts, only to stress the necessity of recognizing a signifier for any speculation on various signified meanings to take place. The time lapse depends somewhat on how close one's ear is to the ground but there is always the risk that by the time academia comes to produce its own texts on a cultural phenomenon (and, in some ways, producing that phenomenon as it will come to be known in academic circles and possibly beyond), that phenomenon will have declined in popularity or at least distinctly changed in character. This inevitable transformation should not, however, render an enquiry redundant. It should merely make us recognize that an 'object' of

study will not wait for us to catch up with it, but will always be in flux
– presenting us with a process (the production of which we are intricately
implicated in) rather than an 'object' in its traditional sense. This might be
particularly true for 'knowledges', popular or otherwise. It may be late, then,
but it is not 'too late' (and as scholars, we might contend that it is never
too late; in fact, a common complaint about cultural studies from historians
is that we approach things too early: that it might not be late enough to
think about the culture we still live in and breathe). There is also a more
'post-structuralist' way of thinking about this which might suggest that we
construct the object in the very act of studying it. This would suggest that we
both arrive too late *and* too early (before the object, so to speak, since we're
also constructing it).

2. *Steamshovel Press*, http://www.umsl.edu/~skthoma/sp16.htm.

3. *Conspiracy Planet*, http://www.conspiracyplanet.com/.

4. Todd Hoffman falls into the trap of attempting to cite an origin for the
appeal of conspiracy theory. At first, Hoffman entertains Ron Rosenbaum's
suggestion that the exposé of Kim Philby as a spy ('who had every reason to
defend the status quo') opened up the possibility of anyone being connected
to a conspiracy despite appearances. However, Hoffman settles on Watergate
as the origin of the appeal (1998: 395). This, of course, can easily be countered
by the many books on historical conspiracy theories. Of note is research by
Bernard Bailyn (1972), David Brion Davis (1971), and J. Wendell Knox (1972)
who have all produced historical accounts of the recurrence of conspiracy
and conspiracy theories in American politics, often making a case for their
central role in the formation of national identity. More recently, Pauline Maier
(1997) directs us to the largely unsubstantiated accusations against the king
in the Declaration of Independence.

5. The magazine *Mondo 2000* links many of these threads in its features,
showing how conspiracy theory cannot be isolated. Launched in 1984
as *High Frontiers* in California (changed to *Reality Hackers* in 1988, and
then to *Mondo 2000* in 1992), *Mondo 2000* filled its pages with articles
on psychedelia and drug culture, cyberpunk, technology, design, hacking,
issues of performative gender, as well as conspiracy theories. These concerns
filtered into the general ethos of the magazine. For a history of *Mondo 2000*,
see Boulware (1995).

6. Stephen Duncombe writes that the two defining influences on zines were
the emergence of science fiction fanzines in the 1930s and the fanzines
produced by fans of punk rock in the 1970s. 'In the early 1980s these two
tributaries, joined by the smaller streams of publications created by fans of
other cultural genres, disgruntled self-publishers, and the remnants of printed
political dissent from the sixties and seventies, were brought together and
cross-fertilized through listings and reviews in network zines like *Factsheet
Five*' (1997: 7).

7. With thanks to Al Hidell of *Paranoia* magazine for providing a background to conspiracy theory zines. Personal email correspondence, 11 May 2000.

8. Kenn Thomas quoted from personal email correspondence, 9 May 2000.

9. John Judge is a Washington DC researcher into assassinations and conspiracies.

10. Mae Brussell hosted a conspiracy theory radio show – *World Watchers International* – from KLRB in Carmel. California. and KAZU, Pacific Grove, California, and was an active researcher into political assassination and political scandal, providing a role model for conspiracy theorists. According to Mark Fenster, her work was publicized by countercultural publication, *The Realist* (1999: 183). Virginia McCullough is the archivist of the Mae Brussell Archive, which is set to be located at the Stanford University Library.

11. See James Daugherty, A-albionic, http://www.a-albionic.com.

12. The Center For The Preservation Of Modern History, *Prevailing Winds* Research, PO Box 23511 Santa Barbara, CA 93121, USA.

13. Al Hidell in personal email correspondence, 11 May 2000.

14. Jim Keith is the author of many conspiracy related classics including *Mind Control, World Control* (1997); *OKBOMB: Conspiracy and Cover-up* (1996); and editor of *Secret and Suppressed: Banned Ideas and Hidden History* (1993).

15. Ron Bonds in personal email correspondence with the author, 8 May 2000.

16. Richard Linklater's film featured a character who was writing a conspiracy book called *Conspiracy A Go-Go*.

17. Conspiracy narratives have, of course, provided a plot device for Hollywood films for over half a century. One only needs to think of 1950s war, spy and science fiction films, or the conspiracy narratives of the 1970s, such as Francis Ford Coppola's *The Conversation* (1974), Alan J. Pakula's 'so-called paranoia trilogy' (Jameson 1992: 52), *Klute* (1971), *The Parallax View* (1974), and *All the President's Men* (1976), and Sydney Pollack's *Three Days of the Condor* (1975). However, conspiracy films of the 1990s can be seen to resonate within a conspiracy theory industry. The 1970s conspiracy film, that is, could be read as a contained conspiracy narrative. This is not to deny the wider, extra-diegetic, political implications of the 1970s conspiracy films, but to observe the ways in which the 1990s films and television programmes are generally more reliant upon the audience's capacity to contextualize the narratives within a wider public discourse of popular conspiracy theories *and* the conspiracies that the 1970s films represented. The 1970s films could be said to emerge from the leftist legacy of conspiracy theory, reacting against a discourse of political denial that stems from the House of Un-American Activities Committee investigations, focusing on the idea of political conspiracy, whereas the 1990s films and television programmes seem reliant upon the particular manifestation and

social inflection of conspiracy theory as a popular knowledge of circulation and exchange. Whereas the 1970s films seem to present conspiracy narratives that respond to a political climate, the 1990s films are dependent upon a commercial form of conspiracy theory that draws on that 1970s political climate, but not exclusively so, rendering any ideology inconsistent. The 1990s films and television serials rely on a particular form of popular narrative: a form that the makers of those 1970s films could surely not have anticipated.

18. Some of the many compendia include Jonathan Vankin and John Whalen, *The Giant Book of Conspiracies* (1995); Jonathan Vankin, *Conspiracies, Cover-Ups and Crimes: From Dallas to Waco* (1996); Doug Moench, *The Big Book of Conspiracies* (1995).

19. Before *The X-Files* ended, Fox Network had a specially dedicated shopping site: *The X-Files* Store online at http://www.fox.com (accessed 21 December 2001).

20. A local Roswell newspaper report in 1997 points towards the commercial gains of being associated with conspiracy theory:

> Michael Anador is high as an alien saucer this week. His business, the Apache Gallery, has increased sales by about 90 percent in the last two weeks, he said, and it's only going to get better. But his normal stock of Mexican and Native American art has gone by the wayside for now. 'This week - anything to do with aliens goes,' he said. Most of his business is in alien jewellery and crop-circle T-shirts, he said. Visitors are welcomed in by an old Army jeep occupied by dummy aliens wearing various head-dress and clothing from his store. UFO and alien buffs have already converged on this normally docile town of about 50,000, and organizers say the gathering is bound to get bigger by the weekend. (Wise 1997: 1)

21. Although, as Matthew Hills points out, Appadurai's configuration of the commodity reductively imposes a logic of identity: 'at point "a" in time the object is purely a commodity, whereas at point "b" in time this same object is purely a non-commodity. The awkward question which then remains, is how and where is the definite division between these events to be located?' (1999: 81). While, therefore, it might be easy for us to identify when a text produced through the optic of conspiracy theory is definitely a commodity, it might be more difficult for us to decide when it is not.

22. Interestingly, Kellner expresses both views in the same paper.

23. A contributor to one of the conspiracy theory discussion boards I monitored at the time of Diana's death (the *Conspiracy Theory Discussion Board*, available http//www.internet-inquirer.com) referred to the Paris deaths as 'Dianagate' with an obvious reference to the Watergate affair, a discursive tactic that has been utilized for many scandals and exposés from 'Irangate' (the Iran-Contra affair) to 'Zippergate' (the Monica Lewinsky affair). This

situates the Diana case within a continuum of scandals and cover ups, each of which became embroiled in legal proceedings and only came to light after extensive investigations. The term 'Dianagate', then, indicates the anticipation of an exposé and sets forth the complexity of the task ahead of conspiracy theorists. By invoking the rhetoric of political exposés, the contributor attempts to accentuate the political significance of contributors' endeavours and to push the boundaries of how and where their theories can resonate (beyond the limits of the board itself); but the playful element is also significant.

24. Inferno, 'Theories and ideas so far – update', *Conspiracy Theory Discussion Board,* 4 September 1997, http://www.internet-inquirer.com/board.htm (accessed 20 October 1997).

25. Donna J., 'Things that make you go hmmm…', *Conspiracy Theory Discussion Board,* 4 September 1997, http://www.internet-inquirer.com/board.htm (accessed 20 October 1997).

26. MZA, 'Re: A Moslem Mother of King of England', *Conspiracy Theory Discussion Board,* 17 September 1997, http://www.internet-inquirer.com/board.htm (accessed 20 October 1997).

27. James Country, 'Survivor', *Conspiracy Theory Discussion Board,* 4 September 1997, http://www.internet-inquirer.com/board.htm (accessed 20 October 1997).

28. Inferno, 'Theories and ideas so far – update', *Conspiracy Theory Discussion Board,* 4 September 1997, http://www.internet-inquirer.com/board.htm (20 October 1997).

29. Peter Knight and Alasdair Spark describe how: 'the assassination provides the "motherlode" for conspiracies (the event at which almost all conspiracies eventually touch base), and therefore 22 November 1963 serves as one of the fractures from which the modern conspiracy era has been dated, and – as important – is back-dated to by the contemporary "reverse mapping" of recent American history as conspiracy led' (1997). This trend is evident in the Internet discussion of Diana. For example, on the *Conspiracy Theory Discussion Board* (http//www.internet-inquirer. com), the *Warren Commission Report* serves as an implicit and explicit point of reference for contributors. One contributor writes how s/he wants the Paris investigation to be different from the 'inane machinations of the Warren Report.' Another refers to the explanation that the car crash was an accident as the new version of the lone gunman theory proposed by the *Warren Commission Report.* Even the names of some of the contributors to the board draw on JFK conspiracy folklore, such as 'Umbrella Woman', whose assumed name refers to the figure reported to have opened his/her umbrella in Dealey Plaza on the day of the assassination as a sign to the other conspirators. One contributor sees the board as a way of stopping 'another JFK'. This refers not only to the mission of the board to prevent

a cover up, but also, ironically, for the board to prevent a proliferation of theories that would result in the event of Diana's death becoming obscured by a series of narratives. References to the infamous *Warren Report*, which endorsed the lone gunman theory over conclusions of a conspiracy, highlight the distrust conspiracy theorists have in reports that do not ratify their own conclusions. While there are few concentrated attempts to trace Diana's death back to that of JFK in the way that Knight and Spark suggest, it is clear that this seminal event permeates and shapes the rhetoric on the board that I considered for my research: the *Conspiracy Theory Discussion Board*.

30. The First Diana Conspiracy Site, 31 August 1997, http://www.healey.com. au/~themagic/di.htm (accessed 15 November 1998).

31. KL, 'Americans knew before the Britons', 31 August 1997. Quoted from a selection of theories posted to alt.conspiracy.princess-diana and uk.current-events.princess-diana collected by http://www.mcn.org/b/poisonfrog/diana/usenet.htm (accessed 21 October 1997).

32. Of course, the Internet has also gained a reputation for being an arena for useless, illegitimate knowledge: 'a vast repository of drivel, pornography, consumption, and gambling' (Dean 2002: 75).

33. 'George', a user of Parascope's Matrix Message board, derides a fellow user by suggesting that 'he probably got his information off the web', 27 October 1997, http://www.parascope.com (accessed 29 October 1997). Other entries on this message board indicate a low tolerance for poorly researched hypotheses.

34. Anonymous, 'Unconvinced but Pondering', *Conspiracy Theory Discussion Board*, 10 September 1997. http//www.internet-inquirer.com (accessed 20 September 1998).

35. James, 'anti-depressants: yeah right', *Conspiracy Theory Discussion Board*, 10 September 1997, http//www.internet-inquirer.com (accessed 20 September 1998).

36. Bang@value.net. 'Re: Dodo Delete', 1 September 1997. Quoted from a selection of theories posted to alt.conspiracy.princess-diana and uk.current-events.princess-diana collected by http://www.mcn.org/b/poisonfrog/diana/usenet.htm (accessed 21 October 1997).

37. 'Four of the hijackers' passports were recovered, including one found on the street minutes after the plane he was aboard crashed into the north tower of the World Trade Center' (Associated Press 2004).

38. Jean Laplanche and Jean-Bertrand Pontalis explain this working through as 'the process by means of which analysis implants an interpretation and overcomes the resistances to which it has given rise. Working-through is taken to be a sort of psychical work which allows the subject to accept certain repressed elements and to free himself from the grip of mechanisms of repetition' (1988: 488).

CHAPTER 3: CULTURAL STUDIES ON/AS
CONSPIRACY THEORY

1. Paul Gilroy, 'History of Cultural Studies,' *Save Cultural Studies Campaign*, available http://myweb.tiscali.co.uk/culturalstudies/history.htm (accessed 2 March 2005).
2. Elaine Showalter, 'Slaying the Hydra', *Conspiracy Cultures Conference* at King Alfred's College of Higher Education, Winchester, 1998.
3. Lyotard writes: 'A wrong results from the fact that the rules of the genre of discourse according to which one judges are not those of the genre or genres judged' ([1983] 1988: 9).
4. One of the most obvious examples of such a challenge can be found in Lyotard's *The Postmodern Condition* ([1979] 1994). In this by now seminal text, Lyotard shows how the legitimating strategy of science – its recourse to philosophy – relies upon that which science professes to be in opposition to, namely narrative knowledge. In this way, 'as resolute a philosophy as that of Descartes can only demonstrate the legitimacy of science through what Valéry called the story of the mind, or else in a *Bildungsroman*' (29). Unlike narrative knowledge, 'a statement of science gains no validity from the fact of being reported' (26). Such an opposition, however, cannot be confined to scientific and narrative knowledge. Indeed, Lyotard's configuration risks a certain homogenization of the latter. The philosophical discourse and Cashinahua oral tradition that Lyotard cites as instances of narrative knowledges, for example, have a less than simple affiliation. I would argue that the relationship between certain 'popular' narrative knowledges, and knowledges that have undergone institutional processes of legitimation such as philosophy may be as problematic as that between science and narrative knowledge.
5. However, it is important to note and take on board the consequences that the same could be said for a 'new' interpretation as well as a 'bad' interpretation. It is this tension that Lyotard sees as one problem with scientific communities of consensus (see below).
6. Eco admires the 'esthetic of the free, deviant, desirous and malicious use of texts' such as the work of Borges, but these are always 'uses' rather than 'interpretations'. More uncertainly, he refers to Barthesian *jouissance* as being on the dividing line between 'the free *use* of a text taken as imaginative stimulus and the *interpretation* of an 'open' text.' While he concludes that this decision would rely on whether *jouissance* was imposed onto the text or found within its own strategy, such arbitration appears highly problematic (1997: 44).
7. To provide another example of this at work, in 'Cogito and the History of Madness', Derrida problematizes the distinction between reason and madness by explaining that although the Cogito apparently ensures reason, it actually

allows for the possibility of madness. The possibility of iterability ensures that the Cogito must be able to be repeated in the event of one's madness, placing madness within the transcendental, ideal 'I' that is invoked in the Cogito and exceeds the totality of what one can think. Thus the 'inside', in this case 'reason', taken to its (il)logical conclusion, will lead beyond its perceived boundary. To think madness from a position of reason is to see the way in which reason is always already outside itself (Derrida [1967c] 1981: 31–63).

8. As an indicator of negative feelings towards cultural studies, comments like the following (which appeared in the supposedly 'left-wing', British newspaper, the *Guardian*) are a commonplace sentiment amongst the chattering classes: 'You need only glance down the list of texts in the burgeoning field of "cultural studies" to bring on a fit of "the world's gone mad" fever' (Brockes 2003).

9. I should point out here that attacks on cultural studies come from differ-ent angles, partly depending on which version of cultural studies is being targeted. In the US, cultural studies is very much associated with theoretical encounters and Sokal seemed to be more concerned with attacking the likes of Althusser, Deleuze, Latour, Lacan, Baudrillard and so on. However, Sokal's essay and the incident in general are linked with Andrew Ross, one of the editors of the cultural studies journal *Social Text*, who would easily be aligned with a more 'British' version of cultural studies.

10. See Official Secrets Act 1989 (c. 6) Section 2 (Defence), available http:// www.hmso.gov.uk/acts/acts1989/Ukpga_19890006_en_2.htm (accessed 1/6/04).

CHAPTER 4: HOT GOSSIP: THE CULTURAL POLITICS OF SPECULATION

1. Various policies have been proposed and implemented by the Blair govern-ment as a direct result of research conducted into the knowledge economy (as outlined in the 1998 DTI White Paper, *Our Competitive Future: Building the Knowledge Driven Economy*).

2. 'An explosion which turned out to be a dam blast in southern Iran sent jitters through financial markets amid speculation that the country's only nuclear reactor had come under attack' (McDowall and Penketh 2005).

3. Biblical references are taken from *The New Oxford Annotated Bible*, New Revised Standard Version, B. M. Metzger and R. E. Murphy (eds), Oxford University Press: Oxford and New York.

4. Qur'anic quotations are adapted from the edition by Abdullah Yusuf Ali, *The Qur'an: With Text, Translation and Commentary*, New York: Tahrike Tarsile Quran, 1998.

5. In legal terms, hearsay is defined as: 'second-hand evidence in which the witness is not telling what he/she knows personally, but what others have said to him/her', and 'scuttlebutt or gossip' (see Hill and Hill 1995).

6. It was, ironically, a previous respondent who suggested I *must* look at Miller and McHoul if I want to talk about non-speculative readings of culture.

7. My discussion of Miller and McHoul's speculation is influenced in part by Jacques Derrida's 'To Speculate – On "Freud"' ([1980] 1987). Not least because the dismissal of philosophy that Derrida observes in Freud's work serves as an exemplary precedent to any attempt to limit speculation. Freud initially puts his hopes in the observation of patients as a way of securing psychoanalysis against the charge of philosophy and I think we can hear echoes of Freud's failure to recognize his debts in cultural studies' recent turn to ethnographic sociology and political economy. Of course, I should say at the outset that Derrida's discussion of the speculative operations at work within *Beyond* is only one element of a painstakingly close reading. And when dealing with an essay that is concerned with borrowing and the trope of debt, it is with no small amount of irony that I am going to borrow and lift from context a small part of Derrida's reading to derive a generality concerning speculation.

8. The pleasure principle, for Freud, is a governing principle that seeks to avoid unpleasure (by reducing or regulating excitations) – and so we can instantly see why the death drive, which is a tendency to the state of inertia (another reduction of excitations, but this time to the point of non-existence), and the fact that we repeat unpleasurable experiences, causes problems for the pleasure principle that Freud needed to address. He attempts to do just this in *Beyond the Pleasure Principle*.

9. Of course, one could argue that this whole book is filled with thetic speculations. But we would have to ask what status that thesis has if it involves a discussion, as it does here, of those aspects of knowledge that prevent it from being a fully sealed, self-identical argument. I am very interested in what exceeds existing discussions of gossip, while knowing that my own reading will be subject to excesses in turn.

10. To be fair, however, the book does seem to aim at a market beyond the strictly academic, which could also account for Mellencamp's theoretically light touch.

11. The report is published online at http://www.number-10.gov.uk/output/Page1470.asp (accessed 2 June 2004). The BBC news article outlining the similarities between the government's document and the doctoral thesis of Ibrahim al-Marashi appears as 'A piece of plagiarism?' *BBC News*, 7 February 2003, available http://news.bbc.co.uk/1/hi/uk_politics/2736149.stm (accessed 2 June 2004).

12. The claim that Saddam Hussein could launch weapons of mass destruction in forty-five minutes was set out as part of its case for war in the government

dossier *Iraq's Weapons of Mass Destruction - The assessment of the British Government,* 24 September 2002, available http://www.number-10.gov.uk/output/ Page271.asp (accessed 3 June 2004).

CHAPTER 5: SEXED UP: GOSSIP BY STEALTH

1. 'Blair's War: Frontline', *PBS*, 3 April 2003, available http://www.pbs.org/wgbh/pages/frontline/shows/blair/prime/blairbush.html (accessed 5 May 2005).
2. *Channel 4 News* obtained a copy of the summary of the confidential legal advice written by the Attorney General Lord Goldsmith and sent to the Prime Minister on March 7th, two weeks before the war with Iraq. The documents reveal that Lord Goldsmith warned Mr Blair that failure to secure a second United Nations resolution explicitly authorizing military action would force the government "urgently" to reconsider its legal case.' 'Complete Legal Documents,' Channel 4 News, 27 April 2005, available http://www.channel4.com/news/special-reports/special-reports-storypage.jsp?id=91 (accessed 4 June 2005).
3. Sean Ley reports that, in a move to distract from his allegiance with America, Blair tried to suggest that ousting Saddam Hussein was simply following 'Labour's moral and long established belief in liberating people from dictators. In other words, Tony Blair is not clinging onto the coat tails of a Republican President playing out the last act of a family revenge drama – as some of Labour's anti-war campaigners believe. Instead, this is a Labour Party leader acting within his party's tradition' (Ley 2003). Such a suggestion fits with my argument here, that the decision wasn't a rupture in any way.
4. It's not clear how far Gilligan escapes this charge of a programmatic decision. On the one hand, he speculated and took a risk whether he was aware of it or not (a recent televised drama of the Kelly/Gilligan affair suggested Gilligan was simply a slipshod journalist who slept in late the morning of his broadcast). The gossip he heard from Kelly perhaps forced a decision upon him. Gilligan didn't know what kind of return his reported gossip would prompt (which was, as it turned out, personally tragic for the Kelly family, disruptive to Gilligan's own career and the BBC as a whole, and highly challenging to the government and its style of doing business). Gilligan said what many thought but dared not say. In this speculation, Gilligan perhaps got more than he bargained for. Though Gilligan didn't have watertight proof, one could say that the 'intelligence' he did rely upon was as at least as uncertain and uncorroborated as the government's case for war and their claim about Saddam Hussein's WMD. But on the other hand, Gilligan's accusations were still contained within a knowable schema in keeping with Gilligan and Campbell's mutual dislike (Campbell allegedly referred

to his nemesis as 'Gullible Gilligan' after the journalist wrote a story about a proposal for a new constitution for the European Union in 2000), or the BBC's marginally anti-war stance.

CONCLUSION: OLD ENOUGH TO KNOW BETTER? THE WORK OF CULTURAL STUDIES

1. A glance at any university prospectus reveals the use of such language, although the pursuit of knowledge is often grounded by a claim to social responsibility. Of course, this apparently self-evident role or identity of the university is not stable. Rather, it is subject to market conditions. A notable attempt to think through this changing identity can be found in Bill Readings' *The University in Ruins* (1996), which finds a modern university devoted to a meaningless or at least commercially driven idea of 'excellence', rather than culture.

Bibliography

Ahmed, K. (2003), 'And on the Seventh Day Tony Blair Created...', *The Observer*, 3 August, available http://observer.guardian.co.uk/politics/story/0,6903,1011460,00.html (accessed 5 June 2005).

al-Awayishah, H. (2000), *Gossip and its Adverse Effects*, trans. H. Khattab, Riyadh: International Islamic Publishing House.

Amin, A. and Thrift, N. (eds) (2004), *The Cultural Economy Reader*, Oxford: Blackwell.

Ang, I. (1985), *Watching Dallas*, London: Taylor & Francis.

Appadurai, A. (1986), 'Introduction: Commodities and the Politics of Value', in A. Appadurai (ed.), *The Social Life of Things: Commodities in Cultural Perspective*, Cambridge: Cambridge University Press.

Apple, M.W. (ed.) (2003), *The State and the Politics of Knowledge*, London and New York: RoutledgeFalmer.

Aristotle (1984), *The Complete Works of Aristotle*, Vol. 2, revised Oxford translation, J. Barnes (ed.), Princeton and Oxford: Princeton University Press.

Associated Press (2004), '9/11 Commission Wants More Time', *CBS News*, 27 January 2004, available http://www.cbsnews.com/stories/2004/02/04/terror/main597957.shtml (accessed 21 October 2004).

Ayim, M. (1994), 'Knowledge Through the Grapevine: Gossip as Enquiry', in R. F. Goodman and A. Ben-Ze'ev (eds), *Good Gossip*, Kansas: University of Kansas Press.

Badmington, N. (2004), *Alien Chic: Posthumanism and the Other*, London and New York: Routledge.

Bailyn, B. (1972), 'The Logic of Rebellion: Conspiracy Fears and the American Revolution', in R. O'Curry and T. Brown (eds), *Conspiracy: The Fear of Subversion in American History*, New York: Holt, Rinehart & Winston.

Baron, R. and Spitzer, N. (1992), *Public Folklore*, Washington and London: Smithsonian Institution Press.

Baudrillard, J. (1983), *Simulations*, trans. P. Foss, P. Patton and P. Beitchman, New York: Semiotext(e).

Baudrillard, J. (1987), *The Evil Demon of Images*, Sydney: The Power Institute of Fine Arts.

Baudrillard, J. (1990), *La Transparency du Mal: Essai sur les Phénomènes Extremes*, Paris: Galilée.

BBC (2003a), 'A Piece of Plagiarism?' *BBC News Online*, 7 February, available http://news.bbc.co.uk/1/hi/uk_politics/2736149.stm (accessed 2 June 2004).

BBC (2003b), 'Schools to Teach Creationism', *BBC News Online*, 28 April, available http://news.bbc.co.uk/1/hi/england/wear/2981663.stm (accessed 22 November, 2004)

Bennett, A. and Kahn-Harris, K. (eds) (2004), *After Subculture; Critical Studies in Contemporary Youth Culture*, London and New York: Routledge.

Bennington, G. (1993), 'Derridabase', *Jacques Derrida*, Chicago and London: Chicago University Press.

Bennington, G. (2000), *Interrupting Derrida*, London and New York: Routledge.

Berger, P. and Luckmann, T. (1966), *The Social Construction of Reality*, New York: Doubleday.

Bergmann, J.R. (1987), *Discreet Indiscretions: The Social Organisation of Gossip*, trans. J. Bednarz, Jr., New York: Aldine de Gruyter.

Bhabba, H.K. (1990), *Nation and Narration*, Routledge, London and New York.

Blackhurst, C. (1997), 'Was Diana Murdered?' *Independent on Sunday*, 19 October, 1–2.

'Blair's War: Frontline' (2003), co-produced by Frontline and Mentorn, aired 3 April on PBS, transcripts available http://www.pbs.org/wgbh/pages/frontline/shows/blair/prime/blairbush.html (accessed 5 May 2005).

Bok, S. (1982), *Secrets: On the Ethics of Concealment and Revelation*, Oxford: Oxford University Press.

Bondanella, P. (1997), 'Interpretation, Overinterpretation, Paranoid Interpretation', in R. Capozzi (ed.), *Reading Eco: An Anthology*, Bloomington and Indianapolis: Indiana University Press.

Boulware, J. (1995), 'Mondo 1995', *SF Weekly*, 14 (35), 11 October, available http://www.sfweekly.com/issues/1995-10-11/feature2.html/page1.html (accessed January 2004).

Bourdieu, P. (1984), *Distinction: A Social Critique of the Judgement of Taste*, trans. R. Nice, Massachusetts and London: Harvard University Press.

Brockes, E. (2003), 'Taking the Mick', *Guardian*, 15 January, available http://education.guardian.co.uk/students/story/0,9860,875003,00.html (accessed 8 December 2003).

Brown, D. (2003), *The Da Vinci Code*, London and New York: Doubleday.

Brown, W. (2000), 'Resisting Left Melancholia', in P. Gilroy, L. Grossberg, A. McRobbie (eds), *Without Guarantees: In Honour of Stuart Hall*, London and New York: Verso.

Brown, W. (2001), *Politics out of History*, Princeton and Oxford: Princeton University Press.

Brunvard, J. H. (1968), *The Study of American Folklore*, New York and London: University of Utah Press.

Bukari, A. (1987), *The Translation of the Meanings of Sahih Al-Bukhari*, trans. M. Muhsin Khan, New Delhi: Kitab Bhavan.

Burt, K. (2001), 'Bitch's Brew', *Guardian*, 2 April, available http://www.guardian. co.uk/Archive/Article/0,4273,4163333,00.html (accessed 4 May 2005).

Channel 4 News (2005), 'Complete Legal Documents', *Channel 4 News*, 27 April, available http://www.channel4.com/news/special-reports/special-reports-storypage.jsp?id=91 (accessed 4 June 2005).

Coombe, R. J. (1992), 'Postmodernity and the Rumor: Late Capitalism and the Fetishism of the Commodity Sign', in W. Stearns and W. Chaloupke (eds), *Jean Baudrillard: The Disappearance of Art and Politics*, London: MacMillan.

Dant, T. (1991), *Knowledge, Ideology and Discourse: A Sociological Perspective*, London: Routledge.

Davies, M. (2003), 'People's Assembly Challenges Blair, *BBC News*, 12 March, available http://news.bbc.co.uk/1/hi/uk_politics/2843961.stm (accessed 7 May 2005).

Davis, D. B. (ed.) (1971), *The Fear Of Conspiracy: Images of Un-American Subversion From the Revolution to the Present*, Ithaca and London: Cornell University Press.

Dean, J. (1998), *Aliens in America: Conspiracy Cultures from Outer Space to Cyberspace*, Ithaca and London: Cornell University Press.

Dean, J. (2002), *Publicity's Secret: How Technoculture Capitalizes on Democracy*, Ithaca and London: Cornell University Press.

DeCurtis, A. (1991), '"An Outsider in This Society": An Interview with Don DeLillo', in F. Lentrecchia (ed.), *Introducing Don DeLillo*, Durham and London: Duke University Press.

Dégh, L. (1994), *American Folklore and the Mass Media*, Bloomington and Indianapolis: Indiana University Press.

DeLillo, D. in interview with Begley, A. (1993), 'Don DeLillo: The Art of Fashion CXXXV', *Paris Review*, 35(128): 274–306.

DeLillo, D. (1997), *Underworld*, New York: Scribner.

Department for Trade and Industry (1998), 'Our Competitive Future: Building the Knowledge Driven Economy', http://www.dti.gov.uk/comp/competitive/main.htm (accessed 4 November 2004).

Derrida, J. ([1967a] 1984), *Of Grammatology*, trans. G. C. Spivak, Baltimore and London: Johns Hopkins University Press.

Derrida, J. ([1967b] 1973), *Speech and Phenomena and Other Essays on Husserl's Theory of Signs*, trans. D. B. Allison, Evanston: Northwestern University Press.

Derrida, J. ([1967c] 1981), 'Cogito and the History of Madness', in *Writing and Difference*, trans. A. Bass, Chicago: University of Chicago Press.

Derrida, J. ([1972a] 1982), 'Signature Event Context', *Margins of Philosophy*, trans. A. Bass, Chicago and London: University of Chicago Press.

Derrida, J. ([1972b] 1981), *Dissemination*, trans. B. Johnson, London: Athlone.

Derrida, J. ([1972c] 1993), 'The Purveyor of Truth', trans. J. Mehlman, in J. P. Muller and W. J. Richardson (eds), *The Purloined Poe: Lacan, Derrida and*

Psychoanalytic Reading, Baltimore and London: Johns Hopkins University Press.

Derrida, J. ([1980] 1987), 'To Speculate – on "Freud"', *The Postcard: From Socrates to Freud and Beyond*, trans. Alan Bass, Chicago: University of Chicago Press.

Derrida, J. ([1991] 1992), *The Other Heading: Reflections on Today's Europe*, trans. P.-A. Brault and M. B. Naas, Bloomington and Indiana: Indiana University Press.

Derrida, J. (1992a), 'Canons and Metonymies: An Interview with Jacques Derrida', in R. Rand (ed.) *Logomachia: The Conflict of the Faculties*, Lincoln and London: University of Nebraska.

Derrida, J. (1992b), 'Passions: An Oblique Offering', in D. Wood (ed.), *Derrida: A Critical Reader*, Oxford and Cambridge, MA: Blackwell.

Derrida, J. ([1992c] 1995), *The Gift of Death*, trans. D. Wills, Chicago and London: University of Chicago Press.

Derrida, J. (1992d), 'This Strange Institution Called Literature', trans. R. Bowlby and G. Bennington, in D. Attridge (ed.), *Acts of Literature*, London and New York: Routledge.

Derrida, J. (2002), 'Force of Law: The "Mystical Foundation of Authority"', trans. M. Quaintance, in G. Anidjar (ed.), *Acts of Religion*, London and New York: Routledge.

Derrida, J. (2003), 'Autoimmunity: Real and Symbolic Suicides', in dialogue with Giovanna Borradori, *Philosophy in a Time of Terror*, Chicago and London: University of Chicago Press.

Dorson, R. M. (1968), 'What is Folklore?' *Folklore Forum*, 1(4): n.p.

Dowbenko, U. (2003), 'WSJ Promotes 9-11 Govt Conspiracy Theory', *Conspiracy Planet*, 23 October, available at http://www.conspiracyplanet.com/channel. cfm?channelid=89&contentid=956&page= (accessed 10 October 2004).

Doyle McCarthy, E. (1996), *Knowledge As Culture: The New Sociology of Knowledge*, London and New York: Routledge.

Du Gay, P. and Pryke, M. (2002), *Cultural Economy*, London: Sage.

Duncombe, S. (1997), *Notes from the Underground: Zines and the Politics of Alternative Culture*, London and New York: Verso.

Eco, U. (1988), *Foucault's Pendulum*, trans. W. Weaver, London: Picador.

Eco, U. (1990), *The Limits of Interpretation*, Bloomington and Indianapolis: Indiana University Press.

Eco, U. (1992), 'Interpretation and History', 'Overinterpreting Texts', 'Between Author and Text', 'Reply', in S. Collini (ed.), *Interpretation and Overinterpretation*, Cambridge: Cambridge University Press.

Editors of *Lingua Franca* (eds) (2000), *The Sokal Hoax*, Lincoln and London: University of Nebraska Press.

Ellis, M. (1998), 'The Diana Conspiracies...', *Evening Standard Magazine*, 6 February, 15-16.

Emler, N. (1994), 'Gossip, Reputation, and Social Adaptation', in R. F. Goodman and A. Ben-Ze'ev (eds), *Good Gossip,* Kansas: University of Kansas Press.

Evans, M. (2005), 'Leak Shows "Blair Set on Iraq War a Year before Invasion"', *Times Online,* 2 May, available http://www.timesonline.co.uk/printFriendly/ 0,,1-18169-1594495-18169,00.html (accessed 1 June 2005).

Fairclough, N. (1995), *Critical Discourse Analysis: A Critical Study of Language,* London and New York: Longman.

Fenster, M. (1999), *Conspiracy Theories: Secrecy and Power in American Culture,* Minneapolis MN: University of Minnesota Press.

Fenves, P. (1993), *'Chatter': Language and History in Kierkegaard,* Stanford: Stanford University Press.

Fischer, C. S. (1995), *America Calling,* Berkeley and Los Angeles: University of California Press.

Fiske, J. (1993), *Power Plays, Power Works,* London and New York: Verso.

Flett, K. (2005), 'What if Gossip was Banned?' 'G2', *The Guardian,* 19 June, 4.

Foucault, M. ([1966] 1992), *The Order of Things: An Archaeology of the Human Sciences,* trans. anon, London and New York: Routledge.

Foucault, M. ([1969] 1994), *Archaeology of Knowledge,* trans. A. M. Sheridan, London and New York: Routledge.

Foucault, M. ([1975] 1977), *Discipline and Punish: The Birth of the Prison,* trans. A. Sheridan, London and New York: Penguin.

Foucault, M. ([1976] 1978), *The History of Sexuality: Volume One,* trans. R. Hurley, London: Random House.

Foucault, M. (1980), 'Two Lectures', in C. Gordon (ed.), *Power/Knowledge: Selected Interviews and Other Writings 1972-1977,* trans. C. Gordon, L. Marshall, J. Mepham and K. Soper, Brighton: Harvester.

Fox, K. (2001), 'Evolution, Alienation and Gossip: The Role of Telecommunications in the 21st Century', *Social Issues Research Centre,* available http:// www.sirc.org/publik/gossip.shtml#top (accessed 1 June 2004).

Freud, S. (1920), 'Beyond the Pleasure Principle', *Vol. XVIII Standard Edition,* trans. J. Strachey, London: Hogarth Press.

Freud, S. (1925), 'An Autobiographical Study', *Vol. XX Standard Edition,* trans. J. Strachey, London: Hogarth Press.

Frow, J. (2005), 'Theory', in T. Bennett, L. Grossberg and M. Morris (eds), *New Keywords: A Revised Vocabulary of Culture,* Oxford, Blackwell.

Furedi, F. (2004), 'Diana Syndrome – We Get the Conspiracies We Deserve', *The Independent,* 11 January, available http://argument.independent.co.uk/low_ res/story.jsp?story=479979&host=6&dir=140 (accessed 9 October 2004).

Gelder, K. and Thornton, S. (eds) (1997), *The Subcultures Reader,* London and New York: Routledge.

Genosko, G. (1994), *Baudrillard and Signs: Signification Ablaze,* London: Routledge.

Gettier, E. (1963), *'Is Justified True Belief Knowledge?' Analysis*: 121–3. Available http://www.ditext.com/gettier/gettier.html (accessed 12 August 2005).

Gilbert, J. (2004), 'Signifying Nothing: 'Culture', 'Discourse', and the Sociality of Affect', *Culture Machine*, Vol. 6, available http://culturemachine.tees.ac.uk/ Cmach/Backissues/j006/articles/gilbert.htm (accessed 5 January 2005).

Gilroy, P. (n.d.), 'History of Cultural Studies', *Save Cultural Studies Campaign*, available http://myweb.tiscali.co.uk/culturalstudies/history.htm (accessed 12 December 2004).

Gluckman, M. (1963), 'Gossip and Scandal', *Current Anthropology*, 4(3): 307–16.

Godzich, W. (1987), 'Afterword: Religion, the State, and Post(al) Modernism', in S. Weber, *Institution and Interpretation*, Minneapolis: University of Minnesota Press.

Goodman, R. F. (1994), 'Introduction', in R. F. Goodman and A. Ben-Ze'ev (eds), *Good Gossip*, Kansas: University of Kansas Press.

Gordon, J. B. (1996), *Gossip and Subversion in Nineteenth Century British Fiction: Echo's Economies*, Oxford: MacMillan.

Gordon, J. B. (2001), 'Hearsay Booked: Fugitive Talk Brought to Justice', in S. I. Salamensky (ed.), *Talk, Talk, Talk: The Cultural Life of Everyday Conversation*, London and New York: Routledge.

Grossberg, L. (2004), 'The Life and Times of Cultural Studies', unpublished paper quoted with author's permission.

Hall, G. (2002), *Culture in Bits*, London and New York: Continuum.

Hall, S. ([1980] 1993), 'Encoding/Decoding', in S. During (ed.), *Cultural Studies Reader*, London and New York: Routledge.

Hall, S. (1981), 'Notes on Deconstructing "the 'Popular"', in R. Samuel (ed.), *People's History and Social Theory*, London and New York: Routledge.

Hall, S. (1992), 'Cultural Studies and its Theoretical Legacies', in L. Grossberg, C. Nelson and P. Treichler (eds), *Cultural Studies*, Routledge: New York and London.

Hall, S. (1996), 'The Problem of Ideology: Marxism Without Guarantees' in D. Morley and K-H. Chen (eds), *Stuart Hall: Critical Dialogues in Cultural Studies*, London and New York: Routledge.

Hall, S. and Jefferson, T. (eds) (1976) *Resistance Through Rituals: Youth Subcultures in Post-war Britain*, London: Hutchinson.

Hamilton, I. (1998), 'Taste, Tact and Racism', *London Review of Books*, 20(2), 22 January.

Harding, L. (1998), 'Bishop Quashes Diana Rumours', *Guardian*, 12 January, p. 4.

Hassan, A. (trans.) (1983), *Sunan Abu Dawud: One of the Six Authentic Collections of the Traditions of the Holy Prophet*, Lahore: Muhammed Ashraf.

Heelas, P. (1996), *The New Age Movement: The Celebration of the Self and the Sacralization of Modernity*, Malden, MA and Oxford: Blackwell.

Heidegger, M. ([1927] 1962), *Being and Time*, trans. J. Macquarie and E. Robinson, London: SCM Press.

Herbert, I. (2005), 'Vigilante Violence: Death by Gossip', *Independent*, 23 March, p. 1.

Hesmondhalgh, D. (2002), *The Cultural Industries*, London, Thousand Oaks and New Delhi: Sage.

Hill, G. and Hill, K. (1995), *The Real Life Dictionary of the Law: Taking the Mystery Out of Legal Language*, Los Angeles: General Publishing Group.

Hills, M. (1999), *The Dialectic of Value: The Sociology and Psychoanalysis of Cult Media*, unpublished Ph.D. dissertation, University of Sussex.

Hills, M. (2002), *Fan Cultures*, London and New York: Routledge.

Hoffman, T. (1998), 'History as Conspiracy', *Queen's Quarterly*, 105(3): 392–406.

Interactivist.net (2004), 'Double Crossing Back: A Review Article of the 2004 Crossroads in Cultural Studies Conference', *Interactivist.Net*, 2 October, available http://info.interactivist.net/article.pl?sid=04/10/02/2021233 (accessed 6 October, 2004).

Jack, I. and Marlow, P. (eds) (1997), 'Those Who Felt Differently', *Granta*, 60 (Winter): 9–36.

Jameson, F. (1988), 'Cognitive Mapping', in C. Nelson and L. Grossberg (eds), *Marxism and the Interpretation of Culture*, Chicago: University of Illinois Press.

Jameson, F. (1992), *The Geopolitical Aesthetic: Cinema and Space in the World System*, Bloomington and Indianapolis: Indiana University Press.

Karpf, A. (2002), 'Uncle Sam's Lucky Finds', *Guardian*, 19 March, http://www.guardian.co.uk/september11/story/0,11209,669961,00.html (accessed 21 October 2004).

Keith, J. (ed.) (1993), *Secret and Suppressed: Banned Ideas and Hidden History*, Los Angeles CA: Feral House.

Keith, J. (1996), *OKBOMB: Conspiracy and Cover-up*, Lilburn GA: IllumiNet.

Keith, J. (1997), *Mind Control, World Control*, Kempton, IL: Adventures Unlimited Press.

Kellner, D. (1999), '*The X-Files* and the Aesthetics and Politics of Postmodern Pop', *Journal of Aesthetics*, 57(2): 161–75.

Kerr, J. (2003), 'Diana Letter Sensation: "They Will Try To Kill Me"', *The Mirror*, 20 October, p.1, available http://www.mirror.co.uk/news/allnews/content_objectid=13533662_method=full_siteid=50143_headline=-DIANA-LETTER-SENSATION--THEY-WILL-TRY-TO-KILL-ME–name_page.html (accessed 18 January 2005).

Kierkegaard, S. ([1846] 1978), *Two Ages: The Age of Revolution and the Present Age, A Literary Review*, trans. H. and E. Hong, Princeton, NJ: Princeton University Press.

Knight, P. (2000), *Conspiracy Culture: From Kennedy to The X-Files*, London and New York: Routledge.

Knight, P. and Spark, A. (1997), 'Conspiracy Thinking and Conspiracy Studying', *Conspiracy Culture*, available at http://www.kwac.ac.uk/research/ccc (accessed 20 December 2001).

Knight, P. and Spark, A. (1998), 'Plots All Over the Landscape', *The Times Higher Education Supplement*, 25 December, p. 22.

Laclau, E. (2005), *The Populist Reason*, London: Verso.

Laplanche, J. and Pontalis, J.B. (1988), *The Language of Psycho-analysis*, trans. D. Nicholson-Smith, London: Karnac.

Latour, B. (2004), 'Why has Critique Run Out of Steam? From Matters of Fact to Matters of Concern', *Critical Inquiry*, Winter, 30(2), pp. 225–8, available http://www.uchicago.edu/research/jnl-crit-inq/issues/v30/30n2.Latour.html (accessed 20 May 2005).

Lawson, M. (1998), 'Never Say Di', *Guardian*, 14 February.

Lawson, M. (2004), 'Seeing is not Believing', *Guardian*, 6 September, available http://www.guardian.co.uk/print/0,3858,5008897-103680,00.html (accessed 20 October 2004).

Le Bon, G. ([1895] 1977), *The Crowd: A Study of the Popular Mind*, New York and Harmondsworth: Penguin.

Leishman, K. (1999), 'Politics is Elsewhere: *Popular Culture and Everyday Life*', *M/C*, 8 June, available http://www.uq.edu.au/mc/reviews/words/popcult.html (accessed 15 April 2004).

Levin J. and Arluke, A. (1987), *Gossip: The Inside Scoop*, New York and London: Plenum.

Ley, S. (2003) 'Blair Makes Moral Case for War' *BBC News*, 15 February, available http://news.bbc.co.uk/1/hi/uk_politics/2765875.stm (accessed 2 May 2005).

Litchfield, J. (1998), 'A tragedy yes, a conspiracy never', *Independent*, 25 August, p. 9.

Lloyd, G. (2005), 'Knowledge', in T. Bennett, L. Grossberg, and M. Morris (eds), *New Keywords: A Revised Vocabulary of Culture and Society*, Oxford: Blackwell.

Lyotard, J-F. ([1979] 1994), *The Postmodern Condition: A Report on Knowledge*, trans. G. Bennington and B. Massumi, Manchester: Manchester University Press.

Lyotard, J-F. ([1983] 1988), *The Differend: Phrases in Dispute*, trans. G. van Den Abbeele, Manchester: Manchester University Press.

Mack, J. E. (1994) *Abduction: Human Encounters with Aliens*, New York: Scribner.

Maier, P. (1997), *American Scripture: Making the Declaration of Independence*, New York: Alfred A. Knopf.

Marcus, G. E. (ed.) (1999), *Paranoia Within Reason: A Casebook on Conspiracy as Explanation*, Chicago and London: University of Chicago Press.

Mardle, E. (2004), 'Gossip – The Original Knowledge Economy', *A Networked World*, 28 January, available http://keynet.blogs.com/networks/2004/01/gossip_the_orig.html (accessed 5 May 2004).

McDowall, A. and Penketh, A. (2005), 'Iran Blast Panics Financial Markets', *Independent Online Edition*, 17 February, available http://news.independent.

co.uk/world/middle_east/story.jsp?story=611816 (accessed 20 February 2005).

McGuigan, J. (1992), *Cultural Populism*, London and New York: Routledge.

McHale, E. (1994), 'Fundamentals of Folklore', in J. Suter (ed.), *Working with Folk Materials in New York State: A Manual for Folklorists and Archivists*, Ithaca, NY: New York Folklore Society.

McLuhan, M. (1965), *Understanding Media: The Extensions of Man*, New York: McGraw Hill.

McNay, L. (1994), *Foucault: A Critical Introduction*, Cambridge: Polity.

Mellencamp, P. (1992), *High Anxiety: Catastrophe, Scandal, Age and Comedy*, Bloomington and Indianapolis: Indiana University Press.

Merck, M. (ed.) (2004), 'Cultures and Economies', *New Formations*, 52 (Spring).

Miller, T. and McHoul, A. (1998), *Popular Culture and Everyday Life*, London, Thousand Oaks, and New Delhi: Sage.

Moench, D. (1995), *The Big Book of Conspiracies*, New York: Paradox Press.

Morello, C. (2004), 'Conspiracy Theories Flourish on the Internet', *Washington Post*, 7 October, p. B01, available http://www.washingtonpost.com/wp-dyn/articles/A13059-2004Oct6.html (accessed 9 May 2005).

Morin, R. and Deane, C. (2001), 'Poll: Americans' Trust in Government Grows – Confidence in Government More than Doubles since April 2000', *Washington Post*, 28 September, available http://www.washingtonpost.com (accessed 18 November 2002).

Muggleton, D. and Weinzierl, R. (eds) (2003), *The Post-subcultures Reader*, Oxford: Berg.

The New World Network (no date given), 'Princess Homicide?' *The Real News*, available http://www.newworldnetwork.com/diana.htm (accessed 15 January 1998).

Obed Brown, H. (1977), 'The Errant Letter and the Whispering Gallery', *Genre*, 10(4): 573–99.

Official Secrets Act (1989) (c. 6) Section 2 (Defence), available http://www.hmso.gov.uk/acts/acts1989/Ukpga_19890006_en_2.htm (accessed 1 June 2004).

Palmer, R. (2005), '94% of You Believe Diana Was Murdered', *Daily Express*, 25 May, p. 1.

Parsons, C. (2001), 'Why We Need Conspiracies', *BBC News Online*, 24 September, available http://news.bbc.co.uk/1/hi/world/americas/1561199.stm (accessed 12 October 2004).

Parish, J. and Parker, M. (2001), *The Age of Anxiety: Conspiracy Theory and the Human Sciences*, Oxford: Blackwell.

Patton, C. (1993), 'Embodying Subaltern Memory: Kinesthesia and the Problematics of Gender and Race', in C. Schwichtenberg (ed.), *The Madonna Connection: Representational Politics, Subcultural Identities, and Cultural Theory*, Sydney: Allen & Unwin.

Pipes, D. and Khashan, H. (1997), 'Diana and Arab Conspiracy', *Weekly Standard*, November 10, available http://www.danielpipes.org/article/290 (accessed December 2003).

Pipes, D. (1997), *Conspiracy: How the Paranoid Style Flourishes and Where It Comes From*, New York: Free Press.

Plant, S. (1995), 'Cultural Studies and Philosophy', *Parallax*, 1: 100–1.

Plato (1987), *Theaetetus*, trans. R. A. H. Waterfield, London: Penguin.

Popper, K. (1966), *The Open Society and its Enemies, Vol.2: The High Tide of Prophecy: Hegel, Marx and the Aftermath*, 5th edition, London: Routledge.

Raban, J. (2004), 'Running Scared', G2, *Guardian*, 21 July, available http://www.guardian.co.uk/uselections2004/story/0,13918,1265653,00.html (accessed 10 January 2005).

Ravitch, D. (2000), *Left Back*, New York: Simon & Schuster.

Readings, B. (1996), *The University in Ruins*, Cambridge, MA and London: Harvard University Press.

Robbins, B. and Ross, A. (2000), 'Response: Mystery Science Theater', in the editors of *Lingua Franca* (eds), *The Sokal Hoax*, Lincoln, NB and London: Nebraska University Press.

Robins, R.S. and Post, D. (1998), *Political Paranoia: The Psychopolitics of Hatred*, New Haven: Yale University Press.

Rongstad, R. and St.John-Smith, T. (1997), 'Diana Conspiracy Talk Spreading Fast', *Sun Tzu's Newswire*, 1 September, available http://www.ccnet.com/~suntzu75/mad_minute/mmindex.htm#index (accessed 15 October 1997).

Rosenbaum, J. B. and Subrin, M. (1963), 'The Psychology of Gossip', *Journal of American Psychoanalytic Association*, 11(October): n.p.

Rosnow, R. L. and Fine, G. A. (1976), *Rumor and Gossip: The Social Psychology of Gossip*, New York, Oxford, Amsterdam: Elsevier.

Ross, A. (1991), *Strange Weather: Culture, Science, and Technology in the Age of Limits*, London: Verso.

Royle, N. (2003), *The Uncanny*, Manchester: Manchester University Press.

Rutherford, J. (ed.) (2002), 'Knowledge/Culture' *Mediactive*, Issue 1.

Saini, A. (2005), 'EU Ban Angers Health Food Makers', *CNN.com*, 13 July, available http://edition.cnn.com/2005/WORLD/europe/07/13/eu.supplements/ (accessed 18 July 2005).

Schein, S. (1994), 'Used and Abused: Gossip in Medieval Society', in R. F. Goodman and A. Ben-Ze'ev (eds), *Good Gossip*, Kansas: University of Kansas Press.

Shleifer, A. (2000), *Inefficient Markets: An Introduction to Behavioral Finance*, Oxford: Oxford University Press.

Showalter, E. (1997), *Hystories: Hysterical Epidemics and Modern Culture*, London: Picador.

Sign of the Times, editorial (2004), 'Shooting the Messenger', *Sign of the Times*, 8 October, available http://signs-of-the-times.org/signs/signs20041008.htm (accessed 20 October 2004).

Skolnick, S. (1997), 'Princess Diana was Assassinated', *Conspiracy Nation*, Vol. 10 (98), September, available FTP: ftp://ftp.shout.net/pub/users/bigred/Vol 10/cn 10-98 (accessed 20 November 1997).

Snoddy, R. (1992), *The Good, the Bad and the Unacceptable: The Hard News about the British Press*, London: Faber & Faber.

Sokal, A. (1996), 'Transgressing the Boundaries: An Afterword', *Dissent*, 43(4): 93-9.

Sokal, A. (2000), 'Revelation: A Physicist Experiments with Cultural Studies', in the editors of *Lingua Franca* (eds), *The Sokal Hoax*, Lincoln and London: Nebraska University Press.

Spacks, P. (1985), *Gossip*, Chicago and London: University of Chicago Press.

Spivak, G.C. (1976), 'Preface' in J. Derrida, *Of Grammatology*, Baltimore and London: Johns Hopkins University Press.

Tempest, M. (2003), 'Blair: Iraq Oil Claim is Conspiracy Theory', *Guardian*, 15 January, available http://politics.guardian.co.uk/foreignaffairs/story/0,11538,875173,00.html (accessed 15 October 2004).

Theophrastus (1953), *The Characters of Theophrastus*, Cambridge, MA: Harvard University Press.

Toelken, B. (1979), *The Dynamics of Folklore*, Boston: Houghton Mifflin.

Turner, P. (1993), *I Heard it through the Grapevine: Rumor in African-American Culture*, Berkeley, CA: University of California University Press.

UK Government (2002), 'Iraq's Weapons of Mass Destruction – The Assessment of the British Government', 24 September, available http://www.number-10.gov.uk/output/Page271.asp (accessed 3 June 2004).

UK Government (2003), 'Iraq – Its Infrastructure of Concealment, Deception and Intimidation', January, available http://www.number-10.gov.uk/output/Page1470.asp (accessed 2 June 2004).

Vankin, J. (1996), *Conspiracies, Cover-ups and Crimes: From Dallas to Waco*, Lilburn, GA: IllumiNet.

Vankin, J. and Whalen, J. (1995), *The Giant Book of Conspiracies*, Bristol: Paragon.

Weber, S. (1987), *Institution and Interpretation*, Minneapolis: University of Minnesota Press.

Wendell Knox, J. (1972), *Conspiracy in American Politics 1787-1815*, New York: Arno Press.

Wheen, F. (2004), 'I Second That Emotion', extract from *How Mumbo-Jumbo Conquered the World*, London, Fourth Estate, in 'Talk of the Town', *Independent on Sunday*, 8 February.

Wilkes, R. (2002), *Scandal: A Scurrilous History of Gossip*, London: Atlantic Books.

Williams, R. ([1958] 1997), 'Culture is Ordinary', in A. Gray and J. McGuigan (eds), *Studies in Culture: An Introductory Reader*, London: Arnold.

Wintour, P. (1998), 'PM's Fury at Tacky "Diana Death Industry"', *Observer*, 15 February, p. 1.

Wise, J. (1997), 'Real or Imagined, Aliens Sell', *Avalanche-Journal*, July, p. 1.

Yarbrough, T. (n.d), 'Suicide through Marginalization: A Manifesto for the Study of Contemporary Culture' *Newfolk*, available http://www.temple.edu/isllc/newfolk/manifesto.html (accessed 19 Jan 2004).

Young, R. (ed.) (1981), *Untying the Text: A Post-structuralist Reader*, Boston, London and Henley: Routledge & Kegan Paul.

Younge, G. (2004), 'Evolution Textbooks Row Goes to Court', *Guardian*, 9 November, available http://www.guardian.co.uk/usa/story/0,12271, 1346678,00.html (accessed 22 November 2004).

Žižek, S. (2002), 'Afterword', *Revolution at the Gates: Selected Writings from Lenin in 1917*, London: Verso.

Zwi Werblowsky, R .J. and Wigoder, G. (eds) (1986), *The Encyclopedia of the Jewish Religion*, New York: Adama Books.

Zwi Werblowsky, R. J. and Wigoder, G. (eds) (1997), *The Oxford Dictionary of the Jewish Religion*, Oxford and New York: Oxford University Press.

Index

DATE DUE

SEP 2 2			
			PRINTED IN U.S.A.
GAYLORD			